STUDIES IN IMPERIALISM

General editors: Andrew S. Thompson and Alan Lester
Founding editor: John M. MacKenzie

When the 'Studies in Imperialism' series was founded by Professor John M. MacKenzie more than thirty years ago, emphasis was laid upon the conviction that 'imperialism as a cultural phenomenon had as significant an effect on the dominant as on the subordinate societies'. With well over a hundred titles now published, this remains the prime concern of the series. Cross-disciplinary work has indeed appeared covering the full spectrum of cultural phenomena, as well as examining aspects of gender and sex, frontiers and law, science and the environment, language and literature, migration and patriotic societies, and much else. Moreover, the series has always wished to present comparative work on European and American imperialism, and particularly welcomes the submission of books in these areas. The fascination with imperialism, in all its aspects, shows no sign of abating, and this series will continue to lead the way in encouraging the widest possible range of studies in the field. 'Studies in Imperialism' is fully organic in its development, always seeking to be at the cutting edge, responding to the latest interests of scholars and the needs of this ever-expanding area of scholarship.

Law across imperial borders

Manchester University Press

Law across imperial borders

BRITISH CONSULS AND COLONIAL
CONNECTIONS ON CHINA'S WESTERN
FRONTIERS, 1880–1943

Emily Whewell

MANCHESTER UNIVERSITY PRESS

The right of Emily Whewell to be identified as the author of this work has been
asserted by her in accordance with the Copyright, Designs and Patents Act 1988.

Published by Manchester University Press
Oxford Road, Manchester M13 9PL
www.manchesteruniversitypress.co.uk

British Library Cataloguing-in-Publication Data
A catalogue record for this book is available from the British Library

ISBN   978 1 5261 4002 9   hardback
ISBN   978 1 5261 8231 9   paperback

First published 2020

The publisher has no responsibility for the persistence or accuracy of URLs
for any external or third-party internet websites referred to in this book, and
does not guarantee that any content on such websites is, or will remain,
accurate or appropriate.

Typeset by Newgen Publishing UK

For my father, Peter Whewell, in memory

CONTENTS

FIGURES

ACKNOWLEDGEMENTS

This book would not have been possible without the support of a number of people and institutions. I became interested in British consular jurisdiction in China during my time as a PhD student at the University of Leicester. My supervisors Clare Anderson and Toby Lincoln inspired me in my quest to study both global and Chinese history. I am grateful for their patience and support. They always encouraged me and I greatly appreciated all the invaluable time spent in discussing my work, which eventually led me to write this book.

I am also thankful for the financial support that has enabled me to undertake such intense archival research. The University of Leicester and the Universities' China Committee in London funded my archival research in London and Shanghai. I am also thankful for the funding provided by the Max Planck Institute for European Legal History, which has allowed me to spend many more days, weeks and months in the archives and libraries. Thanks also go to the archivists, especially at The National Archives and the British Library in London, the Shanghai Municipal Archives for assisting me on multiple occasions, and the Shanghai Academy of Social Sciences for hosting me during 2014 to explore the collections in Shanghai.

I am grateful for the support of many friends, as well as those who have dedicated time to providing advice and reading drafts. My heartfelt thanks go especially to Katy Roscoe and Victoria Barnes. I would like to thank Rachael Buchanan, Emilie Hoang and Emma Hughes, who have always been a source of encouragement. Life is always much easier when you have fantastic friends, and I am grateful for all the excellent times spent together whilst I have been researching and writing.

Thanks also go to all those many who have provided feedback on my work in various forms, such as Stefan Vogenauer, Robert Bickers, Prashant Kidambi and the anonymous reviewers of my article 'Legal mediators: British consuls in Tengyue (western Yunnan) and the Burma-China frontier region, 1899–1931', forming the bulk of my chapter on the Frontier Meetings in Chapter 3. I must thank the anonymous reviewers of the drafts of this book, who provided invaluable comments that helped me to explore new avenues and enrich my book. I am also grateful to Laura Vann for her help with the cartography.

ACKNOWLEDGEMENTS

I would like to say my thanks to my family, who have always supported me throughout writing the book. I wish particularly to thank my mother, who always took great interest in what I was working on and read many drafts without complaint. Finally, my thanks to Caroline, for all her support and her understanding.

ABBREVIATIONS

BPP, HC   British Parliamentary Papers, House of Commons
IOR   India Office Records, British Library
NAI   National Archives of India
SMA   Shanghai Municipal Archives
TNA   The National Archives, London

NOTE ON TRANSLITERATION

Where possible, Chinese names and places are romanised using the standard pinyin form or added in parentheses within quotes that used the older system of Wade-Giles.

LIST OF BRITISH REPRESENTATIVES IN KASHGAR

1891	G. Macartney (Assistant for Chinese Affairs to the Resident in Kashmir)
February 1904	G. Macartney (consul – as recognised by Britain only)
September 1908	G. Macartney (consul; consul-general from 1910)
August 1918	P. Etherton
May 1922	N. Fitzmaurice
July 1922	C. P. Skrine
September 1924	R. A. Lyall
July 1925	G. V. B. Gillan
October 1927	F. Williamson
October 1930	G. Sherriff
September 1931	N. Fitzmaurice
November 1933	J. W. Thomson-Glover
October 1936	K. C. Packman
October 1938	H. H. Johnson
November 1940	E. Shipton
October 1942	M. C. Gillett
March 1925	R. G. Etherington Smith
January 1946–8	E. Shipton

LIST OF TENGYUE CONSULS

July–December 1899	J. W. Jamieson [acting]
January–October 1900	[Unfilled position]
November 1901	G. Litton
March 1902	L. A. McKinnon [acting]
October 1903	G. Litton
January 1906	H. A. Ottewill
November 1908	H. Sly
January 1909	A. Rose
May 1911	C. D. Smith
January 1916	A. Eastes
~ 1918	L. Giles [acting]
February 1919	J. B. Affleck
March 1921	O. R. Coales
November 1923	H. I. Harding
January 1927	S. W. Smith
January 1932	H. I. Prideaux-Brune
April 1934	W. S. Toller
October 1935	R. Hall
July 1938	G. E. Stockley
April 1940–2	M. C. Gillet

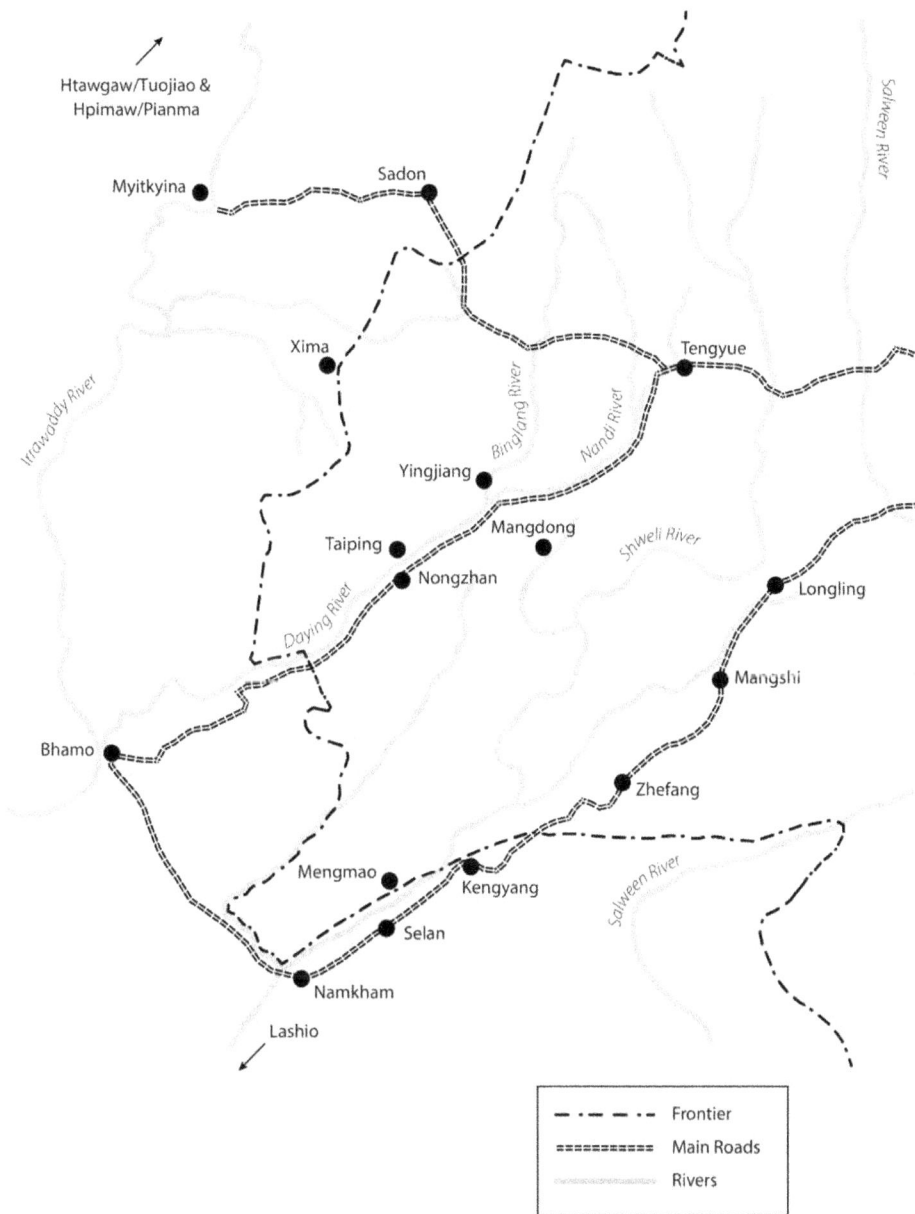

Figure 1 Trade routes from Tengyue to Burma with British-claimed borders c. 1900

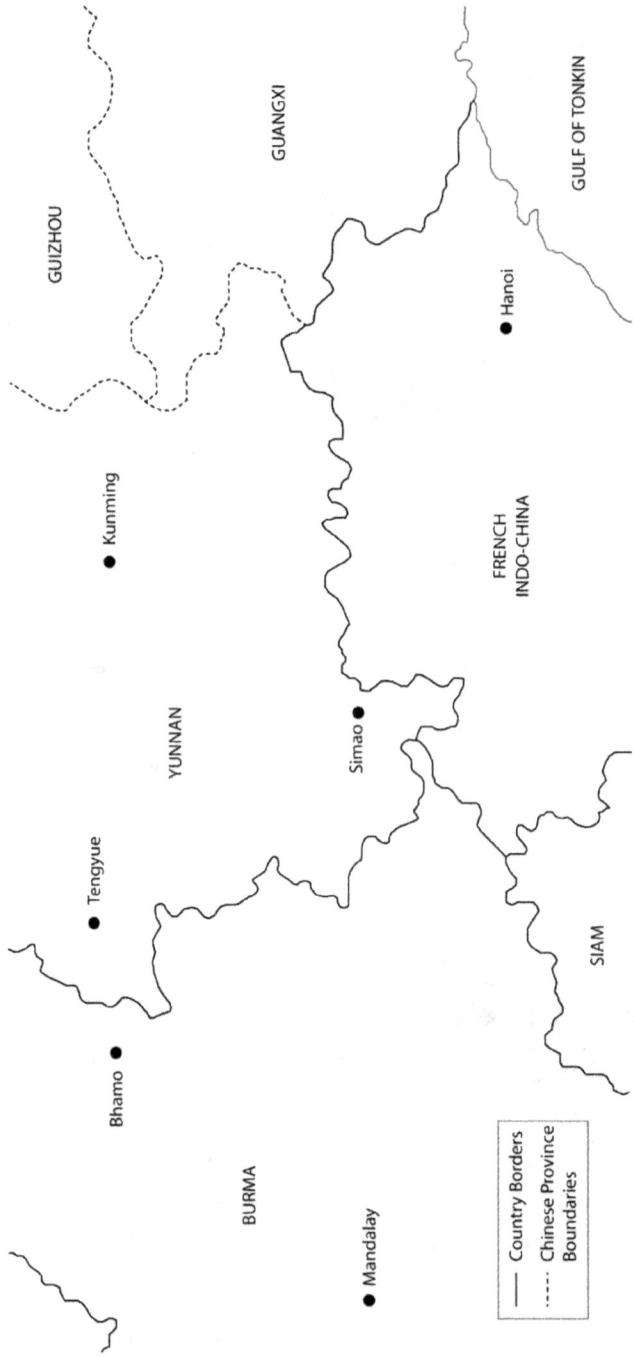

Figure 2 Consular establishments in Yunnan with British-claimed borders, c. 1900

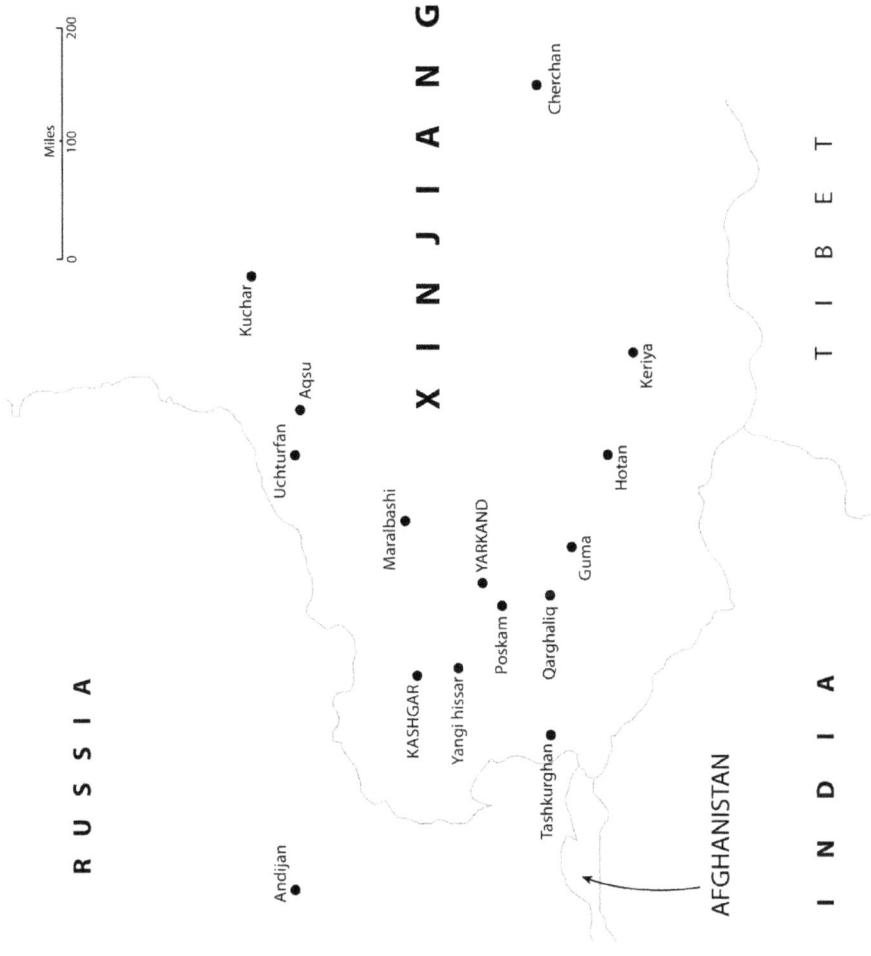

Figure 3 Towns in Xinjiang with British consular and *aqsaqal* representatives

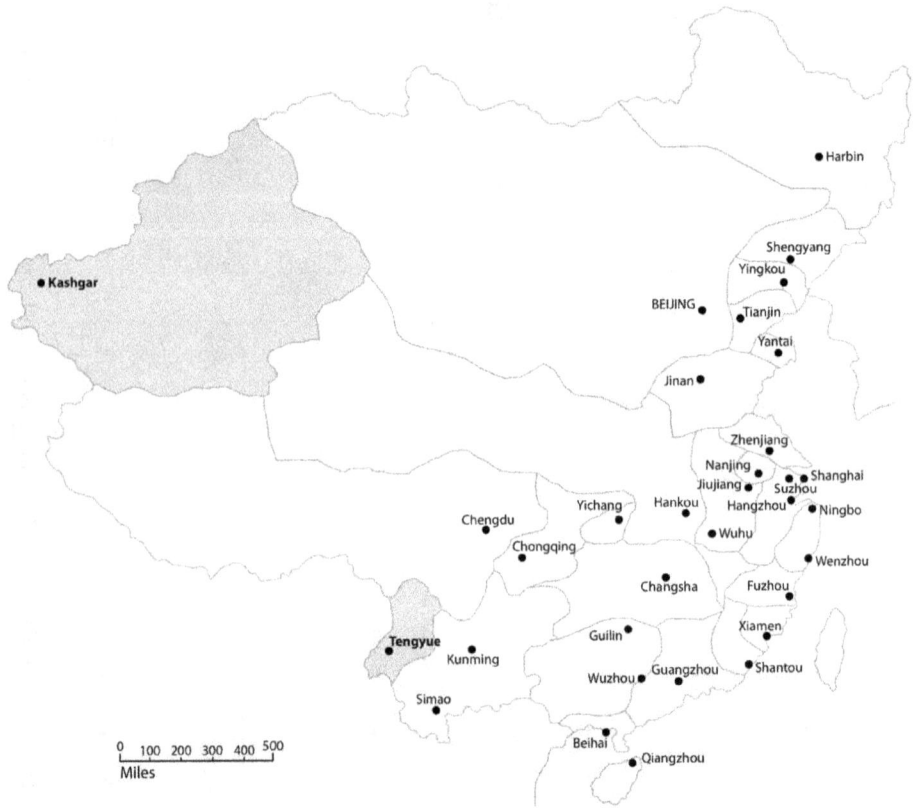

Figure 4 Consular districts in China c. 1911

INTRODUCTION

In 1914, British consular guards arrested and detained Akhtar Muhammed, an Indian-born British subject residing in the far western Chinese province of Xinjiang. He was one of many Indian men who had travelled from the northern regions of British India, crossed the valleys and mountainous terrain, and entered Chinese territory. The British representative stationed in Kashgar, in the west of the province, suspected that Muhammed had committed burglary. His subsequent arrest and trial followed legal precedent and legislation. Metropolitan Orders in Council and Sino-British treaties allowed British representatives to have jurisdiction over British suspects in China. This extraterritoriality empowered British officials to order arrests, detain suspects and exercise English law over such subjects. In Xinjiang, this representative was George Macartney, who was not only a consular official but also a representative of the British Indian colonial government. Macartney tried Muhammed and found him guilty. He sentenced him to serve a term of two years' imprisonment and used his consular powers under Article 88 of the China Order in Council (1904) to deport Muhammed to India according to the Colonial Prisoners Removal Act (1884).[1] Six years later, Macartney's successors could exercise various colonial laws in force in India over British subjects in Xinjiang, and Indian courts assumed appellate jurisdiction. In the Burma-China frontier to the south, consular officers stationed in Tengyue, in the west of the Chinese province of Yunnan, also arrested and detained Indian and Burmese men who had crossed into Chinese territory. Using extraterritorial legislation, consuls could later deport such individuals back across the frontier or send them for trial in Mandalay.

The case of Akhtar Muhammed and similar instances of consular practice suggest that law as applied by consuls was important for British authority in the seemingly remote western frontiers of China.

[1]

The nature of these legal powers transcended what we think of as the boundaries between different jurisdictions of the British Empire. These legal roles of the consuls and their connection to colonial authority have remained hidden in archival documents. This book therefore illuminates these activities of consular representatives in two consular circuits in the frontiers of China from the turn of the twentieth century: the district of 'Kashgar', which covered the province of Xinjiang, and the district of 'Tengyue' in the western part of the province of Yunnan.

I make three arguments in this book. First, I argue that these frontier consuls played a key role in creating forms of transfrontier legal authority. Consuls petitioned various colonial and consular authorities for adaptations to the law that ensured greater legal cohesion between their districts and colonial authority. They also worked alongside, or on behalf of, colonial officials. Second, I demonstrate that the impetus behind these legal adaptations was the perceived challenges brought about by the movement of British subjects and goods across frontiers. Salt and opium smugglers, itinerant Indian and Afghan traders, and local populations who drifted from place to place exposed the jurisdictional gaps between consular and colonial authority. Local and transfrontier mobility therefore defined and shaped British jurisdiction across the frontier. Finally, British authority in the frontiers embraced and worked alongside other local norms and legal structures. The incorporation of indigenous elites and customary law was a distinctive feature of frontier administration, and consular legal practices often required the cooperation of Chinese officials. This book is therefore the story of British consuls at the edge of the British and Chinese Empires and the nature of their legal powers.

Treaty port China and consular jurisdiction

For much of the nineteenth century, the British imperialist presence was confined to the south and east coast of China. Prior to 1833, the East India Company (EIC) traded exclusively in the southerly trading port of Canton. The Qing conferred customary judicial rights to agents of the company, which allowed these agents to exercise jurisdiction in criminal cases where the defendant was a British subject. When the Government of India Act (1833) removed the trade monopoly of the EIC on the Chinese coast, a piece of metropolitan legislation, the Order in Council (1833), provided the first set of written provisions for British judicial rights in China. After the Opium War (1839–42), the Treaty of Nanjing (1842) and the Treaty of the Bogue (1843) contained various rights for British subjects, as well as the 'Most Favoured

Nation' clause. Subsequent Sino-Foreign treaties that gave extraterritorial legal rights to treaty power nations in the territory of China – i.e. the immunity of its subjects from Chinese law – was thereafter automatically conferred to Britain. This allowed representatives of Britain to try British defendants in both criminal cases and civil suits. These agents were consuls, who presided over their consular districts in newly opened treaty ports, which now allowed foreign trade and residence.[2] In due course, the Qing conceded more rights to treaty power nations, including further opened treaty ports, concessions and leases. In some treaty ports, foreign-run Municipal Councils exercised municipal jurisdiction and the Sino-foreign Maritime Customs, headed by a foreign national, exercised revenue control.[3] Alongside extraterritoriality, this complex layering of indirect foreign rights therefore made China a 'semicolonial' legal landscape.[4] Whereas the partial violation of Chinese sovereignty distinguished China from colonial domains (such as the Crown colony of Hong Kong), there existed strong economic, cultural and social connections between the treaty ports and other parts of the British Empire.[5] These included words, ideas, architecture, trade and, of course, people from British India, Hong Kong and Southeast Asia. In this book, I show how legal connections were forged between British consuls in semicolonial China and colonial authority in India and Burma across the frontiers.

By the early twentieth century, many treaty ports had growing numbers of sojourning and resident foreign communities. In particular, the International Settlement in Shanghai hosted a cosmopolitan community.[6] Law underpinned the growth of this community and the development of foreign commercial interests. Extraterritoriality provided British consuls and the British Chief Judge in Shanghai with considerable scope to adjudicate cases that had significant social, economic and political ramifications for British subjects and companies. Despite the importance of British consular jurisdiction, scholarly interest of extraterritoriality has thus far focused more on the beginning and end of the treaty ports and extraterritorial privileges.[7] This is unsurprising as the narrative of foreign legal imperialism during these bookend years of the 'century of humiliation' (*bainian guochi*), i.e. the 1830s and 1840s and 1930s and 1940s, is intertwined with the significant developments and events in the history of modern China. This includes war, Sino-foreign diplomacy and, in the twentieth century, the rise of Chinese nationalism and socialism. As a result, we know much less about the legal practices of consular officials or the extraterritorial system as it functioned between these years.[8] As consuls were one of the key agents of British imperialism in different localities in China, this is a surprising shortcoming in the historiography of Britain in China.[9]

[3]

This shortcoming becomes more apparent when we turn to the Chinese hinterland and inland consulates. The narratives of the establishment of consular districts such as Chongqing and Chengdu in Sichuan, Kunming and Tengyue in Yunnan and Kashgar in Xinjiang are often associated with geopolitical rivalries. Their economic benefit to Britain appeared small or even negligible, and many scholars examining the foreign presence in these regions have tended to focus on the small groups of foreign missionaries and explorers.[10] Consuls appeared in some of these districts to be lonely imperial officials and the stations seemingly had less importance to British interests than the eastern coastal ports.[11] However, this book shows that consuls stationed in Kashgar and Tengyue played an important legal role for British colonial and consular authorities. This involved hearing cases of British subjects in these districts and resolving issues pertaining to transfrontier jurisdiction.

Consuls exercised extraterritoriality, but they had to do so within the parameters of British imperial policy. Consuls were guided by the Foreign Office, who managed consular administration and formulated general policy for British interests in extraterritorial jurisdictions and the Ambassador at Beijing, who was the most senior British diplomat in China. The Chief Judge for Her Britannic Supreme Court for China sitting in Shanghai also had a significant voice in legal arrangements of British extraterritorial powers. Although consuls took into consideration British directives from London, Beijing and Shanghai, they often reformulated how to exercise British rights in their districts. Located at the very edge of the Chinese Empire and at a considerable distance from the east coast of China, consular officials often acted without direct oversight. Instead, they usually only engaged with their administrative superiors in order to report their activities and secure legal ratification for practices they felt were more suitable for the frontier. This book therefore provides a key insight into their legal activities in the frontier as well as their role between British colonial, consular and metropolitan authorities, providing a narrative of the British legal presence in the hinterland of China.

Law in imperial contexts

It is important to ask why law in the British Empire mattered and to whom. In the colonial and imperial world, from North America to the Caribbean, Africa, Asia and Australia, law was part of a British imperialist philosophy. British officials, trade companies and merchants often considered English law – or colonial law as derived in some measure from English law or its principles – as a guarantor of 'liberty'.

[4]

Non-European and non-Christian legal systems, such as in China, were considered inferior, 'uncivilised' and too alien for European or British subjects.[12] Law was also a system of governance, where imperial officials administered justice inside and outside of courtrooms. British officials had the power to discipline its wayward nationals or acquit them of suspected crimes. British merchants and companies also felt a sense of security over their rights with a British legal system that they understood. Therefore, although commerce and the threat of force often underpinned imperialism – such as 'gunboat diplomacy' in China – legal practices supported, regulated and protected imperial interests. Although many indigenous subjects under imperialist rule could benefit from imperial rule, law could also serve imperial power by helping to maintain imperial race, gender and class hierarchies.[13] Law therefore could be simultaneously a symbolic and discursive tool, a system of law enforcement and administration, as well as a series of norms about how people should relate to other people and the world around them.

Law and legal practices were often shaped by pragmatism. Extra-legal practices abounded within and across empire, and many governments were limited financially, which curtailed the extent and scope of their jurisdiction.[14] Nor did colonial and imperial authorities always seek to carve out neat territorially bound jurisdictions. The legal geography of colonial and imperial systems could be 'lumpy' rather than a based upon a defined set of laws and practices conforming to the precise contours of the territory claimed by colonial states.[15] This included the creation of sea-lanes and trade routes that demonstrated how colonial authorities adapted their geographies of law to economic imperatives.[16] In the districts of Kashgar and Tengyue, consuls could not claim jurisdiction over such an expansive area in difficult topographical landscapes. Instead, they focused on key areas, such as trade routes to control and the people within them. Consuls were therefore pragmatic and their legal practices were reflective of the limitations of British authority. Thus, these local officials and ordinary people were also the key actors who were involved in the making, breaking and amendment of law.[17] Examining the thoughts and actions of frontier consuls who framed their practice on their understanding of the actions of claimed British subjects is therefore paramount in this book.

Law in empire was far from a monolithic, centralised system with a clear-cut set of institutions and practices. Colonial authority competed for jurisdiction with existing legal systems. Lauren Benton has argued that this contestation over the same people, goods and natural resources, or 'jurisdictional jockeying' and 'jurisdictional politics', was commonplace.[18] Colonial governments also often delegated authority to different imperial agents.[19] This sometimes included incorporating indigenous elites into imperial administration or allowing them to govern their localities with minimal imperial oversight.[20] Likewise, when the British obtained extraterritorial privileges in China, the China they set foot in was a vast multi-ethnic empire with a plural legal landscape. The Qing permitted minority groups some powers of jurisdiction in minor cases over their subjects and some provisions of the Qing code endorsed different punishments based on ethnicity.[21] The plurality of laws multiplied as the Celestial Empire conceded extraterritorial powers to various other treaty power nations.[22] Although extraterritoriality was therefore just one form of law amongst others, as Pär Cassel has shown, extraterritoriality in China and Japan was not monolithic, but took plural forms itself. The exercise of extraterritoriality was contingent upon its resonance with the indigenous legal order and its evolution.[23] In other words, the local legal landscape shaped Western extraterritorial systems and practices in China and Japan (as well as Japanese extraterritoriality in China). I show how the local legal context of the frontiers shaped British extraterritorial practices. In the consular districts of Tengyue and Kashgar, consuls delegated legal powers to local elites to govern local British communities. Consuls also incorporated customary law into their decision-making in many Sino-British cases. Extraterritoriality therefore involved not only consuls enforcing the provisions of the Orders in Council, but also a wide range of legal practices not defined by metropolitan legislation. Consuls exercising jurisdiction incorporated and accommodated other legal structures, and consuls – on both the east coast and towards the frontiers – continuously redefined the scope and nature of their powers.

Finally, law in empire was also mobile. The movement of people, goods and ideas shaped law across the imperial world and created transnational connections within and between empires.[24] This included law and legal personnel, such as the transnational influence of British Indian legislation, policemen and lawyers in the Indian Ocean region.[25] However, we know far less about the imperial legal connections between semicolonial China and colonial domains. I provide a new perspective, demonstrating how consuls and their roles highlight a type of transnational legal connection across two frontiers in Asia.

Frontiers

Frontiers were sites where imperial authority was most tenuous. More often than not, they were places where the environment prevented colonial regimes from effective administration over local populations.

These geographical features could include mountainous terrain, canyons and ravines, marshland, jungle, tundra or desert land. Many scholars focusing on imperial borders in Asia have shown how people at the margins of empire used these environments and exploited the tenuous reach of the colonial state to challenge state authority or to benefit themselves.[26] State responses included the circulation of imperial discourses characterising the frontiers as sites inhabited by 'lawless' and violent populations, as well as increased state violence.[27] The peripheries of empire can therefore tell us much about imperial anxieties and legal responses to such challenges to state authority.

A focus on the frontiers can also point to imperial state-building efforts and the role of individuals such as local inhabitants and migrants, as well as transfrontier economies and institutions that defined state-frontier relations.[28] Transfrontier smugglers, for example, played an important role in inter-empire politics.[29] China and Southeast Asia scholars have illuminated the various relations between the periphery and the centre, the local and the national, the permeability of borders, 'contact zones' and cultural encounters.[30] They highlight the rich and diverse patterns of relations between the Chinese Empire and local groups, as well as between various actors themselves.[31] In Southeast Asia, James Scott, for example, has argued that people living in the hill regions, which included the Burma-China frontier, were largely autonomous from the control of lowland empires.[32] This is in contrast to the long-held assumption that local elites and local ethnic populations were subsumed incrementally into the Chinese state over time.[33] Patterson Giersch argues instead that the relations between local groups and the Chinese state were complex and inter-mixed. Both indigenous people and the Chinese accommodated the norms of each other, a perspective that this book reflects in the examination of British consular jurisdiction with other legal entities in the frontier.[34]

Scholarship on frontiers has therefore helped to break down the traditional national and territorial lens of historical studies. It has also brought into sharper relief how imperial jurisdictions accommodated multiple legal structures and how the movement of people challenged or shaped imperial policy and law. Whereas the attention on frontiers between India and China, and between Burma and China have focused on the relations of local people to Chinese authority, in this book I offer a British imperial perspective. I show how consuls shaped their jurisdictional practices on the local British communities. This community included many individuals and groups that were mobile – migrants and transitory ethnic group subjects who traversed the frontier. Transnational migrants challenge the idea of impermeable borders in a globalised world and illuminate the spaces between legal authority structures. Such people were therefore at the centre of legal disputes between political entities. This meant that in Xinjiang and Yunnan, British consuls also shaped their legal practices around Chinese authority. In the districts of Kashgar and Tengyue, this led to unique forms of legal practices.

The terminology I use for understanding the site of these colonial-consular connections is important for framing my perspective. I use the term 'frontier' to describe the consular districts of Kashgar and Tengyue. Frederick Jackson Turner famously used 'frontier' to describe a meeting point between two different civilisations.[35] Others have since used the term to indicate a blurred zone of multiple cultural, economic, social and political interactions between local inhabitants, migrants, and competing states and empires. Patterson Giersch, for example, has used the term 'middle ground' in his analysis of the Sino-Southeast Asian frontier.[36] Giersch uses this term to emphasise the mutual adaptation and cultural exchange of ideas and customs, as well as integrated trade relations between local groups and the Chinese state. However, the frontier was also a site of inter-imperial rivalry. When the British established consular authority in Yunnan and Xinjiang, they also contested Chinese claims (and Russian sovereignty in Xinjiang) over the same people, land and resources in the region. Britain also considered a presence in the frontier imperative for limiting the sphere of influence of other European empires.[37] Adelman and Aron use the terms 'frontier' and 'borderland' to distinguish the notion of the coming together of different cultures, and as a site of imperial rivalry.[38] In this book, I subsume both definitions into the singular word of 'frontier'. I believe this term best conveys the concept of a zone of mobility between jurisdictions. British officials – both colonial and consular – also referred to the regions as 'frontiers', referring to its sometimes unclear legal and political dimensions. 'Frontier' therefore appears to most accurately reflect these officials' uncertainty and their sense of being stationed somewhere on the edge of imperial centres.

The Xinjiang and Tengyue frontiers

This book examines two different frontiers to demonstrate the commonalities in British frontier jurisdiction. In the northwest of China, Xinjiang – like Manchuria, Mongolia and Tibet – was a frontier province. It was a large, arid region, ringed by mountains and home to oasis towns. The majority of the population were Turkic Muslims, although growing numbers of ethnic Chinese Muslims, alongside Mongols, Kazakhs and others, inhabited the region. Chinese administration relied heavily on local elites to govern local populations, such as for tax collection and hearing minor disputes. The Silk Road traditionally ran through the region and connected it to other parts of Central Asia and the Indian subcontinent. It therefore attracted many sojourning merchants as well as resident merchants from different backgrounds, including individuals who migrated from the northern parts of British India and Afghanistan. In the southwest of China, the province of Yunnan was considered within the rule of the Qing (1644–1911) and within the Republican era (1912–49) as a part of 'China proper'. However, Chinese rule over its western region, which included the frontier with Burma, held many similarities to the administration of the official frontier provinces of Xinjiang, Mongolia, Tibet and Manchuria. Here, in the tropical climate, lived many different ethnic minorities, including the Shans, Kachins, Lisus and Panthays, amongst others. The region featured mountains, gorges, winding valleys and plains. Like in Xinjiang, successive Chinese governments relied on community leaders for local administration. In return for accepting Chinese sovereignty, China allowed these local elites to arrange local affairs, including exercising customary law in minor disputes amongst their populations.

By the late nineteenth century, British imperial interests turned to the frontiers of China. As the Russian Empire increased its sphere of influence in Central Asia, the British Indian government aimed to station a representative in Xinjiang to protect and promote British Indian interests. From 1891, this representative made his base Kashgar in the west of the province. The fear of Russian influence in Central Asia also made British colonial and consular authorities turn to Tibet. British legal rights were granted in the trade marts of Yadong (1894) and Gyantse and Gartok (1904) following the Sino-British Appended Sikkim-Tibet Convention (1893). The Tibetan trade marts had no consulates, but a British Indian Political Officer had some jurisdictional powers in trade disputes which involved a British defendant.[39] To the southwest, Upper Burma became subsumed into the province of Burma and part of British India in 1885.[40] British interests immediately turned towards the northeastern parts of Burma adjacent to Yunnan. Wary of a French presence in Southeast Asia, the British ensured that the subsequent Sino-British treaties over rights in the Burma-China frontier guaranteed the establishment of a consular presence in Tengyue, on the Chinese side of the frontier. The connection of consuls to colonial interests was therefore evident from the opening of the consulate and its proximity to colonial frontiers.

Although both consular districts were situated on a frontier, they incorporated different spatial and geographical dimensions as well as economic, political and social dynamics. The consular district of

Kashgar covered the whole of the province of Xinjiang. To Chinese and British officials in Beijing, the whole province was a frontier. To consuls stationed in Xinjiang, as the consular district was bounded by the mountains and desert where fewer British subjects lived between the northern reaches of India and that of China, they also considered the whole province as a 'frontier'. One of the most popular appellations for the region in British sources was 'Kashgaria'. This referred to the whole province, but particularly the west and the south, where most of the British communities lived in oasis towns. This included Kashgar and Yarkand to the south and west of the province, which had trade routes connecting them to the Karakoram Pass and northern India, notably through Leh, Chitral and Gilgit.

By contrast, the 'frontier' station of Tengyue included within it a frontier between Burma and China populated by many people. This frontier was over 965 km, stretching from Siam up to Tibet and inhabited by different ethnic groups. For the most part, when Tengyue consular officials talked about the 'frontier', they were reporting on, and referring to, a shorter section of the region with the trade routes between consular and colonial strongholds. This 'middle section' also had the largest number of borders agreed by both Britain and China. Within this section, the stations of Bhamo, Myitkyina and Lashio on the Burmese side and Tengyue on the Chinese side marked the largest outposts of stationed British authority. The main trade routes ran from these centres across the frontier. From Myitkyina, a trade route ran through Sadon and a small path through Sima to Tengyue. However, the most important route went from Bhamo to Tengyue, a distance of approximately 220 km, of which about 82 km lay in Burma and 138 km lay in China. One route ran through Nongzhan, but the most popular route went via Namhkam, Zhefang and Mangshi before reaching Tengyue. Aside from trade paths, there were also prominent Frontier Police Battalions stationed in outposts, such as at Sima, Sadon, Htawgaw (Tuojiao) and later Hpimaw (Pianma). In this book, I focus on this 'middle section' of the frontier, a triangle between Bhamo and Myitkyina to Tengyue.

Sources

Two types of materials provide a rich source base for this book: archival documents and late nineteenth- and early twentieth-century accounts of the frontiers. Archival materials from The National Archives in London, the British Library and the National Archives of India include correspondence between British consular officers in China, colonial officials from Burma and India, and the India Office and Foreign Office in London. Many of these sources are written by the hand of the people in power – consuls, diplomats and judges – reporting on legal issues involving people in the frontiers. However, as Ann Laura Stoler has encouraged, colonial archives can and should be read 'against' and 'along the archival grain'.[41] This can allow the historian to discern the failures of imperial governance as much as official ambitions. Likewise, as Ranajit Guha has argued, one can pinpoint different aspects of imperial rule and individual agency buried within official rhetoric of control[42] (or indeed within the language of formulaic regulations and governance). As the book focuses on the aims and actions of British consuls, it does not attempt to voice the perceptions of the local population through these sources. Nor does it attempt to draw the view of the Chinese authorities, which is beyond the scope of this book. Following Patterson Giersch's warning of the 'misleading paper trial' of Chinese imperial sources on the frontier, I exercise some caution when describing the reach of British imperial authority and its agents' control over local populations.[43] Local resistance to empire authority was a constant feature in the frontier. I emphasise that consuls sought to adapt their powers and that of colonial power to the frontier economy and the values of local people. This demonstrates that British authority – where it could be exercised at all – needed to accommodate local practices, and law was shaped around them. I therefore try to highlight the tenuous nature of British authority in the frontier.

A variety of nineteenth- and early twentieth-century works provide information on the frontiers. Travelogues and ethnographic accounts of the frontiers were forms of colonial knowledge that helped British officers to understand their region and enabled British expansion into previously unknown territories. Information of the geography, local customs and climatic conditions helped officers traverse an unfamiliar domain and categorise unfamiliar people into taxonomies that made sense to them. Some of these accounts were written by the consular officers themselves, providing an insight into their perceived world. Legal handbooks on extraterritoriality and foreign jurisdiction also gave British officers a framework for understanding their powers in a foreign land, elucidating a topic that most legal experts understood poorly. These works provide an insight into what consular officials would have understood about their environment and legal powers. Finally, although there were few reports on the far reaches of the Chinese Empire, I have also consulted the most widely read English-language newspaper in treaty port China, the *North China Herald* (*NCH*), and *Shenbao*, which was the most widely read Chinese newspaper.

Structure

The book is divided into two parts, which proceed broadly chrono-
logically in each. As the two case studies have a different history –
featuring different inhabitants and migrants, frontiers, and legal
environments – they do not mirror each other in chronology or subject matter. Instead, I draw out similar themes through the work of
consular officials in each. The first part focuses on the Burma-China
frontier. Chapter 1 traces the establishment of British authority (1899–
1911). As the provisions of the treaties were key legal documents,
I show how the Tengyue consuls understood the rights of British and
Chinese smugglers in two key transfrontier trades: salt and opium. The
movement of illicit goods was integral for the frontier economy and
local populations. Tengyue consuls reimagined consular rights based
on their understanding of the these local considerations and imperial
policy. I explore two key smuggling cases to show how consuls were
mediators amongst a number of different British colonial and consular
authorities in London, India, Burma and China on legal rights. The
chapter is therefore concerned with how consuls understood the overlapping frameworks and tensions of different layers of law: Sino-British
treaties, Burmese territorial law and extraterritoriality. Chapter 2
demonstrates how the movement of different people, such as migrant
labourers and itinerant domiciled subjects, shaped colonial and extraterritorial law (1911–25). Consuls petitioned for greater powers of
deportation to remove unwanted Indian migrants across the frontier. Consuls also petitioned the metropolitan, Indian and China consular authorities to enable Burmese officers to exercise colonial law
across borders by virtue of extraterritoriality. This chapter is therefore concerned with the relationship between borders, colonial law and
extraterritoriality. Chapter 3 explores how Tengyue consuls worked in
a court to resolve Sino-British cases involving local populations (1909–
35). The court was a reflection of the coming together of local laws
and British and Chinese jurisdiction. The consular role was to work
alongside Chinese officials and act as linguistic and cultural mediators
between these officials and their Burmese counterparts. They therefore balanced British imperial objectives – such as furthering colonial
claims to land – with efforts to ensure Chinese cooperation in the resolution of transfrontier cases.

The second part of the book turns to the northwest frontier of
Xinjiang and its connection to the Raj. Chapter 4 examines the establishment of extraterritorial jurisdiction in the province (1880–1918).
There, no treaty existed defining consular rights in the province. As
a result, the consular official George Macartney carved out his rights

through adjudicating Sino-British cases and by diplomatic negotiation with the Chinese authorities. As Macartney worked for the Indian government and, after 1908, was also a China consular official, he therefore bridged the colonial and semicolonial world. From 1918, his legal powers were derived from consular frameworks, but he could apply colonial laws from British India. He also sent suspects and convicts to India, creating an administrative and judicial fusion between the consular and colonial system. In Chapter 5, I examine court cases in Xinjiang (1912–25). Consular officials worked a compromise between administering consular law, carrying out imperial objectives and allowing the jurisdiction of local custom over British subjects. Consuls were aided by *aqsaqals*, senior merchants who resolved minor disputes of the British communities in various towns. Consuls not only incorporated this indigenous administrative practice into British administration, but also arranged the *aqsaqal* system and had clear influences from Indian community organisation. I therefore show how Indian communities and Indian influences shaped British administration in Xinjiang. Finally, in Chapter 6, I trace the decline of British jurisdiction in the province (1917–39). The Chinese authorities in Xinjiang challenged British consular rights, and consuls responded by managing this erosion of their powers. Consuls based their approach to managing this decline on the needs of the British community living in Xinjiang, as well as on practical and political considerations. I end by showing how the trading community that moved between India and Xinjiang declined rapidly and thereafter ended consular rights in the province.

Notes

1 TNA: FO656/136 J. Jordan, Ambassador at Beijing, to H. de Sausmarez, His Majesty's Britannic Supreme Court for China, 2 November 1915.

2 In 1865, an Order in Council provided for the establishment of Her Britannic Majesty's Supreme Court for China and Japan in Shanghai. The Chief Judge acted as a higher and appellate judge to any case or suit involving a British defendant. Although the Chief Judge was therefore an important legal official, the majority of cases involving British subjects were summary court cases. Outside of Shanghai, consuls were therefore the legal official who heard these cases.

3 On the Shanghai Municipal Council, see: I. Jackson, *Shaping Modern Shanghai: Colonialism in China's Global City* (Cambridge: Cambridge University Press, 2017). On the Maritime Customs, see: H. van de Ven, *Breaking with the Past: The Maritime Customs Service and the Global Origins of Modernity in China* (New York: Columbia University Press, 2014).

4 On the complexity of the 'semicolonial' landscape, see: T. Barlow, 'Colonialism's career in postwar China studies', *Positions*, 1 (1993), 224–67; B. Goodman and D. Goodman, 'Introduction: colonialism and China' in B. Goodman and D. Goodman (eds), *Twentieth-Century Colonialism and China* (London: Routledge, 2012), pp. 1–22. In this book, I use the term 'semicolonial' as a description of pertaining to law.

This entailed the partial infringement of Chinese sovereignty due to the immunity of treaty power individuals as defendants in cases and suits.

5 See, amongst others: R. Bickers, *Britain in China: Community, Culture and Colonialism, 1900–1949* (Manchester: Manchester University Press, 1999); R. Bickers, *Empire Made Me: An Englishman Adrift in Shanghai* (London: Allen Lane, 2003); R. Bickers and C. Henriot (eds), *New Frontiers: Imperialism New Communities in East Asia 1842–1953* (Manchester: Manchester University Press, 2000).

6 On the British presence and foreign community in China, see: Bickers, *Britain in China*; Bickers, *Empire Made Me*; R. Bickers, 'Shanghailanders: the formation and identity of the British settler community in Shanghai 1843–1937', *Past and Present*, 159:1 (1998), 161–221.

7 See, for example: T. Kayaoğlu, *Legal Imperialism: Sovereignty and Extraterritoriality in Japan, the Ottoman Empire, and China* (Cambridge: Cambridge University Press, 2010); W. Fishel, *The End of Extraterritoriality in China* (New York: Octagon, 1974); L. Chen, *Chinese Law in Imperial Eyes: Sovereignty, Justice and Transcultural Politics* (New York: Columbia University Press, 2016).

8 On British extraterritoriality, see: E. Whewell, 'British Extraterritoriality in China: The Legal System, Functions of Criminal Jurisdiction and its Challenges, 1833–1943' (PhD dissertation, University of Leicester, 2015); D. Clark, *Gunboat Justice: British and American Law Courts in China and Japan (1842–1943)*, vols 1–3 (Hong Kong: Earnshaw Books, 2015). More general works on extraterritoriality and especially the US extraterritorial system include: P. Cassel, *Grounds of Judgment: Extraterritoriality and Imperial Power in Nineteenth-Century China and Japan* (Oxford: Oxford University Press, 2012); G. An, *xifeng luori: lingshi caipan quan zai jindai zhongguo de queli* [*Consular Jurisdiction: Its Background and Course of Establishment in China*] (Shanghai: falü chubanshe, 2012); E. Scully, *Bargaining with the State from Afar: American Citizenship in Treaty Port China, 1844–1942* (New York: Columbia University Press, 2001).

9 The most comprehensive work on consuls to date remains that of Coates: P. D. Coates, *The China Consuls: British Consular Officers in China, 1843–1943* (Oxford: Oxford University Press, 1988).

10 See, for example, on missionaries: J. Wyman, 'Foreigners or outsiders? Westerners and Chinese Christians in Chongqing 1870s–1900', in R. Bickers and C. Henriot (eds), *New Frontiers: Imperialism's New Communities in East Asia, 1842–1953* (Manchester: Manchester University Press, 2000), pp. 75–87. On explorers, see: J. Dabbs, *A History of the Discovery and Exploration of Chinese Turkestan* (The Hague: Mouton, 1963); D. Glover et al. (eds) *Explorers and Scientists in China's Borderlands, 1880–1950* (Seattle: University of Washington Press, 2011); E. Mueggler, *The Paper Road: Archive and Experience in the Botanical Exploration of West China and Tibet* (Berkeley: University of California Press, 2011). On politics, see: L. Nyman, *Great Britain and Chinese, Russian and Japanese Interests in Sinkiang, 1918–1934* (Malmö: Esselte studium, 1977); C. Skrine and P. Nightingale, *Macartney at Kashgar: New Light on British, Chinese and Russian Activities in Sinkiang, 1890–1918* (Oxford: Oxford University Press, 1987).

11 Coates, *The China Consuls*, pp. 253–319. An exception was 'Hankow' (Wuhan) with a larger foreign community including merchants: Coates, *The China Consuls*, pp. 269–70.

12 On the imperial discourses of Chinese law, see Chen, *Chinese Law in Imperial Eyes*.

13 On law and imperial violence in British India, see, for example: E. Kolsky, *Colonial Justice in British India: White Violence and the Rule of Law* (Cambridge, Cambridge University Press, 2010).

14 On customary kidnapping practices, see: B. Miller, *Borderline Crime: Fugitive Criminals and the Challenge of the Border, 1819–1914* (Toronto: University of Toronto Press, 2016). On bribery, see: J. Saha, *Law, Disorder and the Colonial State: Corruption in Burma c. 1900* (Basingstoke: Palgrave Macmillan, 2013).

15 L. Ford, *Settler Sovereignty: Jurisdiction and Indigenous People in America and Australia, 1788–1836* (Cambridge, MA: Harvard University Press, 2010); L. Benton,

A Search for Sovereignty: Law and Geography in European Empires, 1400–1900 (Cambridge: Cambridge University Press, 2010).

16 Benton, *A Search for Sovereignty*.

17 *Ibid.*

18 *Ibid.*

19 *Ibid.*

20 L. Benton, *Law and Colonial Cultures: Legal Regimes in World History, 1400–1900* (Cambridge: Cambridge University Press, 2002); Benton, *A Search for Sovereignty*; S. E. Merry, 'Legal pluralism', *Law and Society Review*, 22:5 (1988), 869–96; Ford, *Settler Sovereignty*.

21 See, for example: D. Sutton, 'Violence and ethnicity on a Qing colonial frontier: customary and statutory law in the eighteenth-century Miao pale', *Modern Asian Studies*, 37:1 (2003), 41–80.

22 Treaty power nations included: the United States (1844), France (1844), Sweden/Norway (1847), Russia (1851), Germany (1861), Portugal (1862), Denmark (1863), the Netherlands (1863), Spain (1864), Belgium (1865), Italy (1866), Austria-Hungary (1869), Japan (1871) (revised by the Sino-Japanese Treaty of Commerce and Navigation (1896)), Peru (1874), Brazil (1881), Mexico (1899) and Switzerland (1918).

23 Cassel, *Grounds of Judgment*.

24 See especially on the movement of people: Z. Laidlaw, *Colonial Connections, 1815–1845: Patronage, the Information Revolution and Colonial Government* (Manchester: Manchester University Press, 2005); D. Lambert and A. Lester (eds), *Colonial Lives across the British Empire: Imperial Careering in the Long Nineteenth Century* (Cambridge: Cambridge University Press, 2006). On connections between treaty port China and India, see, for example, on Indian policemen: I. Jackson, 'The Raj on Nanjing Road: Sikh policemen in treaty-port China', *Modern Asian Studies*, 46:6 (2012), 1672–704.

25 On the movement of Indian policemen and law, see: T. Metcalf, *Imperial Connections: India in the Indian Ocean Arena, 1860–1920* (Berkeley: University of California Press, 2007). On Indian policemen in Shanghai, see also Jackson, 'The Raj on Nanjing Road'.

26 E. Beverley, 'Frontier as resource: law, crime and sovereignty on the margins of empire', *Comparative Studies in Society and History*, 55:2 (2013), 241–72; M. Ellenberg, 'Evading colonial authority: rebels and outlaws in the borderlands of Dutch West Borneo 1850s–1920s', *Journal of Borderlands Studies*, 29:1 (2014), 1–15; W. van Schendel and E. de Maaker, 'Asian borderlands: introducing their permeability, strategic uses and meanings', *Journal of Borderlands Studies*, 29:1 (2004), 1–9.

27 E. Kolsky, 'The colonial rule of law and legal regime of exception: frontier "fanaticism" and state violence in British India', *American Historical Review*, 120:4 (2015), 1218–46; M. Condos, 'Licence to kill: the Murderous Outrages Act and the rule of law in colonial India, 1867–1925', *Modern Asian Studies*, 50:2 (2015), 479–517.

28 See, for example: B. Guyot-Réchard, *Shadow States: India, China and the Himalayas, 1910–1962* (Cambridge: Cambridge University Press, 2016); T. Simpson, 'Bordering and frontier-making in nineteenth-century British India', *Historical Journal*, 58:2 (2005), 513–42; A. Arsan, *Interlopers of Empire: The Lebanese Diaspora in Colonial French West Africa* (New York: Oxford University Press, 2014).

29 E. Tagliacozzo, *Secret Trade, Porous Borders: Smuggling and States along a Southeast Asian Frontier, 1865–1915* (New Haven, Yale University Press, 2005).

30 P. K. Crossley (ed.), *Empire at the Margins: Culture, Ethnicity, and Frontier in Early Modern China* (Berkeley: University of California Press, 2005); D. Lary (ed.), *Chinese State at the Borders* (Vancouver: University of British Columbia Press, 2007). On transcultural phenomena on the Indian–Tibetan frontier, see: M. Viehbeck (ed.), *Transcultural Encounters in the Himalayan Borderlands: Kalimpong as a 'Contact Zone'* (Heidelberg: Heidelberg University Publishing, 2017). On Xinjiang, see: J. Millward, *Beyond the Pass: Economy, Ethnicity and Empire in Qing Central Asia, 1759–1864* (Stanford: Stanford University Press, 1998); P. Perdue, *China Marches*

West: The Qing Conquest of Central Eurasia (Cambridge, MA: Harvard University Press, 2005).

31 See, for example, the work on 'New Qing Imperial History': J. Millward, R. Dunnell, M. Elliot and P. Forêt (eds), *New Qing Imperial History: The Making of Inner Asian Empire at Qing Chengde* (New York: Routledge, 2004).

32 J. C. Scott, *The Art of Not Being Governed: An Anarchist History of Upland Southeast Asia* (New Haven: Yale University Press, 2009).

33 In Chinese, see most prominently: Y. She, *zhongguo tusi zhidu* [*China's Tusi System*] (Shanghai: shangwu shuju reprint, 1947). In English, see: H. Wiens, *China's March towards the Tropics* (Hamden: Shoe String Press, 1954).

34 P. Giersch, *Asian Borderlands: The Transformation of Qing China's Yunnan Frontier* (Cambridge, MA: Harvard University Press, 2006). On the broader region, see also: B. Davis, *Imperial Bandits: Outlaws and Rebels in the China-Vietnam Borderlands* (Seattle: University of Washington Press, 2017); M. Condos and G. Rand, 'Coercion and conciliation at the edge of empire: state-building and its limits in Waziristan, 1849–1914', *Historical Journal*, 61:3 (2018), 695–718.

35 F. Turner, 'The significance of the frontier in American history', *Report of the American Historical Association for 1893* (1894), 199–227.

36 Giersch, *Asian Borderlands*.

37 A. Lamb, *British India and Tibet 1766–1910* (London: Routledge, 1986); A. Lamb, *The McMahon Line: A Study in Relations between India, China and Tibet 1904–1914*, vol. 1 (London: Routledge, 1966).

38 J. Adelman and S. Aron, 'From borderlands to borders: empires, nation-states, and the peoples in between in North American history', *American Historical Review*, 104:3 (1999), 814–41.

39 Unlike Kashgar and Tengyue, these Tibetan treaty marts were not consular districts and were not governed by China Orders in Council. I have not included an analysis of the Tibetan trade marts in this book for this reason.

40 In 1937, Burma became a British colony independent of British India until independence. In this book I refer to the imperial political entity there before and after 1937 simply as 'Burma'. I describe the political structure there as British 'colonial authority'.

41 A. L. Stoler, *Along the Archival Grain: Epistemic Anxieties and Colonial Common Sense* (Princeton: Princeton, University Press, 2009).

42 R. Guha, *Elementary Aspects of Peasant Insurgency in Colonial India* (Delhi: Oxford University Press, 1983).

43 Giersch, *Asian Borderlands*, p. 12.

PART I

The Burma-China frontier

CHAPTER ONE

Treaty-making and treaty-breaking: transfrontier salt and opium, 1904–11

In 1885, Britain annexed 'Upper Burma' as part of British India, an area comprising the central plains and northern region of present-day Myanmar. In order to secure its sovereignty, Britain required not only the compliance of local headmen in parts of Upper Burma, but also legal recognition from Burma's tributary sovereign: China. After signing the subsequent 'Convention relating to Burma and Thibet' (1886), China formally accepted British sovereignty. A further amendment, the 'Convention between Great Britain and China, giving effect to Article III of 24th July 1886 relative to Burma and Thibet' (1894), outlined the basis of Sino-British frontier relations. The amendment that followed in 1897 added further provisions for Sino-British economic relations on the frontier and the establishment of British consulates in the neighbouring Chinese province of Yunnan. The treaties provided a framework of legal relations between China and British Burma, but were far from a clear statement of legal rights. Subsequently, Chinese and British officials wrangled over the interpretation of its provisions over the next several decades. The first legal dispute related to the right to seize illegal goods crossing the frontier and the punishment of smugglers. In particular, there were two legal questions. First, were frontier treaties the authoritative legal documents over seizure and punishment rights or were territorial laws inviolable? Second, how did the principle of extraterritoriality fit into these transfrontier legal arrangements of seizure rights on the frontier?

In this chapter, I show how British consuls stationed at Tengyue, situated in western Yunnan on the edge of the Burma-China frontier, were key actors who tried to work out these questions and tensions of law. By highlighting their role, I demonstrate that although Tengyue consuls were initially stationed for political and economic reasons, their continued presence was also due to managing frontier affairs concerning legal issues. Consuls worked with Burmese colonial officials, and petitioned the consular authorities in Beijing and colonial authorities in Rangoon on these legal concerns. They were therefore key legal actors who attempted to work out transfrontier rights between colonial and consular jurisdictions.

An important part of the consul's role was to balance three considerations: imperial policy aims, what was practical for the frontier, and how provisions of the treaties applied alongside extraterritoriality and territorial law in Burmese territory. The treaties dealt with two main issues. The first was border demarcation, which was an important objective for the Burmese government. A number of scholars have focused on the issue of borders, documenting Sino-British disputes.[1] In many parts of the frontier, there had been few, if any, demarcated borders previously. British officials felt a clear delimitation of their jurisdiction was necessary in the region of winding hills and dense jungle, but Chinese officials often disagreed over their placement.

The other important set of provisions were those regarding commerce. As well as the promotion of Sino-British trade, the treaties outlined the control of the transfrontier trade of salt and opium. These two commodities were of central importance to many frontier communities and their regulation was essential to both British Burma and China. As legal questions pertaining to these two commodities opened up the debate about how to apply law in the frontier, I examine the legal debates that took place between 1904 and 1911. The principal tension was between the frontier treaties and territorial law of Burma and China in relation to the rights of seizure and punishment of smugglers. The former was silent on the rights of punishment other than seizure, whereas the territorial law of China and Burma required the punishment of smugglers. It was also unclear what treaty right either Burma or China had as regards the seizure of whole caravans.

As Eric Tagliacozzo has argued, the movement of illicit transfrontier goods, imperial economic objectives and the creation of borders were inter-related in the China-Burma-Siam frontier.[2] In this chapter, I show how Tengyue consuls reconfigured their understanding of the relationship between the frontier treaties, territoriality and extra-territorial powers through these cases of salt and opium smuggling. Their understanding of the frontier economy and imperial policy, which dictated peace on the frontier, shaped their legal viewpoints. Transfrontier smugglers and their illicit goods were therefore at the centre of a heated legal contestation between British and Chinese authority, and forced consuls to reformulate ideas about imperial rights in the frontier.

[20]

I first detail the establishment of British authority in the region, out-lining the British colonial and consular institutions on either side of the frontier. This gives a background to the local imperial actors, the setting and their relations to the frontier. I then examine the Ma Sheng case concerning transfrontier salt and the ensuing debates that centred on the interpretation of the frontier treaty and its amendments. Finally, I examine the Ma Chun opium case that reopened the dispute over the case of Ma Sheng. I demonstrate how the Tengyue consul, Archibald Rose, petitioned for the treaties to be considered the authoritative legal document governing Sino-British relations on the frontier. Although the Burmese government rejected his petition by favouring territorial rights, I show how Rose implemented his ideas about how to resolve the tensions of law within his consular district. This reflected how he shaped his legal practices in relation to both imperial policy and the local conditions of the frontier.

Establishing British legal authority

Following the Treaty of Nanjing (1842), the Treaty of the Bogue (1843) and the Treaty of Tianjin (1858), various towns and cities were opened for British trade and residence. The bilateral treaties also provided the framework for extraterritorial jurisdiction. This allowed British officials to adjudicate in cases where a British subject was a defendant in any case or suit. Opened ports allowed Britain to station consuls to exercise these extraterritorial powers in the locality. Reflecting the importance of maritime trade, most of the places were port-cities or located on an inland river that led to the coast. The name later given to this system of rights – treaty port China – was an accurate reflection of where foreign privileges were exercised and the association with mari-time commerce.

By the late nineteenth century, this began to change with the opening of cities and towns for foreign trade in China's hinterland, alongside the establishment of inland consulates. Following the Chefoo Convention (1876), China allowed British representatives to watch trade in Chongqing, in the western Chinese province of Sichuan, and a later treaty in 1890 opened it as a treaty port.[3] The opening of other inland stations demonstrated Britain's desire to station consuls in the hinterland for economic and political purposes. British merchants and officials envisioned a terrestrial trade connection between British India and the Chinese interior, with British officials also hoping to oversee the development of a lucrative market of local products such as regional teas.[4] Several missions across the southwestern province of Yunnan and the Burma-China frontier, such as the missions of Edward

Sladen in 1868 and 1875, had already provided information on possible trade routes and ethnographical information.[5]

British interest in the Chinese interior was also geopolitical. In an era of intense imperial competition in Asia, a British presence in the Chinese hinterland aimed to limit the increasing influence of other European empires. The rivalry with France was particularly strong in southwest China.[6] Following the conclusion of the Sino-French war and the Tianjin Accord (1884), France made present-day south Vietnam a French colony, 'Cochin China'. 'Annam', 'Laos' and 'Tonkin' were French protectorates and the latter two bordered Yunnan. A French presence also extended into China with a consulate in 1889 in Longzhou, located in the southwest province of Guangxi.[7] From 1898, France also acquired the leased territory of Guangzhouwan on the south coast of Guangdong. In Yunnan, French imperial interests were focused on exploiting mineral resources and establishing transport routes. The construction of the Hanoi-Kunming railway from 1910 thereafter increased France's economic and political influence.

As Britain annexed Upper Burma, policy-makers therefore aimed to insert a provision for the opening of consulates in Yunnan into a Sino-British treaty and to clarify sovereign claims and transfrontier rights. The subsequent 1886 Treaty (Article XIII) sanctioned the stationing of several consulates. To delineate Burmese claims to lands, the convention stated the necessity of a Delimitation Commission to demarcate a boundary (Article III). The treaty emphasised Britain's desire to encourage Sino-British transfrontier trade (Articles II and IV). Later the 1894 Treaty fleshed out more precisely political and economic relations between Britain and China on the frontier. More exact border claims were outlined (Articles I–VII), and most items were sanctioned to pass across one side to the other duty free (Article VIII). However, the treaty prohibited the transportation of opium across the frontier in either direction, except small quantities for personal use (Article XI). The importation of salt into China was also prohibited, but duty-free salt could pass from China to Burma through certain trade routes (Articles VIII–XI).

The treaties appeared to clarify the trade relations between Britain and China, but the first priority of the Burmese government was to establish authority on the Burmese side of the frontier. The Commissioner in Mandalay was the central administrative nucleus of Upper Burma forming the top of the administrative hierarchy. Below this post, Burma was divided into districts with a British Deputy Commissioner and a police garrison in each. Towards the northeast, there were Deputy Commissioners in the towns of Bhamo and Myitkyina. Superintendents and Assistant Superintendents administered sub-divisional areas and

Frontier Officers oversaw government interests in the small towns nearer the frontiers. Military battalions with police posts attempted to create a sense of authority in the more remote areas. Two districts covered the Burma-China frontier. The first was the 'Kachin Hills' to the north with rolling green hills and winding valleys. The area was populated by many Kachins (some governed by headmen called *duwa*) living mostly in the hills.[8] Other inhabitants included Lashis, Marus, Lisus and Muslim Panthays. To the south were the 'Northern Shan States' and 'Southern Shan States' (and after 1922 consolidated as the 'Federated Shan States'). In reality, the Shan States were a series of different polities (populated mostly by Shans with local headmen called *sawbwa*).[9]

The political relations of these ethnic groups to lowland authority was one characterised by strong autonomy. Before 1886, many of these groups paid tribute to the former King of Burma, Thibaw Min. In return, local headmen maintained control over their population. When the British Burmese military battalions arrived shortly after 1886, the colonial aim of the 'pacification' of local groups entailed helping local political agents to establish the same sort of suzerainty over local leaders as the former Burmese monarchy had enjoyed.[10] However, establishing authority – or rather the acknowledgement of British sovereignty in Burma – was a slow, incremental and patchy process.[11] British officers and military regiments visited various areas in the valleys and hills to meet with local groups. In some places, local leaders resisted the British claim to sovereignty for some time before acknowledging British suzerainty. In other areas, local groups never accepted British authority.

Where the acknowledgement of sovereignty was achieved, the colonial government thereafter formally granted local leaders local autonomy. Headmen could exercise customary law for resolving minor civil disputes amongst their populations and arrange local political affairs. Willem van Schendel and later James C. Scott, amongst other scholars, consider this general autonomy from lowland empires as reflective of a continued history of the larger upland region of Southeast Asia of 'Zomia'.[12] Such local autonomy was necessary in the region as the environment limited the ability of British officials to exercise authority. The topography included mountains, winding hills and valleys, stretches of jungle and lowland plains. Frontier Officers did not have the knowledge, language skills or finances to administer the regions directly. Malaria in the hilly regions also prevented many non-inhabitants – such as army recruits and officers of both Burma and China – from being stationed in the region in certain seasons or for long periods.[13] These factors all contributed to a tenuous Burmese sovereignty over parts of the region, a legal landscape that would soon become familiar to a British consul from the China side of the frontier.

Consuls and consulates

As provided in the treaties, from the turn of the century, two consulates and a consulate-general opened in Yunnan.[14] The consulate-general in Kunming, established in 1902, oversaw British interests in the more prosperous central and eastern parts of the province. It supported the Simao and Tengyue consuls by taking up more serious frontier issues that affected Sino-British relations with the provincial Yunnan authorities in Kunming.

A consul in Tengyue, western Yunnan, was tasked with overseeing British interests across the Burma-China frontier. The consulate opened in 1899 in the town (which today is named 'Tengchong') at the edge of the Yunnan Plateau.[15] The town was situated close to the frontier and the Qing saw Tengyue as a frontier post inhabited mostly by 'civilised' Han people.[16] The British marked a consular district around Tengyue incorporating the west of the province, which included a series of valleys in the Burma-China frontier. One of the immediate priorities of the Burmese government was to reinforce and draw boundaries to assert British sovereignty with the help of the Tengyue consuls. The consuls also provided information on the local politics of the valley and hill populations, producing intelligence reports for consular authorities in Beijing and the colonial government in Rangoon. Other reports included travel accounts, providing ethnographic information and reviews of trade development and trade routes.[17] The latter stated the nature of the transfrontier trade, which consisted of imported goods (principally Burmese cotton from the Shan States) heading to the larger regional town of Dali and beyond, with tea and metals exported to Burma.[18] This trade appealed to British officials, who hoped to increase commercial links with the Burmese town of Bhamo and its resident Deputy Commissioner stationed seven days' travel from Tengyue.

Despite the hopes for a lively transfrontier trade, foreign visitors and consuls voiced their disappointment on arrival at Tengyue. In 1900, consul Jamieson found to his great displeasure that the local *pu'er* tea, which he hoped British merchants could develop a market for, was 'not suited to foreign palates'.[19] In 1902, the Australian traveller George Morrison was surprised by the lack of industry and commerce in Tengyue. He described the settlement scathingly as 'more a park than a town', consisting largely of 'waste land or gardens'.[20] Travelling to and from Tengyue was time-consuming and sometimes hazardous. The Burma trade routes to the west were mostly steep pony tracks

[24]

and the routes east towards the provincial capital Kunming featured a series of ascents reaching over 2,000 metres. Typically, a caravan travelling from Dali, a city 386 km to the north of Tengyue, to the provincial capital took thirteen days.[21] The British consular official and traveller, Edward Colborne Baber described the hardship of the region with reference to a traditional Chinese proverb: when travelling, one had to 'eat the bitterness of Yunnan' (*chi Yunnan ku*).[22] Consuls quickly realised that prospects for transfrontier trade would be too limited for British interests. Hill tracks could only service a small-scale transit of goods. The rainy season from June to September also rendered some of the existing tracks unserviceable. In 1908, consul Archibald Rose spoke of the isolation of the consulate. He reported that 'the city [of Tengyue] enjoys all the fiscal and commercial privileges of a Treaty Port, [but], there is no navigable water within nine days' journey and the trade of the district is dependent entirely on four mule roads, all of them leading up from Burma across difficult mountainous territory'.[23] Later consuls described Tengyue as a 'treaty mart' rather than a treaty port, emphasising its distance from maritime connections.[24] By 1910, British prospects in Yunnan appeared limited and the fate of the proposed Mandalay to Yunnan railway reflected this overall disappointment. Despite the initial fanfare, surveyors and policy-makers eventually deemed a railway unviable and the tracks were never constructed.[25]

Notwithstanding the disappointment of economic prospects, the stationing of consuls remained important for British interests in the region. Their duty of informing the consular authorities of Chinese activities and designs over the frontier was apparent, and the consuls replaced the Advisor on Chinese Affairs in Burma from 1904. Consuls carried out this role largely without direct support. The most senior British representative in China who provided advice on British policy in China – the Ambassador at Beijing – was located near the northeast coast, with correspondence taking many weeks or sometimes months to arrive. A Chief Judge of Her Majesty's Supreme Court for China provided legal advice and acted as a higher and appellate court judge in Shanghai, but was likewise located on the east coast of China. Tengyue consuls therefore assumed much individual responsibility in their capacity as British representatives in their district. Untrained in law and without a speedy means of communication to their administrative superiors, consular reports over the decades demonstrated that they relied on their local knowledge when they reacted to legal issues and defended British interests.[26] This knowledge included their understanding of the environment and local people, as well as their relationship with Chinese officials.

Consuls also spent much of their time on frontier issues because there were few British subjects and British trade interests elsewhere in western Yunnan. Compared to some of the eastern treaty ports with hundreds or thousands of foreign residents and sojourners, the registered British population living in western Yunnan was astonishingly small. When the American traveller William Geil passed through the Tengyue shortly after its opening, he noted that it did not even have a small community of intrepid foreign missionaries.[27] This made Tengyue an uncomfortable place for 'unripe' travellers, as they relied on Chinese for company and housing.[28] In fact, the consulate itself during this time – a 'native two-story building with an enclosure' – appeared to house only the consul, an Indian doctor, a Chinese man (presumably a consular writer), a goat, a pony and two dogs.[29] A Commissioner of Customs also resided at the Imperial Chinese Customs House in Tengyue from 1902, although one of the first to serve in this post was removed from his position shortly after his appointment due to persistent 'intoxication'.[30]

A decade after the opening of the consulate, the numbers of foreign subjects remained few. The estimated population in Tengyue was 10,000 people, of which just seven were foreign subjects.[31] Few British merchants ever made their way to the region. In the sporadic census reports, there are scarce reference to traders. For example, at the end of 1917, there was only one merchant in the district working as a sales agent of the British-American Tobacco Company in Dali.[32] Without economic incentives, most of the small number of British subjects later drawn to the region came to preach. A number of these missionaries toured temporarily in the north of the province and some in the frontier. Alongside proselytisers, a small number of geological surveyors, as well as expeditionary men and scientists – such as the botanist George Forrest – travelled to the region.[33]

Before arriving in post, Tengyue consuls had some experience of working in China which would be necessary for them working as a British representative in its territory. Consuls were first trained as part of the China Service to become proficient in reading, writing and speaking Chinese. Although many local inhabitants in the frontier could not speak Chinese, others could speak a little, with many of the headmen having a more proficient ability. Chinese language skills were also essential for conversing with local people in other areas of the consular district away from the frontier and especially for communicating with local Chinese officials. Consuls also learned how to behave with the expected custom and decorum necessary for engaging with the local Chinese authorities. They became familiar with the formal and informal operation of the Chinese administrative system, helped by their experience in various consular roles in China prior to their Tengyue posting. For example, the first resident consul, George John L'Establere Litton, served as a cadet in the Straits Settlements in 1891 and entered the China Consular Service as a student interpreter in Beijing in 1895. Afterwards he became acting consul in the inland station of Chongqing in 1898–9. He then became involved in the southwest frontier through his role in the Burma-China frontier Delimitation Commission in 1899–1900 and served as acting consul at Simao in 1900. He served as a Tengyue consular officer in 1901–2, for Kunming during 1902–3 and again for Tengyue during 1904–6. Litton therefore had a number of years of experience of the southwest. The next Tengyue consul who served for more than a brief period was Archibald Rose (1909–11). Like all those entering the China Consular Service, he started his career as a student interpreter at the British Legation in Beijing in 1897. Like Litton, he was appointed consul at Chongqing, but also served as a consular representative at stations on the east coast (Yantai, Ningbo and Hangzhou), before arriving at Tengyue in 1908. He had a curiosity for the unknown, travelling extensively around parts of China, Mongolia and Central Asia both before and after his Tengyue appointment. Both Litton and Rose therefore had Chinese language skills, an understanding of Chinese culture and experience of representing British subjects. This made them suitable mediators between Burmese and Chinese officials, and soon to be key actors attempting to resolve 'one of the burning problems of the frontier': the issue of transfrontier salt smuggling.[34]

Frontier policy and salt smuggling

Although Tengyue consuls were without direct administrative supervision, they were guided by the general parameters of British consular imperial policy. In 1905, Ernst Satow, the Ambassador at Beijing, urged that friendly relations with China were paramount for British imperial aims in the frontier.[35] As many parts of the region remained without fixed borders, good relations with local Chinese officials would help with the negotiations over the placement of border pillars. In 1909, John Jordan reiterated his predecessor's position.[36] He also emphasised that consuls should try to help prevent social unrest amongst local populations in the frontier.[37] A peaceful frontier was necessary to help British administration and to further the border demarcation project. Consuls were therefore left to formulate their understanding of the frontier within this general framework of the imperial policy. This was soon to be put to the test with cases concerning the transfrontier trade.

The Tengyue consuls were aware of the importance of transfrontier items. Burmese, Chinese and various local ethnic groups traded products such as tea, cottons, bullocks, ponies, animal hides, sugar, potatoes, jade, metals, opium and salt. The latter was a valued commodity across the Chinese Empire. The Qing monopolised the production and commerce throughout its territory and the government employed a regionalised system of salt production and trade. Yunnan was one of these regions, with a rich source in the west of the province, although it did not rival the output of the Sichuan and coastal regions.[38] The Qing naturally had a vested economic interest in developing salt quarries in the province, but it also served political interests. Salt mining led to more Han immigrants and closer relations with local headmen. Government agencies oversaw this monopoly with private merchants and taxed salt at the site of production in Yunnan.[39] The Qing also controlled various salt wells in the frontier.[40] Much of the product was then transported to other parts of western China for sale. Alongside its income from the maritime customs and land tax, salt taxation was an important source of government revenues.[41] This was especially valued in an era when the Qing had spent much on its army and navy in costly wars in the late nineteenth century and in reparation payments following the Boxer Rebellion (1900–1).

Controlling salt production and its trade was therefore a priority for the Qing, who had long banned the import of foreign salt to protect its monopoly and revenues. Unsurprisingly, the Qing requested that the 1886 Treaty included a provision that restated the illegality of transporting salt into China from Burma. It therefore reiterated the unlawfulness of the existing lively trade, which had long been an intrinsic part of the frontier economy.[42] This was due to the cheaper and better-quality Burmese 'sea salt' (haiyan) and the demand for it on the Chinese side of the frontier. Consuls were conscious of this trade and its market, and pointed to the disjuncture between the official prohibition and the local practices of smuggling. By 1911, for example, the Kunming consul-general, Pierce O'Brien-Butler, claimed that the inferior-quality Chinese salt in Tengyue was three times as costly as Burmese sea salt.[43] This created a market for illicit salt in Yunnan.

Tengyue consuls soon became more acquainted with what they saw as the disjuncture between the frontier economy, local administration and legal provisions. The first resident consul at Tengyue, George Litton, spent time travelling around the frontier and enquired into the existence of the banned commodity in his meetings with the local sawbwa, Chinese officers and traders.[44] He concluded that Chinese frontier officials were often complicit in the illicit commerce.[45] This meant that whilst the Viceroy in Kunming condemned the illegal trade with '"tremble and obey" proclamations' and ordered periodic arrests of smugglers, frontier officials ignored the transport or sometimes helped to move the product with smugglers.[46] Litton drew greater attention to the state of affairs after accusing the head of the local Chinese Salt Preventative Regiment, a man surnamed Lin, of possessing sea salt in his quarters and allowing sea salt into China.[47] Lin admitted the salt was intended for him and his soldiers, and the Yunnan Viceroy, Li, ordered his arrest and replaced him with another official. However, Litton claimed the import of sea salt 'went on as usual' and emphasised that the tension between local practice and periodic seizures could cause social unrest as frontier inhabitants depended on illegal salt.[48] Though Viceroy Li had recently ordered the opening of more offices to supply the product through the main trade route, there remained a shortage of Chinese-produced salt. As a result, for the year ending March 1904, a staggering 1,088 tonnes of salt was registered as leaving from Myitkyina and Bhamo with intent to be sold across the border.[49] Although Litton suspected a far smaller amount actually passed through into Chinese territory, it nonetheless indicated that there was a great demand for salt on the Chinese side of the frontier that domestic production could not supply. As salt was a key commodity used in everyday life, the absence of the product threatened the primary British imperial objective of preventing social unrest in the frontier.

In January 1905, Litton wrote to Ernest Satow for guidance. Satow advised Litton to encourage the local Chinese officials to supply more government salt.[50] This would meet local demands and reduce the illicit trade. Litton should then press the Chinese authorities on the topic of making regular arrests of smugglers. Satow's advice was careful; he did not want the Tengyue consuls to challenge the provincial authorities too aggressively on their responsibility for preventing smuggling or on the issue of the complicity of local Chinese officials in the illicit trade. His instruction therefore reflected the importance he placed on maintaining amicable Sino-British relations.

Whilst Litton followed Satow's advice, he was also sceptical about whether it would help resolve the tension between Chinese imperial policy and frontier smuggling. He suspected that the provincial authorities would continue to fail to provide enough salt on its side of the frontier and that frontier officials would continue to allow salt to be smuggled into the Chinese Shan States.[51] He predicted that in the near future there would be British subjects who would protest to him on the seizure of their caravan. In such a case, he felt that Burma should claim compensation on behalf of these subjects. He put forward four reasons for this. First, as the Chinese *sawbwa* taxed the salt, the product thereby became a licit commodity and these headmen were therefore bound to protect the salt traders from robbers. Although some of the smuggling took place on the high passes and were not taxed, Litton also understood that much of it was passing through official trade routes. Second, as the Chinese government had not supplied official salt to local populations who required the product, Litton felt that Britain should protect Burmese caravans importing the product as much as possible. Third, Burmese claims of redress would therefore be legitimate because China had also failed in its 'treaty duty' that China 'keep its tribes in a peaceable condition'.[52] Finally, Litton stated that it was necessary for British officials to claim redress for a seizure of a whole caravan of a salt smuggler. This was because if they did not, Chinese officials would have carte blanche to seize the caravans of all British subjects travelling across the borders, with the justification that they were salt smugglers. In July, Charles Pennell, the Under Secretary to the Government of Burma, acknowledged Litton's proposal and noted that the Lieutenant-Governor concurred in the policy suggested by Litton.[53] In other words, even if caravans carted illicit salt, the British colonial and consular authorities would raise a claim for compensation in the event that any goods (other than salt) were seized.[54]

In the following years, the transfrontier trade not only continued, but flourished, with the value of salt gradually increasing from 1905 to 1908.[55] Consuls continued to believe (or at least maintained the narrative) that the Chinese authorities did not prevent the illicit trade or provide official supplies of salt. The trade had 'gone on its accustomed way, never admitted in theory, flourishing as a matter of fact, [with salt smugglers] paying ... squeezes [bribes] to Sawbwas and others, and satisfying everybody'.[56] This meant that periodic arrests threatened the peaceful relations in the frontier. In February 1908, Chinese officials seized an entire caravan of a British man, which consisted of sixty-two animals laden with salt.[57] The Salt Preventative Department and Tengyue officials kept the animals as a reward. Consul Herbert Ottewill was alarmed as he felt that such cases could lead to discontent amongst frontier populations, as British Shans, rather than Chinese, ran the salt caravan. As many smugglers had previously transported their illicit salt with ease across the same route, Ottewill suspected that Chinese frontier officials wanted to curry favour with the new Tengyue *daotai* (circuit intendant) who was vehemently opposed to the British presence in the region. With building tensions over salt seizures, it was therefore only a matter of time before the first major dispute over seizure rights arose.

The flashpoint occurred six months later in August 1908. A British Shan man had taken salt across the frontier and had his items seized.

On 15 August, the sub-prefect of Longling wrote to Ottewill, reporting the seizure by the Salt Preventative Department in Mangshi.[58] Ottewill responded to the sub-prefect on 27 August in Chinese, claiming that the seizure of the whole caravan was contrary to Article XI of the Burma Convention.[59] As such, he viewed the seizure as a robbery. Hugh Thornton, the Superintendent of the Northern Shan States, wrote to Ottewill to provide more evidence from the case.[60] The British Shan man, Ma Sheng, intended to sell forty loads of sea salt and brought in the same caravan four loads of cotton yarn as well as pack animals. Ma Sheng stated that Chinese men (working on behalf of the Preventative Department) robbed his caravan.[61] Thornton described the story as follows:

> On 6th August 1908, one Man Hseng [Ma Sheng] a Shan of Bam Sawn Village in Muse with 45 bullocks and 5 men, took salt and cotton goods intended for sale in China via Chefang [Zhefang] and Mong Hkeun (Mong Hsih) [Mangshi]. On the 12th August while camped near a Shan village named Hue Yok, they were attacked by 11 Chinese dacoits, who fired on the Shans and drove away all 45 animals. Report was made to Mong Hkawn Sawbwa of this attack but he appears to have done nothing.[62]

Thornton stressed that as Ma Sheng paid tolls on his salt, it was unjust that the Chinese thereafter seized his caravan.[63] On 9 November, the sub-prefect replied to Ottewill, noting that it was his treaty right to confiscate all of the items.[64] Furthermore, owing to the illegal salt trade, Chinese government sales in the district had suffered an annual fall of 105,000 *taels*. The sub-prefect therefore claimed that seizing the salt and goods would pay towards this deficit.[65]

Acting consul Henry Sly, Thornton and the Tengyue *daotai* Liu Jun held a joint enquiry at Namhkam during January 1909.[66] The case did not deal with the issue of salt seizure, but with the seizure of the cotton and animals. Thornton testified that Ma Sheng had revealed that the Mangshi *sawbwa* had refused to pay "squeeze" (bribes) to emissaries of the Salt Preventative Department stationed in Mengpan, another Shan State. Thus, the caravan – including the salt – was taxed and allowed to pass into Chinese territory by the *sawbwa* before being seized and confiscated by the Salt Preventative Department. Thornton claimed that China should pay compensation to Ma Sheng for the confiscation of his cotton yarn and the animals. Liu nevertheless rejected these claims.[67]

The deadlock frustrated Sly, as he believed that leaving the case unresolved would result in 'a general disturbance of frontier trade and of the frontier states'.[68] He referred the *daotai* to the wording of Article XI of the 1894 Treaty, stating that the provision only allowed for the confiscation of the prohibited goods:

Smuggling or the carrying of merchandize through Chinese territory by other routes than those sanctioned by the present Convention shall, if the Chinese authorities think fit, be punished by the confiscation of the merchandize concerned.[69]

In reply, Liu countered that in the Chinese version of the treaty, the provision conveyed the meaning of China's right to seize all goods. This was because of the use of the character 'suo', as a part of the word 'suoyou' meaning 'all' (i.e. all goods).[70] Looking to the Chinese version in response, Sly interpreted the same character, 'suo', to mean the phrase 'souyou zhihuo', which meant the 'above mentioned' or 'the concerned' goods.[71] Further, the use of 'gai' in the phrase 'gaihuo' conferred the meaning of the seizure of only 'specified' goods (i.e. salt).[72] Like Litton before him, Sly pointed to what he saw as China's treaty obligation for policing the frontier. He believed that Article VII of the 1894 Treaty was significant, which stated that frontier posts were 'necessary for preserving peace and good order in the frontier districts', which he felt in turn 'imposes upon China the responsibility for the maintenance within its territories of good order and for the tranquillity of the tribes inhabiting them'.[73] In other words, he claimed that China had broken the terms of the treaty.

Although the stalemate continued, Archibald Rose, now acting consul, and Liu agreed that evidence of the numbers of animals and quantity of yarn seized should be collected. Thereafter, Liu would refer to his superiors in Kunming for instruction.[74] Rose was happy with this recourse as he felt that the provincial authorities would not want to damage Sino-British relations. This would mean that an amicable outcome was more likely. However, as the months passed, it became clear that there was no forthcoming answer and the issue remained unresolved.

The Ma Sheng salt case had therefore opened up the debate over legal rights within the provisions of the 1886 and 1894 Treaties. For the British officials, the situation was delicate. On the one hand, coinciding with a change of British imperial policy in China, a more conciliatory nature of claiming legal rights was preferred. However, the Tengyue consuls pointed to the tension between the frontier economy and Chinese policy on the transfrontier salt traffic. Consuls – Litton, Ottewill and Sly – all claimed that China had violated its treaty obligations. As China could not produce enough salt, frontier communities relied on the illicit transfrontier trade for their supply. By seizing illicit salt periodically, consuls believed China was failing to maintain peace in the frontier, as local populations might riot without an adequate supply. In addition, local headmen loyal to the Chinese were liable for the protection of caravans if they also taxed the smugglers. The Ma Sheng case remained unsolved for the time being, but the question of British legal rights, Chinese treaty violation and the liability of local headmen loyal to China arose once more in a case concerning opium the following year. This time, it would include the question of how territorial rights and extraterritoriality fitted into the framework of transfrontier governance over the opium and salt trades.

Opium

Alongside salt, opium was a key transfrontier trade commodity in China. Despite its illicit status, the drug across China had a wide and popular appeal as a medicinal aid and as a relaxant used for leisurely purposes. During the nineteenth century, the influx of opium reached a new zenith when foreign merchants trafficked the drug into China. When the Chinese Imperial Commissioner Lin Zexu ordered the seizure of British opium on the south China coast in 1839, it served as one of the key flashpoints leading to the 'Opium War' (1839–42). This led to the Sino-foreign treaties and China conceding extraterritorial rights to foreign treaty power nations; opium and its seizure was of no small importance in the history of modern China.

Aside from its maritime connections, the imported opium trade was important to local economies in the interior of China and the western frontiers of the Chinese Empire.[75] As David Bello explores, during the eighteenth and nineteenth centuries, the Qing had limited success in prohibiting the trafficking and sale of opium across the Burma-China frontier and within Yunnan.[76] Opium was cultivated across the province, but many fields were out of reach for Qing officials, especially those located in the frontier. This included Kokang, a Chinese Shan State to the east of the Salween River and the autonomous Wa region, where *yuntu* ('Yunnan mud', i.e. opium) was grown and trafficked into China.[77] Partly because of the inaccessible environment in the higher regions, the Qing often focused prohibition efforts on the trade away from the frontier, leaving transfrontier commerce to thrive. Although the Qing repealed prohibitions during the later nineteenth century as a result of foreign pressure, by the first decade of the twentieth century, the Qing again ordered the suppression of opium. Market forces increased its import demand as eradication campaigns in neighbouring provinces such as Sichuan – a formerly leading site of production in China – had proved quite successful.[78] Provincial proclamations from Kunming in July 1908 outlined a renewed campaign for the eradication of opium cultivation.[79] Despite this, it appeared that opium – both grown and distributed in the frontier and in the province as a whole – remained a key part of the local and regional economy.

The opium trade was also a key part of the British Empire in Asia.[80] In Burma, Indian opium was imported regularly, but there was also home-grown cultivation. The British colonial authorities partly legalised opium. The Opium Act (1878) and its amendment (1891, Article XII) prohibited the use of opium except for medical purposes. Licenced shops sold Indian opium, but those in receipt could not sell it. However, this provision did not include the Shan States and other local areas in Upper Burma during this period, where the colonial government permitted the cultivation of the poppy and a cultivator could sell their produce to any non-Burmese subject.[81] As Ashley Wright explores, this partial legalisation was due to both racial discourses on labour production and practical concerns.[82] The Burmese government discouraged ethnic Burmese from consuming the drug in the belief that it made them less productive. Conversely, the government tended to facilitate opium consumption of other ethnic minorities in Burma because it was thought to make these ethnic groups (who also often had manual labour jobs) work harder.[83] The government also felt that supressing the drug entirely was not achievable in certain regions, such as the Shan States, which were harder to police.[84] By the first decade of the twentieth century, British officers noted the extensive cultivation of opium on the high hills, with the seed sown in late October and its cultivation ready in March.[85]

Like other parts of the British Empire, this legalisation of opium came under increasing scrutiny. Organisations such as the Society for the Suppression of the Opium Trade were critical of the negative moral and health implications accompanying the consumption of opium. To address these public concerns, the Royal Opium Commission of 1895 prepared a long report on the use and trade of the drug. Amongst other conclusions, it downplayed the immorality of the opium trade and its detrimental physical and mental effects on individuals, with the Commission on Burma emphasising the productivity effect of opium on Indian, Chinese and other minority groups in Burma.[86] Thereafter, although the Burmese government was more cautious about supporting home-grown opium and the imports into Burma, it continued to sanction the production process in the frontier. However, British imperial officials adopted a more cautious position on the sale of opium in China due to increasing international criticism and its decreasing trade.[87] In due course, in the 1908 Anglo-Chinese Ten Year Opium Suppression Agreement, Britain promised to reduce Indian exports of opium to China.

Burmese officials allowed a certain amount of Yunnan opium into Burma. As early as 1869, it was believed that the quality of opium in Yunnan was not too inferior in comparison to imported Bengal opium.[88]

The colonial government welcomed the import of small quantities of Yunnan opium for licensed individuals and for its sale in licensed Burmese shops.[89] Chinese officials seemingly allowed the drug to pass through the frontier if taxes were paid.[90] By 1902, Yunnan opium could be found in shops in the Bhamo, Myitkyina and Ruby Mines Districts.[91] It was cheaper than Indian opium and Burmese officials assumed that the local populations in the frontier were more accustomed to this drug. The Burmese colonial government also felt that banning Yunnan opium would only serve to encourage more smuggling. Although there were no specific statistics for consumption in the frontier, between 1895 and 1914, the rates of opium consumption within Burma as a whole increased.[92]

It therefore came as no surprise that the Burmese frontier officials and Tengyue consuls argued that – like salt – opium was a key part of transfrontier trade and life. George Litton argued that trade should be encouraged and lamented that poor trade routes for opium and other goods were the 'principal obstacle to the development of our trade in West Yunnan'.[93] Across the frontier, some paths could not be used in rainy seasons and the constant use of poorly built bridges resulted in their frequent collapse. As one traveller noted, the Chinese proverb 'good for ten years and bad for ten thousand' was an idiom that resonated with foreign observers.[94] During 1903–6, the Tengyue consuls and the Burmese Frontier Officers pressed Ernest Satow to enter into negotiations with the Qing on the topic of some form of regularisation of the trade. Both the India Office and Foreign Office supported the policy as a way to increasing regional commerce.[95] However, Satow's political concerns overshadowed their economic enthusiasm. Since the Boxer Rebellion and subsequent anti-foreign riots in various treaty ports in China, Satow advocated the implementation of a cautious China policy. He was unequivocal, stating that British consular and colonial officers should refrain from pressurising the Yunnan authorities on the idea of permitting the passage of Yunnan opium in bond through Burma.[96]

Although the Burmese government welcomed small amounts of opium from China that they could tax and license, smuggled opium continued to flow across the frontier. Successive consuls invoked the trope of Chinese complicity in their arguments for legalisation, and certainly, as Magnus Fiskesjö notes, some Chinese frontier officials directly taxed opium grown in the Shan States.[97] Opium also appeared to have a similar financial appeal to local cultivators as salt. Ottewill claimed that the crop earned harvesters up to forty to fifty *taels* per acre compared to ten to twenty *taels* for all other types of produce.[98] He further claimed (perhaps with some exaggeration) that there was a clear demand for the crop on the Chinese side of the frontier, with up to 90 per cent of population in Yunnan regularly smoking opium.[99] Part of this illegal cultivation and trade was due to the absence of police, which facilitated crime across the frontier.[100] Stationing Chinese police was no easy task, as many Chinese died in the tropical conditions of the frontier without medical and sanitary precautions.[101] Some autonomous groups in the frontier, such as the Wa, were also known for growing and trading opium, and used Shan and Chinese men as transfrontier merchants to sell their product.[102]

At the same time, the Qing continued in the campaign to limit the production of opium. International attention also turned towards the suppression campaign, and in February 1909, the first international conference to discuss the problem of the narcotic was held in Shanghai.[103] The Qing was adamant about the need to eradicate opium production and consumption, but the Qing's success remained uncertain at the time. The British explorer and official Alexander Hosie claimed that he had seen evidence of the success of the Qing's campaign, but he still found poppy fields ready for cultivation on the high roads of Yunnan.[104] As the Burmese government welcomed small amounts of opium crossing into Burma, the Deputy Commissioners issued permits to their subjects to purchase opium in China and convey it across the frontier. One consular report noted that 'the value of opium thus imported during 1908 was Rupees 1,51,340, with a total value of Rupees 7,28,407 for the past three years'.[105] Despite Qing efforts, the transfrontier opium trade was an important one for both the local and, most likely, regional economy.

The Burmese authorities therefore regulated a limited transfrontier opium trade from Yunnan into Burma through licences and taxation, but strove to eliminate illegal trafficking. Inevitably, when the Burmese police seized an illegal Chinese caravan in Burmese territory in 1909, it once more opened up the debate on the legal rights that surrounded the Ma Sheng salt case. A low-ranking Chinese military official, Ma Chun, asked the Tengyue *daotai* Liu Yuanpi to forward his petition to consul Rose. His petition ran as follows:

> In the 12th moon of last year (January 1909) Kuei Yü-Ching, a native of Sung-ming Chou in the Prefecture of Yunnanfu [Kunming], was going to Burma on business and, as he had not yet completely broken himself of the opium habit, he secretly carried with him about 400 ounces of the drug for his own consumption. At the same period I was thinking of going to Burma myself, so we arranged to travel in company, Kuei providing 2 of his animals for my use, one of which I rode, carrying my baggage on the other. Unknown to me however, Kuei packed his stock of opium on the animal which he had allotted to me. On the 13th of the moon we

[36]

started from Tengyue and on the 6th of the last moon (about January 21st) we were on the Peng-chi-tsai Road in Burma, when we were met by a Kachin policeman, who seized Kuei's opium and made us go to the Office of the Burma Official at Man-mu (Old Bhamo). I stated my case, explaining that the pony belonged to Kuei and that the opium had been brought by him. The Officer however would not believe my story and said that in smuggling opium I had offended against Treaty provisions, and the opium and 'other things' were accordingly confiscated, whilst in addition I was imprisoned for three months, and fined Rupees 100 ... Although I am but a small military official I am nevertheless aware that I come under the law in this matter and, as I was reckless enough to omit examining the pack of my horse which was certainly laden with opium, I was not in a position to repudiate the charge brought against me ... I now present my humble petition, begging that you will lay my case before the Consul and will request him to look into the matter and have the fine refunded and the money and other things returned.[106]

Several letters passed between Liu Yuanpi, the Burmese Frontier Officers and acting Tengyue consul Henry Sly.[107] Liu stated that the opium had been rightfully seized, but that the punishment was 'in excess of the Treaty provisions'.[108] Moreover, he felt that:

[The] justice of the case demands not only that the fine, the money and the missing property be returned to my petitioner but that, in view of the fact that he is an officer of the empire and has lost considerably in the prestige by his confinement, he should be fittingly compensated for this wrongful imprisonment.[109]

Despite these appeals for the return of the possessions to Ma Chun and the loss of face, the Burmese authorities did not act upon the request. Instead, Rose, now consul, emphasised the parallels to the Ma Sheng salt case, where the Chinese authorities had both allowed the taxation of the illicit product before seizing it and all the other items in the caravan.[110]

Sensing a stalemate once more, on 22 June, Rose turned to the Ambassador at Beijing, John Jordan. He suggested reopening diplomatic negotiations on the regularisation of the salt trade (i.e. that Burma make an annual purchase of salt and opium from China) and outlined the existing legal complications.[111] The issue was that Article XI of the 1894 Treaty made the movement of salt and opium across the frontier illicit and liable to confiscation. However, no provision existed which stated the infliction of any further punishment on the offender or for the seizure of the whole caravan of a smuggler. Both Burmese and Chinese officials had confiscated a whole caravan of goods. In doing so, the Burmese officials stated that the application of the Opium Act (1878) applied to Burmese territory. The Chinese officials (conscious of the principle of British extraterritoriality in Chinese territory) did not claim they had a right to apply territorial laws, but that the treaties conferred the right for them to confiscate all the goods of a British smuggler in China. Rose urged for 'the advisability of a uniform procedure on both sides of the frontier', which would bring 'the advantages of a mutual adherence to the terms of the Burma Convention, which is essentially a frontier Treaty and therefore the most suitable machinery for dealing with cases arising out of purely frontier questions'.[112] In other words, Rose advocated for the suspension of territorial law and extraterritorial jurisdiction. Instead, the treaty provisions should apply which granted only the seizure of illicit goods.

In a demi-official letter to Jordan on the same day, Rose revealed that the Lieutenant-Governor of Burma could not assent to withdrawing the exercise of the Opium Act over Chinese smugglers in Burma.[113] However, for the time being, the Lieutenant-Governor had deferred the question to the Government of India.[114] Unrestrained by formal style, Rose continued in his letter to Jordan, describing the Burma Convention (1894) as an 'amazing document'.[115] He clearly valued the provisions in the treaty, but still lamented that there was no provision for a limited government-sanctioned trade between China and Burma. As a result, he felt that 'until we are blessed with some new Treaty it seems better to stand by its provisions'.[116] He was resolute in his belief to stand by the terms of the treaties alone, despite the reservations of the Burmese government.

Next, Rose wrote to Walter Francis Rice, Chief Secretary to the Government of Burma.[117] He reminded him that the salt and opium cases were of no small importance, with the annual value of these two items of frontier traffic calculated at a sum of £20,000.[118] Furthermore, if the Burmese government insisted on applying territorial law and China reciprocated on its side of the frontier, the principle of British extraterritoriality added a further complication. If smugglers were to be punished for smuggling, British suspects in China would be handed over to him, but there would be no way to claim compensation for the seized goods in the consular court. All this circled back to a better solution: that both empires suspend territorial law over smugglers and enforce the 1894 Treaty, which only called for the seizure of the illicit goods on the frontier.[119] Not only would it work in the best interests of both Burma and China, but it would also be of value for 'impressing on the Chinese provincial and district officials the necessity of the invincibility of Treaties with Foreign Powers'.[120] For Rose, the treaties were the authoritative documents on transfrontier legal rights. They supported British imperial policy on the frontier that required the preservation of peace and supported the continuing state of affairs regarding the transfrontier economy.

At this point, the Kunming consul-general E. C. Wilton waded into the debate against Rose, stating that it was 'quite clear that the Burma Government and the Yunnan authorities have the right to frame rules for the punishment of opium and salt smugglers within their respective territories'.[121] He added that British subjects were not bound by Chinese laws in China and therefore China could only apply the provisions of the treaty in cases involving British smugglers.[122] In other words, Rose's argument that both Burma and China use the treaties alone was a moot point in Chinese territory, as China could not exercise its territorial authority over British subjects. Although Rose recognised this legal position, he also knew that the crux of the problem was not simply the tension between territorial law, extraterritorial privilege and treaty provision, but that the Chinese officials still understood their treaty right as seizing a whole caravan. Taking into consideration frontier policy, Rose considered that it would be 'impolitic' to petition the Chinese authorities should they confiscate a British smuggler's goods.[123] Bilateral agreements also stated the right of China to adopt whatever measures to prevent their revenue suffering from fraud or smuggling. Salt, for example, was explicitly declared to be contraband according to the rules of trade supplementary to Article III of the Treaty of Tianjin, as was the movement of 'clandestine trade' by Articles XLVII and XLVIII.[124] Rose felt this might give China a legal claim to seize not only the salt but also the conveying vessel. For the frontier, such vessels were pack-animals. Rose clearly saw the importance and implications of bilateral treaties as a guiding framework of legal rights for both Britain and China in the region.

Addressing the difficulties of applying extraterritorial jurisdiction, Rose pinpointed three alternative solutions.[125] In the first, the smuggler would be at liberty to appeal to the local *daotai* and consul sitting together. The judgment would lie in the hands of the *daotai*, requiring only the presence of the consul to ensure that all possible evidence had been presented. In the second alternative, after seizing contraband, the Chinese authorities could arrest the offender and hand him over to the consul for trial and punishment. In the consular court, the suspect would be dealt with under the provisions of the Order in Council (1904) (Section 70, II). The maximum penalty provided under this provision for intentional smuggling was imprisonment with hard labour for six months and a fine of £100. However, there could not be any redress in this court for the confiscation of the contraband. These two alternatives would reduce the flourishing traffic and as there was no consular constable or jail, offenders would be held in a Chinese cell while awaiting transfer to either Rangoon or Shanghai. In the third alternative, British subjects would only be subject to the treaty, with the provisions applied either by Rose or a Chinese representative. He pointed to Article XVIII of the 1894 Treaty, in which it stated that the treaty was 'consented to with a view of adapting them to local conditions and the peculiar necessities of the Burma-China overland trade'.[126] In effect, Rose conceded that both empires could exercise territorial law, but found a way to insert the authority of the treaties through the application of his extraterritorial jurisdiction. He advocated this application to the two cases, stating that the 'test cases are of unusual importance and that their satisfactory settlement would prove a distinct land-mark in our border policy'.[127]

By 25 September 1909, John Jordan approved Rose's suggestion.[128] In the meantime, Rose and Liu each appealed for compensation to be paid to Ma Sheng and Ma Chun for the loss of their possessions.[129] Jordan in principle agreed with the regularisation of both trades, but underlined the persistent attitude of the Chinese authorities against such measures. This meant it was unlikely that there would be a revision of the frontier treaties.[130] By November 1909, the Government of Burma sent a private copy of a long printed dispatch to Tengyue regarding a fixed policy.[131] After consulting the Government of India and meeting with their approval, the Lieutenant-Governor Herbert White stated that Burma and China were free to invoke territorial laws for the punishment of smugglers.[132] In Chinese territory, British subjects were under the jurisdiction of the consul, as China had relinquished its rights over British subjects through the Sino-British treaties. White further stated that Burma's claim for compensation on account of Ma Sheng's caravan should be abandoned. In addition, the claim of the Chinese authorities to recover compensation on account of the lawful penalties which Ma suffered under the Opium Act (1878) should be rejected. Rice, the Under Secretary for Burma, also stated that any legalisation of the salt trade required Chinese acquiescence for an amendment to the frontier treaty and it was clear that China would not enter into such negotiations. It was a disappointment to Rose, but he had expected this outcome. His proposal to make the frontier treaties the authoritative legal documents was not a solution that the government officials in Burma or India wanted.

Thereafter, Rose claimed that the stance of China was to increase its penalties against smugglers, including the punishment of summary execution for smugglers and those possessing illicit salt.[133] A case that followed shortly afterwards confirmed the new Chinese policy. On 17 September 1910, a body of Kachin porters – 'Shang Lao-wu and his eight associates' – were stopped when passing a Chinese frontier post near Burmese Sadon.[134] They were carrying over 150 kg of salt to a market to exchange for rice when military police arrested and sent them to the *yamen* (courthouse) of the Tengyue sub-prefect. The sub-prefect, Wen

Liangyi, tried the group, found them guilty of smuggling and sentenced them to death. It so happened that Rose had recently sent a supply of quinine and other medicines to the soldiers of the district where the arrest occurred. One of the officers, in acknowledging the gift, reported the incident to him. Rose could not ignore his message, which he quoted as follows from the soldier: ' "I have recently taken certain salt smugglers, much against my wish, but is more than my post is worth to let them pass; the poor fellows will surely lose their heads, but they may be British subjects." '[135] Having already heard of the judgment, Rose made private enquiries and the Tengyue *daotai* immediately hurried to see Rose with the men. Finding that two of them spoke broken Chinese, Rose conducted a brief enquiry and found they were 'undoubtedly Burma subjects from the district of Sadon'.[136] The men admitted they had crossed with salt, but that they had done so openly in daylight and by the main road. As salt was brought frequently across the frontier, they had no knowledge that they had broken the law. On learning that the men were British subjects, Wen handed the men over to Rose.[137]

The subsequent actions of Rose bore out his ideas about the role of the treaties. He did not exercise extraterritorial law, but punished the group by the treaty stipulations – seizure of their salt – alone. Later, the Ambassador added his endorsement of Rose's actions.[138] The incident demonstrated that in the end, Rose enforced his proposal in practice. He referred to the 1886 Treaty as his guidance rather than the Orders in Council governing consular jurisdiction. Rose was satisfied with the outcome, noting that it was 'the first instance of which I can trace any record in which an actual settlement has been affected in such a case'.[139] It appeared to be a defining moment. In relation to opium, the Qing campaign against the cultivation of the drug had pushed up prices of the crop to such a degree in Yunnan that the opium market in the province reduced the lure of transfrontier trade.[140] In turn, the Burmese government also introduced the Opium Rules (1910), which provided further restrictions to the movement of opium from the Shan States into Burma.

It appeared as though there was a temporary solution to the questions of opium and salt smuggling, but on the frontier, consular officials reported instances of social disruption from the salt seizures. A year later, the Tengyue intelligence report noted that a disturbance had taken place in 'Hsiao Lungchuan' (Xiao Longzhuan) as a consequence of the Chinese authorities preventing the import and sale of foreign salt.[141] Local Kachins attacked and killed Chinese soldiers attempting to seize their salt, then blockaded their villages, with two to three thousand repelling Chinese forces; the transfrontier salt trade was still of great importance to local communities.

The question of a regularised trade therefore reared its head once more between the various colonial and consular officials. The Under Secretary of State for India left the question to the Foreign Office and consular authorities in Beijing.[142] The Foreign Office felt that the British representative in Beijing, William Max-Müller, was the most suitable candidate for starting diplomatic negotiations.[143] However, Max-Müller was certain that the Chinese authorities in Beijing would not listen to such proposals.[144] Instead, he suggested that the Tengyue consul should attempt to obtain an agreement with local officials.[145] In turn, Rose appeared to make some headway with a newly appointed Salt Commissioner in Tengyue on the proposal of Burma buying annual supplies of salt and opium. However, when the Kunming consul-general, Pierce O'Brien-Butler, attempted to further discussions in the provincial capital with the Salt Administration, he noted that they regarded his proposal 'most unfavourably and were strongly opposed to any change'.[146] Viceroy Li gave an unequivocal rejection to the proposal. Li stated that the Minister of the Salt Office in Beijing had petitioned the throne on the issue and an imperial decree outlined the Qing's opposition. The decree stated that salt was a government monopoly in China and that its import and export were forbidden by treaty, meaning that 'hence-forth no matter what nation proposes any modification in favour of any kind of salt, Treaty stipulations are to be strictly adhered to, and any compromise is forbidden'.[147] China, he claimed, was abiding by treaty regulations, whereas Britain was seeking to break the terms of the treaties. The Chinese Ministry of Foreign Affairs – the *waijaobu* – then instructed the Provincial Yunnan authorities to stop any such local negotiations. It appeared to be the end of the discussion of the salt and opium trade.

Conclusion

The decree sounded the death knell for the proposal of partly legalizing the salt and opium trade. In July 1911, the Foreign Office and Ambassador eventually agreed 'to allow this question to drop'.[148] It brought to an end an era of intense discussion on the legal, economic and political issues raised by the salt and opium smuggling cases. The Sino-British treaties were key legal documents outlining the regulation of the transfrontier salt and opium trade, but their provisions left questions as to the rights of seizure and the punishment of smugglers by territorial law. Cases demonstrated how British officials – especially the Tengyue consuls – worked through these legal tensions. These tensions were framed within the understanding of the local economy, China's treaty duties and British imperial policy for the frontier.

The question of legal rights was also not simply one that displayed the conflicts between British and Chinese officials; it also revealed the differing views of the Tengyue consuls and other British authorities. Although the salt and opium cases demonstrated that Tengyue consuls were important negotiators on behalf of the Burmese authorities, as the correspondence of Archibald Rose showed, consular views did not align with the Burma Lieutenant-Governor, the India Office or the Kunming consul-general. In the end there was a tenuous equilibrium worked out between territorial law and treaty rights. Territorial law remained authoritative in the Burmese side of the frontier, but in the end, Rose appeared to mete out his version of justice in his consular district based on his views on the authority of the frontier treaty.

Tengyue consuls were key to this debate among different British authorities in London, China, Burma and India. As officials located close to the frontier, they had a greater understanding of local activities and the local economy, and had closer relations with local Chinese officials. They balanced imperial policy, which emphasised the need to maintain a peaceful frontier, with the needs of the local economy and rights of British subjects. In turn, these experiences of the salt and opium cases would continue to shape the Tengyue consular officers' ideas of transfrontier legal rights. In the next era, this would involve jurisdictional questions relating to transfrontier migrants and fugitives.

Notes

1   See, for example: T. McGrath, 'A warlord frontier: the Yunnan-Burma border dispute, 1910–1937' *Ohio Academy of History Proceedings* (2003), 7–29; M. Norins, 'Tribal boundaries of the Burma-Yunnan frontier', *Pacific Affairs*, 12:1 (1939), 67–79. For a short overview in Chinese, incorporating a Chinese perspective, see: Xie Benshu, 'Cong Pianma shijian dao Banhong shijian: zhong main bianjie lishi yange wenti' [From the Pianma incident to the Banhong incident: the historical evolution of the Sino-Burmese border] *Yunnan shehui kexue*, 4 (2000), 208–30.
2   E. Tagliacozzo, 'Ambiguous commodities, unstable frontiers: the case of Burma, Siam, and imperial Britain, 1800–1900' *Comparative Studies in Society and History*, 46:2 (2004), 354–77.
3   'Chunking Agreement 1890: Additional Article to the Agreement between Great Britain and China of 13th September 1876', Article I.
4   W. Walsh, 'The Yunnan myth', *Far Eastern Quarterly*, 2:3 (1943), 272–85.
5   E. B. Sladen, *Official Narrative of the Expedition to Explore the Trade Routes to China via Bhamo* (Rangoon: British Burma Press, 1870); J. Anderson, *Mandalay to Momein: A Narrative of the Two Expeditions of 1868 and 1875 under Colonel Edward B. Sladen and Colonel Horace Browne* (London: Macmillan and Co., 1876).
6   On French consular activities in Yunnan and the region, see, for example: A. François, *Le Manadrin Blanc: Souvenirs d'un Consul en Extréme-Orient, 1886–1904* (Paris, Calmann-Lévy, 1990). Amongst others, for a general and short overview of this Anglo-French rivalry, see: J. Christian, 'Anglo-French rivalry in Southeast Asia: its historical geography and diplomatic climate', *Geographical Review*, 31:2 (1941), 272–82.

7 D. Lary, '"A zone of nebulous menace": the Guangxi/Indochina border in the Republican period', in D. Lary (ed.), *The Chinese State at the Borders* (Vancouver: University of British Columbia Press, 2007), pp. 181–97.

8 British travelogues and reports often categorised 'Kachins' as one large ethnic group, with many sub-groups.

9 British officers used the Burmese name 'sawbwa' and less frequently the Shan name 'saohpa'.

10 For the account of 'pacification' by the Chief Commissioner of Burma (1887–90), see: C. Crosthwaite, *The Pacification of Burma* (London: Edward Arnold, 1912).

11 For a revisionist account of the campaign to establish British authority, see: M. Aung-Thwin, 'The British "pacification" of Burma: order without meaning', *Journal of Southeast Asian Studies*, 16:2 (1985), 245–61.

12 W. van Schendel 'Geographies of knowing, geographies of ignorance: jumping scale in Southeast Asia', *Environment and Planning D: Society and Space*, 20:6 (2002), 647–68; J. C. Scott, *The Art of Not Being Governed: An Anarchist History of Upland Southeast Asia* (New Haven: Yale University Press, 2009); J. Michaud, 'Editorial – Zomia and beyond', *Journal of Global History*, 5 (2010), 187–214.

13 D. Bello, 'To go where no Han could go for long: malaria and the Qing construction of ethnic administrative space in frontier Yunnan', *Modern China*, 31:3 (2005), 283–317.

14 As part of the Britain's Most Favoured Nation clause, following the Sino-French 1895 Convention (Article III), the Qing conceded to Britain the right to place a consular officer in Simao and a customs station at Mengzi. However, the Simao consulate closed shortly afterwards as there were few economic prospects and little political advantage to its stationing, and thereafter only maintained a customs officer.

15 British travellers also referred to the Tengyue as 'Momein'.

16 P. Giersch, *Asian Borderlands: The Transformation of Qing China's Yunnan Frontier* (Cambridge, MA: Harvard University Press, 2006), p. 25.

17 Some of these reports were published, for example: A. Rose, *Lisu Tribes of the Burma-China Frontier* (Calcutta: Baptist Mission Press, 1910); G. Litton, 'Journey on the Upper Salween, October–December 1905', *Geographic Journal*, 32 (1908), 239–66.

18 *Maritime Customs Decennial Reports: 1912–1921* (Shanghai: Statistical Department of the Inspectorate of General Customs, 1924), pp. 387–9.

19 BPP, HC: 1902, [Cd.786–45] *Diplomatic and Consular reports. China. Report for the Year 1900 on the Trade of Ssumao and Mengtse*, p. 4.

20 G. Morrison, *An Australian in China: Being the Narrative of a Quiet Journey across China to Burma* (London: Horace Cox, 1902), p. 245.

21 W. Geil, *A Yankee on the Yangtze: Being a Narrative of a Journey from Shanghai through the Central Kingdom to Burma* (London: Hodder & Stoughton, 1904), p. 234.

22 E. C. Baber, *Travels and Researches in Western China* (London: J. Murray, 1882), p. 183.

23 TNA: FO 228/1733 'Report on the Trade of Tengyueh for the year 1908, by Mr Archibald Rose, acting consul', 30 March 1909.

24 TNA: 228/3275 'Tengyueh intelligence report for the three months ending September 1921'.

25 On the proponents of British economic designs on Yunnan and this disappointment of prospects, see: Walsh, 'The Yunnan myth'.

26 It was unusual for a consul to be trained in law. Exceptions included Pierce O'Brien-Butler, who was called to the Bar in 1895 and later served as consul-general in Kunming.

27 Geil, *A Yankee on the Yangtze*, p. 272.

28 *Ibid*.

29 Geil, *A Yankee on the Yangtze*, p. 268. A Commissioner of Customs was stationed in the consular district.

30 TNA: FO228/1733 – Various reports.
31 *Maritime Customs: Returns of trade and trade report, 1911, part II. – port trade statistics and reports, vol V. – Frontier Ports* (Shanghai: Inspector General of Customs, 1912), p. 840; *Maritime Customs Decennial Reports: 1912–1921*, p. 390.
32 TNA: FO228/3275 'Tengyue Intelligence Report, ending 31st Dec, 1917'.
33 For an account of these botanical explorers, see: E. Mueggler, *The Paper Road: Archive and Experience in the Botanical Exploration of West China and Tibet* (Berkeley: University of California Press, 2011).
34 IOR: L/PS/10/208/2 A. Rose, to Ambassador at Beijing, 24 September 1910.
35 TNA: FO228/1598 E. Satow, Ambassador at Beijing to G. Litton, 18 April 1905.
36 TNA: FO228/1733 J. Jordan, Ambassador at Beijing to H. Sly, Tengyue consul, 15 January 1909.
37 *Ibid.*
38 T. Chiang, 'The salt trade in Ch'ing China', *Modern Asian Studies*, 17:2 (1983), 199–200; T. Chiang, 'The production of salt in China, 1644–1911', *Annals, American Association of Geographers*, 66 (1976), 516–30; J. E. Spencer, 'Salt in China', *Geographic Review*, 25:3 (1935), 359–61.
39 This practice of Qing 'monopolization' appeared to rely on intermediaries and private merchants. Although some scholars highlight the problems and corruption of this system, others attempt to see it as a flexible way of governance that had its benefits for the Qing. See, amongst others, T. Metzger, 'The organizational capabilities of the Ch'ing state in the field of commerce: the liang-huai salt monopoly, 1740–1840', in W. E. Willmott (ed.), *Economic Organization in Chinese Society* (Stanford: Stanford University Press, 1972), pp. 9–45
40 Giersch, *Asian Borderlands*, pp. 46–7.
41 From 1913 to 1949, a Sino-Foreign Salt Inspectorate aimed to recoup foreign indemnities from salt taxation.
42 J. Ma, 'Salt and revenue in frontier formation: state mobilized ethnic politics in the Yunnan-Burma borderlands since the 1720s', *Modern Asian Studies*, 48:6 (2014), 1637–69.
43 IOR: L/PS/10/208/2 O'Brien-Butler, consul-general at Kunming, to Li Jingxi, Viceroy of Yunnan and Guizhou, 24 May 1911.
44 TNA: FO228/1562 G. Litton to E. Satow, Ambassador at Beijing, 29 December 1904.
45 *Ibid.*
46 *Ibid.*
47 *Ibid.*
48 *Ibid.*
49 TNA: FO228/1562 G. Litton to E. Satow, Ambassador at Beijing, 29 December 1904.
50 TNA: FO228/1700 G. Litton to E. Satow, Ambassador at Beijing, 5 January 1905.
51 TNA: FO228/1733 G. Litton to the Chief Secretary to the Government of Burma, 9 January 1905.
52 *Ibid.*
53 TNA: FO228/1733 C. Pennell, Under Secretary to the Government of Burma, to the Superintendent of the Northern Shan States, 6 July 1905.
54 *Ibid.*
55 TNA: FO228/1733 A. Rose to W. Rice, Chief Secretary to the Government of Burma, 22 June 1909.
56 TNA: FO228/1700 H. Ottewill to J. Jordan, Ambassador at Beijing, 14 April 1908.
57 *Ibid.*
58 TNA: FO228/1733 H. Sly to J. Jordan, Ambassador at Beijing, 23 January 1909.
59 TNA: FO1080/248 H. Ottewill, Tengyue consul to Longling sub-prefect, 27 August 1908.
60 TNA: FO228/1733 H. Thornton, Assistant Superintendent Northern Shan States to Tengyue consul, 7 September 1908.
61 *Ibid.*
62 *Ibid.*
63 *Ibid.*

64 TNA: FO1080/249/1 and 2, Longling sub-prefect to H. A. Ottewill, Tengyue consul, 9 November 1908.
65 *Ibid.*; TNA: FO228/1733 H. Sly to J. Jordan, Ambassador at Beijing, 23 January 1909.
66 TNA: FO228/1733 H. Sly to J. Jordan, Ambassador at Beijing, 23 January 1909.
67 *Ibid.*
68 *Ibid.*
69 Convention between Great Britain and China, giving effect to Article III of 24th July 1886 relative to Burma and Thibet (1894), Article XI.
70 TNA: FO228/1733 H. Sly to J. Jordan, Ambassador at Beijing, 23 January 1909.
71 *Ibid.*
72 *Ibid.*
73 *Ibid.*
74 *Ibid.*
75 Today the Burma-China frontier forms part of the 'Golden Triangle' (southwestern China, northeastern Burma, northern Thailand and western Laos) known as a world hub of opium cultivation.
76 D. Bello, 'The venomous course of southwestern opium: Qing prohibition in Yunnan, Sichuan, and Guizhou in the early nineteenth century', *Journal of Asian Studies*, 62:4 (2003), 1109–42.
77 M. Fiskesjö, 'The Fate of Sacrifice and the Making of Wa History' (PhD dissertation, University of Chicago, 2000), pp. 193–4; the term *tu*, 'mud', was a common expression referring to opium, as the raw product looked like mud. The name of the province where it was cultivated was often added as a prefix. See E. Slack, *Opium, State, and Society: China's Narco-economy and the Guomindang, 1924–1937* (Honolulu: University of Hawaii Press, 2000), p. 15.
78 J. Wyman, 'Opium and the state in late-Qing Sichuan' in T. Brook and B. T. Wakabayashi (eds), *Opium Regimes: China, Britain and Japan, 1839–1952* (Berkeley: University of California Press, 2000), pp. 212–27.
79 TNA: FO228/1733 'Report on the Trade of Tengyueh for the year 1908, by Mr Archibald Rose, acting consul', 30 March 1909.
80 See, *inter alia*: C. Trocki, *Opium, Empire and the Global Political Economy* (London: Routledge, 1999).
81 The colonial government phased out this policy by limiting the legality of the drug incrementally following the Shan States Opium Order (1923). The autonomous Wa states also continued to freely export their opium across into China. On the opium question of the British Shan States during the later period of 1937–48, see: R. Maule, 'British policy discussions on the opium question in the Federated Shan States, 1937–1948', *Journal of Southeast Asian Studies*, 33:2 (2002), 203–24.
82 A. Wright, *Opium and Empire in Southeast Asia: Regulating Consumption in British Burma* (Basingstoke: Palgrave Macmillan, 2013).
83 *Ibid.*
84 *Ibid.*
85 G. W. Dawson, *Burma Gazetteer: The Bhamo District* (Rangoon: Government printing, 1912; reprint 1960), p. 44.
86 The Royal Opium Commission, 1895. For an analysis of the report, see: J. Richards, 'Opium and the British Indian Empire: the Royal Commission of 1895', *Modern Asian Studies*, 36:2 (2002), 375–420; P. Winther, *Anglo-European Science and the Rhetoric of Empire* (Oxford: Lexington Brooks, 2003); Wright, *Opium and Empire in Southeast Asia*.
87 See: Y. Zhou, *Anti-drug Crusades in Twentieth-Century China: Nationalism, History, and State Building* (Lanham: Rowman & Littlefield, 1999); R. K. Newman, 'India and the Anglo-Chinese opium agreements, 1907–1914', *Modern Asian Studies*, 13:3 (1989), 525–60.
88 J. Anderson, *A Report on the Expedition to Western Yunnan via Bhamo* (Calcutta: Asiatic Society, 1871), p. 72.
89 TNA: FO228/1598 G. Litton to E. Satow, Ambassador at Beijing 'Intelligence report, Tengyueh', 30 January 1905.

90 *Ibid.*
91 IOR: L/PS/10/208/2 W. Rice, Chief Secretary to the Government of Burma to the Secretary to the Government of India, Foreign Department, 19 October 1909.
92 Wright, *Opium and Empire in Southeast Asia*, pp. 95–107.
93 TNA: FO228/1562 G. Litton to E. Satow, Ambassador at Beijing, 24 November 1904.
94 Geil, *A Yankee on the Yangtze*, p. 278.
95 TNA: FO371/35 Various correspondence: India Office, Foreign Office and Ambassador at Beijing, January–May 1906.
96 TNA: FO371/27 'Memorandum of Information received during the months of May 1906, regarding external affairs relating to the North-East Frontier, Burma, Siam and China'.
97 M. Fiskesjö. 'The Fate of Sacrifice and the Making of Wa History' (PhD dissertation, University of Chicago, 2000), p. 201.
98 TNA: FO228/1669 H. Ottewill to the Chief Secretary to the Government of Burma, 23 January 1907.
99 *Ibid.*
100 TNA: FO228/1669 H. Ottewill to J. Jordan, Ambassador at Beijing, 26 January 1907.
101 *Ibid.*
102 L. Shakespear, *History of Upper Assam, Upper Burmah and the North-Eastern Frontier* (London: Macmillan and Co., 1914), p. 187.
103 The conference (the Shanghai Opium Commission, 1909) laid the groundwork for the subsequent international drug control agreement of the International Opium Convention of The Hague, 1912.
104 A. Hosie, *On the Trail of the Opium Poppy: A Narrative of a Travel in the Chief Opium-Producing Provinces of China, Vol II* (London: George Philips and Son, 1914), pp. 65–75.
105 TNA: FO228/1733 A. Rose to W. F. Rice, Chief Secretary to the Government of Burma, 22 June 1909.
106 TNA: FO228/1733 Liu Yuanpi, Tengyue daotai, to A. Rose 18 June 1909.
107 TNA: FO228/1671 Liu Yuanpi, Tengyue daotai, to H. Thornton and Davidson, 17 January 1909; TNA: FO228/1671 H.A Thornton, Davison and Sly to Liu Yuanpi, Tengyue daotai, 22 January 1909.
108 TNA: FO228/1733 Liu Yuanpi, Tengyue daotai, to A. Rose, 18 June 1909.
109 *Ibid.*
110 TNA: FO228/1733 A. Rose to Liu Yuanpi, Tengyue daotai, 22 June 1909.
111 TNA: FO228/1733 A. Rose to J. Jordan, Ambassador at Beijing, 22 June 1909.
112 *Ibid.*
113 TNA: FO228/1733 (demi-official letter) A. Rose to J. Jordan, Ambassador at Beijing, 22 June 1909.
114 IOR: L/PS/10/208/2 R. Richie, India Office, to the Governor of India in Council, 12 August 1910.
115 TNA: FO228/1733 (demi-official letter) A. Rose to J. Jordan, Ambassador at Beijing, 22 June 1909.
116 *Ibid.*
117 TNA: FO228/1733 A. Rose to W. Rice, Chief Secretary to Government of Burma 22 June 1909.
118 *Ibid.*
119 *Ibid.*
120 *Ibid.*
121 TNA: FO228/1733 E. Wilton, Kunming consul-general to J. Jordan, Ambassador at Beijing, 19 July 1909.
122 *Ibid.*
123 TNA: FO228/1733 A. Rose to J. Jordan, Ambassador at Beijing, 10 August 1909.
124 'Agreement Containing Rules of Trade, Made in Pursuance of Article XXVI of the Treaty of 26th June 1858', No.3 (1858).
125 TNA: FO228/1733 A. Rose to J. Jordan, Ambassador at Beijing, 10 August 1909.
126 *Ibid.*

127 *Ibid.*
128 TNA: FO228/1733 A. Rose to the Government of Burma, 25 September 1909.
129 IOR: L/PS/10/208/2 A. Rose to Liu Yuanpi, Tengyue daotai, 1 June 1909; IOR: L/PS/10/208/2 Liu Yuanpi. Tengyue daotai. to A. Rose, 18 June 1909; TNA: F0228/1671 Liu Yuanpi, Tengyue daotai, to A. Rose, 'Transfrontier trade in opium: claim for compensation arising from false imprisonment under Opium Act', 22 June 1909; FO228/1671 A. Rose to Liu daotai, 'Transfrontier claim for compensation arising from seizure', 22 June 1909.
130 TNA: FO228/1733 A. Rose to the Secretary to the Government of Burma, 25 September 1909.
131 TNA: FO228/1733 A. Rose to J. Jordan, Ambassador at Beijing, 10 November 1909.
132 TNA: FO228/1733 A. Rose to J. Jordan, Ambassador at Beijing, 10 November 1909; IOR: L/PS/10/208/2 India Office to Under Secretary of State, Foreign Office, 8 July 1910.; IOR: L/PS/10/208/2 Foreign Office to India Office, 26 July 1910.
133 IOR: L/PS/10.208/2 A. Rose to Ambassador at Beijing, 24 September 1910.
134 IOR: L/PS/10.208/2 A. Rose to Wen Liangyi, Tengyue daotai, 23 September 1910.
135 IOR: L/PS/10.208/2 A. Rose to Ambassador at Beijing. 24 September 1910.
136 *Ibid.*
137 IOR: L/PS/10.208/2 A. Rose to Ambassador at Beijing. 24 September 1910; see also IOR: L/PS/10.208/2 A. Rose to Wen Liangyi, Tengyue daotai, 'Minutes of an Enquiry held at His Majesty's Consulate, Tengyueh, on Friday, the 23rd of September, 1910', 23 September 1910.
138 IOR: L/PS/10.208/2 W. Max-Müller to E. Grey, Foreign Office, 1 November 1910.
139 IOR: L/PS/10.208/2 A. Rose to Ambassador at Beijing, 24 September 1910.
140 IOR: L/PS/10.208/2 A. Rose to Chief Secretary to the Government of Burma, 24 September 1910.
141 TNA: FO228/1807 C. Smith to J. Jordan, Ambassador at Beijing, 'Tengyue Intelligence Report April–June 1911', 1 July 1911.
142 IOR: L/PS/10/208/2 R. Ritchie, India Office to Foreign Office, 8 July 1910.
143 IOR: L/PS/10/208/2 F. Campbell, Foreign Office to the Under Secretary of State for India, 25 July 1910.
144 IOR: L/PS/10/208/2 M. Müller to O'Brien-Butler, Kunming consul-general, 4 October 1910.
145 *Ibid.*; L/PS/10/208/2 H. Thompson, Chief Secretary to the Government of Burma, to the Secretary to the Government of India, 26 July 1911.
146 IOR: L/PS/10/208 P. O'Brien-Butler, Kunming consul-general, to H. Thompson, Chief Secretary to the Government of Burma, 13 June 1911.
147 IOR: L/PS/10/208/2 Li Jingxi, Viceroy of Yunnan and Guizhou to O'Brien-Butler, Kunming consul-general, 31 May 1911.
148 IOR: L/PS/10/208 Foreign Office to Under Secretary of State, India Office, 11 September 1911; IOR: L/PS/10/208c J. Jordan, Ambassador at Beijing, to E. Grey, Foreign Office, 7 July 1911.

CHAPTER TWO

On the move: people crossing
the frontier, 1911–25

[A]t some parts of the frontier a man walking along paddy-bunds might cross from China to Burma and from Burma to China a dozen times without being aware … that there had been any frontier to cross.[1]

During the first decade of the twentieth century, the movement of illicit goods forced British consuls to reformulate their understanding of how to apply laws related to seizure rights. Although the Tengyue consul Archibald Rose understood the frontier treaties as the authoritative framework for legal relations and enforced them within his district, the Burmese government emphasised the inviolable right to exercise its laws within part of the frontier claimed as the territory of British Burma. It was the first example of how legal questions relating to transfrontier jurisdiction were resolved between British colonial and consular representatives. By the second decade of the twentieth century, consuls started to see another problem relating to transfrontier movement – the migration, drifting and fleeing of people across the frontier. In many areas, there were no boundaries and Burmese colonial officials were unsure of their right to exercise law. In other places where the Burmese government erected boundaries, the inhabitants disregarded them, were unaware of their existence or purposely crossed them to avoid jurisdiction. Territorial jurisdiction and borders therefore did not always suit British administration in the frontier, which was characterised by the frequent transfrontier movement of people. At the same time, consuls were often unable to exert their authority in parts of their consular district furthest from Tengyue. This chapter explores how the British colonial and consular authorities adapted their legal practices in response to the movement of such people across jurisdictional borders.

A range of different people travelled across the frontier. They included non-domiciled Indian, Burmese and Chinese migrants attracted by economic opportunities. The frontier was also home to inhabitants with itinerant lifestyles and some who were more firmly rooted to the land, such a grain farmers, who did not care for or were unaware of borders that cut across their lands or villages. Others crossed the frontier for their own legal advantage, including fugitives and those escaping taxation, as the highlands of the frontier offered a natural place of refuge.

Working alongside their Burmese counterparts, consuls recognised the importance of migrant crossings, itinerant lifestyles as well as the frequency of fugitives fleeing across the frontier. As James Scott has highlighted, the reach of lowland empires over local populations was indeed, in many instances, limited in the highlands of Southeast Asia.[2] The free movement of people in this region was one such characteristic of this autonomy. Certainly, regarding law, imperial regimes often struggled to impose their authority. As Lauren Benton has argued, jurisdictional holes were common features of the legal landscape of India and other parts of the Empire.[3] These were places where imperial authority was limited or could not be exercised. Across the Burma-China frontier, consuls understood the nature of the jurisdictional gaps that existed between British colonial authority, extraterritoriality and Chinese jurisdiction. These gaps became obvious through cases and incidents of transfrontier crime and migration. Local people and economic migrants therefore exposed the limits of colonial authority and consular authority, and consuls thereafter were forced to think of new ways to exercise law across the frontier.

In this chapter, I first outline how the Burmese government attempted to establish territorial authority in the frontier. Second, I show how the limitations of borders, as evidenced by the movement of migrants, prompted consular officials to petition for greater powers of deportation to their consular superiors. This allowed them to deport unwanted migrants across the frontier. Finally, I demonstrate how consuls enabled Burmese officials to exercise colonial law over British subjects who had committed crimes in Chinese territory and had returned to Burma. This extension of colonial law across established borders into the consular district of Tengyue enabled colonial officials to exercise a form of transfrontier jurisdictional power.

Colonial administration, political borders and territorial law

Following the annexation of Upper Burma in 1885, the Burmese government attempted to create a structure of authority through a mixture of territorial administration and indirect relations with local groups. Jurisdiction as defined by territoriality allowed British officials to understand clearly what lands they had the right to tax, which resources they could claim and which people were subject to their sovereignty. Colonial laws attempted to reflect the territorial division of frontier regions. For example, the Kachin Hill-Tribes Regulation (1895) defined the geographical application of criminal law over the Kachin Hills.[4] Deputy Commissioners situated in two main towns near the frontier – Bhamo and Myitkyina – as well as their subordinates, enforced these regulations and collected taxation revenue. Although local groups in the frontier did not have geographically discrete territories, maps, names and administrative infrastructure reflected the colonial attempt at carving parts of the frontier and northeast Burma into territorial entities that clearly denoted colonial authority.

At the same time, colonial officials conferred powers to local leaders to continue with their long-standing custom of exercising local authority over their populations.[5] This included legal powers allowing local headmen to resolve civil disputes amongst their population according to local custom. Over the next several decades, the relationship between the Burmese officers and local groups varied. Some headmen continued to acknowledge British sovereignty, whilst others recognised Chinese sovereignty. A number of group leaders acknowledged both Chinese and Burmese suzerainty and switched allegiance when they deemed it politically expedient or divided their loyalties equally between both empires. In a few instances, some – such as the ethnic Wa in the Wa States – continued to have no allegiance to either China or Burma, remaining entirely autonomous in what the Burmese officials called 'unadministered areas'.

Burmese Frontier Officers often explained their success or failure of maintaining relations with groups by pointing to the structure of ethnic authority. Some groups, for example, had a single clear headman, while others had no clear central authority. The latter caused the British 'no end of trouble for some years' as it made establishing and maintaining relations much more difficult.[6] The perception of the friendliness of certain groups towards British authority also drew upon ethnic stereotypes. A number of Western explorers and Burmese frontier officials provided various types of ethnographic information.[7] British consuls in Yunnan also contributed to the collection of ethnographic 'knowledge' within their accounts of their travels across the frontier.[8] For these British observers, the largest identified ethnic group was the population of Shans. They had less iterant lifestyles compared to other groups, lived in lowland areas and grew crops, such as rice in irrigated fields. They tended to be Buddhists, have higher rates of intermarriage with Burmese and Chinese populations, and some adopted Burmese or Chinese customs. Western observers detailed their appearance as one key marker of their ethnicity. The American traveller William Geil, for example, noted that the Shan men he encountered were 'nice, spry, intelligent-looking fellows', whilst he noted less favourably that the women 'wear monster turbans made out of black cloth, and bright colours about their ankles, with teeth ash black'.[9] In comparison, the most numerous highland population was the Kachins (and their various sub-groups). They were often considered less 'civilised' in comparison to the Shans. Geil remarked that the Kachins he saw were 'wild men of the mountains', with some of the women 'repulsive looking, with great mops of uncombed hair', who were 'gaudily dressed, chewing betelnut'.[10] Tengyue consul Archibald Rose on his tour of the frontier in 1909 added similar sentiments, describing the Kachins as a 'wild and warlike race', whilst the Shans were 'quiet and peace-loving folk', 'of fair complexion, and unlike their mountain neighbours, are clean and attractive in appearance'.[11] The 'wildest' ethnic populations above all were the 'headhunting' groups such as the Wa.[12] These types of characteristics remained consistent in the reports of consular officers over the years, although in reality, many people of different ethnicities adopted the customs of other groups or intermarried.[13] This hierarchy of 'civilised' local groups was not unlike that propounded by Chinese observers, who saw an ethnic hierarchy of Han Chinese at the apex, with chieftain local groups relegated below, followed by 'savage' clans (such as the Lisu, Mang and Lahu).[14] The level of sinicisation often played a role in the classification of different ethnic groups.[15] Despite this hierarchy and classification, the distinction between groups (and sub-groups) could sometimes be hard to discern.[16]

The Burmese administrative feature of delegated authority was also a feature of Chinese frontier governance. In some areas, the Chinese authorities conferred titles upon headmen. In places claimed by China, these headmen owed allegiance to China in return for exercising powers of civil and petty criminal jurisdiction over their people. This practice (often referred to as the *tusi* system) made hereditary chiefs both part of and partly autonomous from Chinese administration.[17] Unlike Britain, the Chinese understanding of sovereignty was not so strongly tied to geographical lines, but was modelled more on ideas of culture and ethnicity. For example, the term 'outer territories' (*waidi*) was used to describe frontier regions, whereas the 'inner lands' (*neidi*) described Han-administered areas largely populated by Han Chinese.[18] This reflected the politico-ethnic division of authority as an important understanding of the geography of empire rather than precise cartographic conceptions.[19] Despite this binary distinction, there was often a zone of ambiguity at the farthest reaches of the Qing Empire over the 'inner' and 'outer' regions.[20]

Although the concept of territorial jurisdiction was not as clearly defined in the Chinese understanding of the frontier, Chinese interest in the region shared many similarities with British imperial object-ives. The Yunnan provincial authorities, during the reign of the Qing, maintained a keen economic and political interest in the region. After the overthrow of the Qing in 1912, the semi-autonomous Provincial Government of Yunnan with its Governor, Tang Jiyao (1913–27), continued using the *tusi* system for frontier administration. As well as economic interests, Chinese political thinkers and central govern-ment officials during this period saw the frontier as a buffer against encroaching foreign empires.[21] Throughout the 1910s and 1920s, the most widely read Chinese newspaper of the time – *Shenbao* – warned of the foreign presence on the frontier and highlighted the dangers of giving too much independence to frontier people, as they were considered culturally, politically and economically unable to protect (*pingfan*) China.[22]

This concept of a buffer zone and geopolitical rivalry led to protracted disputes between Britain and China.[23] Prior to the British annex-ation of Upper Burma, Siam, Burma and China had overlapping non-territorial claims of sovereignty.[24] As a result, there were few borders and the British started frontier negotiations as early 1892, leading to the 1894 Treaty. The joint Delimitation Commission struggled to obtain Chinese agreement over proposed borders at the turn of the century, and by 1911, only around half of the 965 km of the frontier between Burma and China land had bilaterally agreed pillars.[25] In some instances, Chinese frontier officials also retracted their recognition of some borders.[26] In the 'middle passage', where there were more Sino-British borders, the arbitrary nature of the designation of some of the boundaries raised other problems. Consul Archibald Rose described the boundary in one area as following 'an imaginary line through irri-gation channels and changing paddy-fields' and that 'on every ground, political, administrative and commercial, it is in the highest degree inadvisable that we should be dependent on a zigzag and indefinite line marked only by shifting river beds and artificial boundary pillars'.[27] In other words, British officials on both sides of the frontier strove to demarcate the frontier, yet at the same time, these political bound-aries were not always reliable or useful markers of sovereignty. Whilst British imperial policy-makers continued to focus on the border demar-cation project, consular officers began to concentrate on another issue. This involved the more pressing concern of how to eliminate vacuums of power that existed between British colonial and consular authority as a result of the establishment of borders. They also began to con-sider the limitations of consular jurisdiction on the Chinese side of the frontier. The movement of people across the frontier – Burmese subjects crossing into Chinese territory and non-demarcated territory – brought this issue to light.

Migrants and deportation

In the nineteenth century, the southwest region of China experienced a large population growth, with increasing numbers of Han Chinese immigrants from China settling in the region.[28] In Yunnan province, James Lee shows that from 1750 to 1850, the registered population surged from nearly two million to over seven million, with the rise in population due to commercial and industrial expansion.[29] Some of these people headed to western Yunnan and settled in the region.[30] Many therefore brought local frontier markets into a wider community of networks.[31] At the same time, migrants moved across the frontier. British reporters commented upon the population of Chinese living in the northeastern Burmese towns, with some having settled after making their fortunes through the Burma-China trade.[32] In 1901, the India census report for Burma confirmed that there were 524 immigrants living in the districts of Bhamo and 638 living in Myitkyina, who were described as having been born outside of Burma, but were not Indian-born subjects.[33] The Qing remained keen to expand its interests in mineral extraction enterprises in the frontier regions as well as various tea and salt trades and encouraged migration to the frontier. This population would also have included many immigrants who settled in mountainous areas to escape revenue taxes, grow opium or to seek refuge from justice.[34] The Qing often referred to these Han immigrants as 'guest people' (ke min) or 'floating people' (liu min).[35]

On their tours, consuls reported on the liveliness of the frontier trade routes from Tengyue to the Burmese towns of Bhamo and Myitkyina. George Litton, for example, reported what he saw on the trade route to Bhamo. The route started via Longling across the steep ascents and descents to the Mangshi plain and town in the valley of the tributary of the Shweli River (29 km), then through the Zhefang plain to Zhefang (74 km). The road then ascended again above the Mengkwan River, then crossed 'Wan Teng' (112 km). The route continued through 'well cultivated country', proceeding then to the main valley of the Shweli, through the British-claimed Shan State towns of Muse (140 km), Selan (149 km) and Namhkam (169 km). Finally, the route went into the Kachin hills for four stages and through to Bhamo. On his travels, he saw in the 'cold season' (i.e. the busiest season, from October to May), 100 mules from China passing daily on this path, carrying iron pans, straw hats and walnuts amongst other items. Coming from Burma, he saw Chinese traders with 50 mules carrying yarn and cotton goods daily.[36] He reported seeing over 100 other people per day on this route, including Chinese artisans, sawyers, stone masons, iron workers, smiths and carpenters.[37] Chinese migration and trade was certainly a key feature of the frontier.

By the turn of the twentieth century, growing numbers of Indian and Burmese migrants coming from the opposite direction crossed the frontier for economic opportunities.[38] There was a long history of Indian traders and moneylenders in the western and southwestern parts of China.[39] Although we have little evidence of the reasons why these new migrants came, it is reasonable to assume, similar to the Indian migration to the east coast of China, that these migrants included businessmen, manual labourers and those looking for policing and guard work.[40] Indeed, many who had migrated via the sea to Hong Kong and Shanghai later 'wandered into the interior' for better economic opportunities.[41] Whether from crossing the frontier or coming via Shanghai, their migratory lifestyle and occasional unemployment was a source of concern for the consular authorities. Since they preferred to remain itinerant, these migrants often did not register at consulates.[42] They were thus hard to track down when consular or British Indian courts issued warrants for their arrest.[43] Most consuls did not know exactly how many Indian men were residing in their consular district. Instead, evidence of Indian men in the interior is provided by only small snippets from consular reports. For example, in November 1906, the Hankou (Wuhan) consul estimated that there were 109 British Indian subjects in his district.[44] Of these, forty-nine were employed in the Municipal Police. Twenty-six worked in foreign firms, eleven in British firms and ten in Chinese firms. Seven worked for railway companies and six either worked in other miscellaneous jobs or were suspected to be unemployed.[45] This inability to easily track Indian migrants most likely compounded existing fears about the tenuous reach of imperial rule in places away from metropolises. These suspicions about 'lawlessness', for example, were prominent in imperial discourses of the frontiers of British India.[46]

Indian (and Burmese) men also made their way into the southwestern provinces of Yunnan and Guizhou. In July 1903, acting Kunming consul-general George Litton wrote to the British ambassador at Beijing, Ernest Satow, with Satow forwarding his letter to the Foreign Office.[47] Litton viewed the rising number of Indian men in Yunnan and Guizhou as problematic and outlined four proposals on special powers to deal with criminal suspects from these communities. First, he asked whether he could deport suspects for trial in Burma. Article 67 of the Order in Council (1865) stated that subjects in China could be sent to trial in Hong Kong if deemed expedient. Litton requested that Burma was added to this article. Second, Litton asked whether Article 72 of the Order could be applied to cases involving British Indians in Yunnan and Guizhou. This article allowed the Supreme Court in Shanghai the right to determine how and where a case could be heard. In particular, Litton wanted the Supreme Court at Mandalay to be an appellate court for the Yunnan consular courts. Third, he argued that Burma should be added to Article 79 as a place where, if deemed expedient, convicts could be sent for terms of imprisonment. Finally, he asked whether Burma could be added to Article 107, which stated that Hong Kong and England were places where suspects could be deported without their consent.

The Chief Judge of Her Britannic Majesty's Supreme Court for China, Frederick Bourne, provided his opinion.[48] He agreed that it would be expedient to send suspects for trial and those convicted to terms of imprisonment to Burma. He also consented to empowering Yunnan consuls to deport such persons to Burma. However, he thought it was unnecessary to allow special powers for the Yunnan courts.[49] He therefore rejected the suggestion that the Supreme Court in Mandalay could have appellate powers over the Yunnan consular courts.

Two months later, the Ambassador at Beijing, Ernest Satow, reviewed the proposal. He felt that there was 'no doubt as to the necessity for some special legislation with regard to British Indian subjects in Yunnan'.[50] He believed that a separate Order in Council could give Litton some of his desired powers. He acknowledged that Litton had written his proposal in anticipation that a serious case involving Indian subjects may soon arise. Indeed, British officials during this era appeared to suspect that Indian communities were unruly. For example, the Chief Judge of His Majesty's Supreme Court for China, Havilland de Sausmarez, concluded after a prominent murder case (R. v. *Chanda Singh, Sultan Singh and Verdava Singh*), that there was a 'great deal of lawlessness' within certain Indian communities.[51] Satow felt that the consular justice system would encounter difficulties should a serious case between Indian men arise. The Supreme Court in Shanghai would assume jurisdiction, but sending written documents took two months from the consular district to Shanghai and nearly four months before an answer would be received in return. Finally, Satow noted that the new draft Order in Council included a clause that allowed the deportation of British subjects to a place in some part of His Majesty's dominions to which the person belonged (i.e. previously domiciled or born). This clause would allow consuls to send British Indian subjects to India, and Burmese subjects to Burma.[52]

An Order in Council for Yunnan was not drafted, but the next year, the new China Order in Council (1904) included the new deportation powers. Alongside the pre-existing provision that allowed suspects to be sent to Hong Kong, Article 50 stated that a consul or the Chief Judge could send a suspect for trial in Mandalay.[53] Article 83(4) empowered consuls and the Chief Judge to send deportees to any place in the dominions of which the person was born within or previously domiciled, or to any other place to which a receiving government consented.[54] The Order reiterated the use of the Fugitive Offenders Act (1881) and the Colonial Prisoners Removal Act (1884) to apply to China as if China were a British possession.[55] This allowed consuls to deport suspects and convicted prisoners with warrants from requesting colonial governments. These legislative changes provided for greater inter-imperial legal powers, which allowed for the forced removal of Indian migrants to Burma and India. Consuls could deport not only those charged with minor offences, but also those who could not provide security of their future 'good behaviour'.[56] The presence of Indian migrants in southwest China therefore led to legislative changes and facilitated a greater legal and penal connection between consular authority in the southwest of China and colonial authority across the frontier.

With the new legislation, consuls had an opportunity to use their powers. As deportation did not involve a formal hearing, there are few records showcasing these practices. However, one particular incident illustrates how Tengyue consuls used their powers. In 1925, the Tengyue consul, Harold Harding, ordered the arrest of a Madrassi Indian man surnamed Ramya.[57] Harding described Ramya as a 'vagrant' and asked the local Chinese police to arrest him and have him escorted to Tengyue. On executing the orders, the Chinese court runners took him to the jail at the local Chinese Magistrate's *yamen* (courthouse). Here he was to await his deportation to Burma. In jail, Ramya's health deteriorated and the guards allowed him to go to the local hospital. Whilst being transferred, he escaped from the guards and fled across the frontier. Hearing of his escape, Harding made a warrant for Ramya's arrest and Burmese police officers later found and arrested him. Ramya was again detained, but once more managed to escape.

The incident of twice-lucky Ramya would have gone unrecorded had it not been for a later series of correspondence between Harding and the Chief Judge in Shanghai, Skinner Turner. Harding had noticed that there were changes to the procedure of deportation in the new China Order in Council (1925). Article 54 stated that consuls required the Chief Judge to confirm orders of deportation. He therefore asked Turner to provide a set of blank confirmation sheets for deportation orders. Harding stated that he could use these when he wanted to deport an individual rather than wait for a confirmation from the Chief Judge of the Supreme Court. Harding outlined the necessity of having these blank confirmation sheets for a speedy deportation and pointed to the Ramya incident as an example of the problems of waiting for a confirmation order. As the Tengyue consulate had limited financial resources and no consular jail, the consul had no choice, as the Ramya incident showed, but to send British subjects for detention in the Tengyue Magistrate's *yamen* jail. Harding had followed past procedure by issuing a warrant to send Ramya to Burma for trial using Article 50. He did not provide evidence of his alleged crime or check if the alleged crime was also an offence in Burma or India. Harding conceded that Ramya's infraction for vagrancy was a 'trivial' offence, but was nevertheless a misdemeanour that justified deportation. In defending his actions, Harding stated that his disregard for legal procedure was necessary. He used his own maxim using pidgin English – English adapted for Chinese speakers – to convey his sentiments: the consul had to 'maskee [nevermind] the law, and take his wigging [scolding] for it'.[58] Skinner Turner duly delivered his 'wigging', condemning Harding for his improper and over-zealous use of deportation.[59] Nor was Harding the first consul to 'maskee the law' in such a way. Turner reminded Harding that the new provisions of the Order in Council were intended to stop consular officials' frequent misuse of deportation powers.

The Ramya incident and the correspondence between Harding and Turner reflected two important points. First, following legislative changes in 1904, Tengyue consuls not only exercised deportation powers, but also appeared to use them liberally. Second, consuls in the seemingly remote southwest region were successful in their petitions for legislative changes. Migrants from the colonies – people like Ramya who drifted across the frontier – were the reason for these legal amendments. The Yunnan consuls understood that the frontier was a place of migration, a meeting place and a gateway from one territory to another where people sought opportunity. Consuls therefore reformulated their understanding of law and legal practices based on these migratory practices and their assumption of the lawless character of migrants.

Although Tengyue consuls deported British subjects over the frontier, deportation practices were not a one-way process. In the other direction, Chinese subjects crossed into Burma and the colonial authorities deported many back into China. The Burmese government used the Indian Foreigners Act (1864) to deport 'undesirable' Chinese subjects from Burma. As Osada has noted, between 1909 and 1921, there were forty-five deportations.[60] Most of these people were suspected of either being a member of a secret society or of being without employment.[61] However, by 1925, when Ramya was due to be deported to Burma, the Burmese government was deporting over 100 aliens (presumably Chinese subjects) per year.[62] This practice was not without its problems as the Tengyue consul admitted that the Chinese authorities would 'have a legitimate grievance if they become aware of the fact that we are deporting our undesirables across the frontier into their territory'.[63] It was also clear that deporting 'undesirable' colonial subjects of Chinese heritage was a practice with only short-term benefits for British imperial actors. As the Tengyue consul wrote to the Chief Secretary to the Government of Burma:

> As soon as ... ['Burmese undesirables'] ... cross into Yunnan they come strictly speaking under my jurisdiction and control, and if the Chinese authorities attempted to arrest and punish them ... I should have to lodge a protest in defence of the principle of extraterritoriality. On the other hand, if the Chinese authorities handed them over to me, I should have to send them back to Burma, and so they would go on circulating. The best course appears to me to keep Burma frontier suspects as far from the frontier as possible and under some kind of police supervision, if practicable ... For extraterritorial reasons it is manifest that we cannot hand Burma subjects over into the custody of the Chinese authorities, even if the latter were willing to accept them.[64]

Deportation was therefore not a satisfactory practice for those implementing imperial British policy. Consular and colonial practices of deportation helped to remove subjects from Burma and China. Yet at the same time, it helped to sustain a circulation of 'undesirables'. It remained a short-term solution to the problem of porous borders and unwanted migrants.

Adapting colonial jurisdiction

As the Ramya case showed, consuls detained certain migrants in the southwest of China and deported them across the frontier. Although this was a short-term practice intended to help consular officials to remove unwanted migrants, limited resources hampered consular jurisdictional practices. As the Tengyue consul, C. D. Smith, summarised:

> Having neither constable nor jail, nor consulate guard, nor any means of effecting an arrest at a distance, detaining a prisoner in safe custody, or conveying him from place to place, he [the Tengyue consul] is entirely dependent upon the good-will of the Chinese in all these respects. Even supposing the accused person [British subject] to have been successfully arrested, brought to Tengyueh and kept safe (inevitably in the Chinese jail), it is still necessary to bring in the complainant and the witnesses

on both sides, and further, since the complainant, accused and witnesses between them might easily speak three or four distinct languages, the requisite number of interpreters must also be found.[65]

The absence of a consular jail and limited personnel were not the only constraints. Consuls were limited in their jurisdictional capacity as they could only deport suspects of crimes constituting a term of twelve months' imprisonment or less. This was clearly inadequate for the frontier, where offences such as kidnapping, village raids and grievous assaults resulting from acts of vengeance were common. In these instances, the Tengyue consul had to allow the Chief Judge in Shanghai to assume jurisdiction. Smith outlined the implications of this limitation:

> either the parties, witnesses and interpreters must be sent to Shanghai, or a Judge of the Supreme Court must come to Tengyueh on circuit. Either course inevitably involves great inconvenience and expense, and the latter involves the absence of one of the judges from Shanghai for more than two months unless a judge is specially appointed *ad hoc*. Supposing the parties to be sent to Shanghai there might be much difficulty in securing the attendance there of the witnesses or even the complainant. ... In any case the cost of the proceedings would be excessive.[66]

Smith therefore felt that Burmese Frontier Officers were more suitable candidates to exercise legal authority over British subjects across the frontier. They had more financial resources and personnel at their disposal and were more familiar with frontier languages.[67] The environment also prevented the consul from travelling during the rainy season (May–October) and sending suspects to Mandalay added a heavier financial burden.

The Tengyue consuls realised that the Burmese Frontier Officers were best placed to assume jurisdiction, but borders curtailed their powers. It was readily apparent that the establishment of pillars demarcating territorial sovereignty was important for the Burmese government. Yet the effect of jurisdiction was paradoxical: as much as borders consolidated colonial sovereignty within its limits, it also excluded its powers outside of it. These borders were also porous and the movement of people characterised everyday life across the frontier. By the second decade of the twentieth century, British officials feared that the social, economic and political instability in Yunnan following the decline of the Qing Empire would also affect the frontier. After 1911, a semi-autonomous governor, Cai E (1911–13), followed by Tang Jiyao (1913–27), ruled as head of the Kunming government. The Yunnan military focused on securing political power towards the east and the north of the province. As a result, Chinese policing numbers decreased in the frontier and some of the former Qing armies that had disbanded sought refuge in the frontier alongside other loyalists.

This political and social disruption presented other problems on the frontier for British authority. The Tengyue consul depended upon Chinese police to arrest British subjects in Chinese territory. Burmese officials also relied upon the Chinese police to prevent suspects entering China and to arrest those suspected of criminal activity. The local Sino-British Manai Agreement (1902) stated that both Burma and China should retain adequate forces on demarcated sides of the frontier. Thereafter the Burmese government created various military posts and stationed regiments. Bhamo, for example, had a 1,000-strong sepoy regiment and a mountain battery of 800 soldiers, which included Sikhs and Punjabis.[68] The Burmese authorities also had military and civil police regiments filled with Shan recruits outside of the city.[69] Smaller divisions of military police in the frontier included 500 Kachin men and 400 Indian men.[70] Whilst Burmese officers claimed that they had followed the word of the agreement, consuls accused the new government in Kunming of failing to provide police and detectives in the Shan States. In 1919, consul Affleck claimed that the Agreement had become a 'dead letter', with the 'last of their few garrisons opposite to our posts on the frontier [having] disappeared at the time of the Revolution in 1911 since when no attempt has been made to replace them'.[71] Inadequate policing allowed crime to multiply and helped Burmese fugitives to escape over the frontier with ease.[72] As former Qing troops disbanded and fled to the frontier, successive consuls reported that many of these former soldiers had become 'brigands' plundering villages in lieu of a livelihood. Aside from ex-military men, consuls felt that without satisfactory policing, the frontier attracted the 'riff-raff' of the Chinese population, who engaged in illegal activities such as opium cultivation.[73] The role of stationed military police was not simply to arrest petty criminals. On many occasions, local groups of Shans, Kachins and others rebelled against British and Chinese sovereignty, and military police attempted to suppress uprisings.[74] The veracity of some of these claims by consuls on the extent of criminality is questionable, but the narrative of 'lawlessness' was a key part of their petitions to their superiors for enhanced legislative powers.

During January 1911, the Deputy Commissioner of Bhamo W. H. L. Cabell, the Superintendent of the Northern Shan States H. Thornton and the Tengyue consul Archibald Rose wrote a proposal together on the need to reformulate legal practices in the frontier.[75] As they were the principal British officers working in the region, they had witnessed the shortcomings of British authority across borders and presented ideas on what they felt would ameliorate this jurisdictional shortcoming. In particular, they highlighted the limitations of frontier jurisdiction over British Burmese subjects who committed offences in Chinese frontier territories. There were two inter-related points of concern. One involved incidents of elopement and another on the general issue of British subjects committing crimes in China. On several occasions, China had requested that Burmese officers find and extradite couples who had eloped from Chinese to Burmese territory. The British officers remarked that Kachin custom regarded an unmarried girl as 'chattel, a marketable commodity'.[76] The man who would marry her had to pay a certain price as a wedding present to her parents. If he did not and he enticed her to run away with him, Kachin groups would consider this as a type of theft. The British officers understood the seriousness of the contravention of this local custom to local communities, but it was not an offence in the treaties or according to colonial or consular law. If the elopement had been an abduction, an extradition request could be made or an order of deportation, but in all of the cases brought up to the officers, the woman had been of age and a consenting party. The man therefore was not a 'criminal' as stated in Article XV of the Burma-China 1886 Treaty or an offender according to the Order in Council (1904). The three British officers therefore suggested that an arbitrator should be appointed from Burma and China to consider the case and fix compensation in cases of transfrontier elopement. The Lieutenant-Governor of Burma, the Secretary of State for India and the Ambassador at Beijing agreed to the suggestion of arbitrators.[77] Thereafter the Ambassador, John Jordan, allowed acting consul Smith to begin negotiations with the local Chinese officials on hearing these cases in the Frontier Meetings.[78]

Whereas cases of transfrontier elopement revealed the disjuncture between local custom and imperial law, the three British officers were also aware of the difficulties of prosecuting British subjects for transfrontier crimes as defined by the treaties and the Order in Council. In such instances, the consul in Tengyue assumed jurisdiction, but it was often impractical to send suspects and witnesses there from some parts of the frontier. The consul could also only hear cases that involved a maximum sentence of twelve months of imprisonment. The only recourse for family members and local headmen was to appeal for compensation in the so-called 'Frontier Meetings'. These were courts that awarded compensation in Sino-British cases on the frontier. 'The Gilbertian situation' was that the Government of Burma was forced to pay compensation for the wrongful act of its subject across the frontier at the Meetings, although the Chinese officers usually knew the identity and whereabouts of an offender and could even produce him if they wanted.[79] The three officers therefore suggested two possible solutions.

The first suggestion was to empower the Burma officers and Chinese officials at the Frontier Meetings with criminal jurisdiction. The second suggestion was to give the consul greater jurisdictional powers so that he could try a British subject in Chinese territory of any offence, sitting as a consul with extraterritorial powers at the Meetings.[80]

In the meantime, Rose wrote an additional letter to Jordan outlining his preference for the second proposal by highlighting the drawbacks of the first.[81] He suggested that allowing the Chinese and British officers in the Frontier Meetings to have jurisdictional powers over these British subjects was problematic. This was because it would allow Chinese officials to become co-judges with jurisdictional powers over British subjects. In addition, as Rose had experienced in relation to the question of salt smuggling in 1908–9, neither the Burmese authorities in Rangoon nor consular authorities in Beijing would agree to dispose of the principle of extraterritoriality in Yunnan or Burmese territorial jurisdiction. This therefore left the second option – to empower him with full powers of criminal extraterritorial jurisdiction at the Frontier Meetings – as the only viable option.

Whereas Jordan supported his proposal, the Foreign Office stated that it was impractical to amend current legislation as the issue was not urgent.[82] Further, consuls had no judicial training. Empowering lay legal officials to pass sentences of capital punishment contravened the principles of the China Orders.[83] Despite the Foreign Office rejecting the proposal resoundingly, the next Tengyue consul, C. D. Smith, took up the issue three years later. Having reviewed his experience of frontier cases and affairs, he felt it was imperative to reformulate and strengthen British powers in the frontier.[84] Rather than empower consular officials, he proposed that Burmese officers should have extended powers of jurisdiction over British subjects who had committed crimes across the border and had returned to Burma.[85] In justifying his proposition, he drew attention to the jurisdictional limitations of consular jurisdiction in the frontier and the problems of arbitrary borders. Not only were the Shans, Kachins, Lisus and others often unaware of borders imposed on their lands, but in many instances, their family members lived on both sides of the border. This meant that local populations moved between China and Burma on a daily basis and consular administration was not suitable. He stated:

> To require a Burmese Shan peddler, for instance, to obtain a passport from the consul in Tengyueh before he should be permitted to cross from Hsenwi to Mongmao (which is technically in the 'interior' of China), or a Kachin or Lisu or other tribesman to do the same before visiting his relations in Chinese territory, is too grotesquely impossible to be gravely considered.[86]

Smith also considered how the familiarity with legal cultures should determine the application of law. For him, the underlying rationale for extraterritoriality was to exempt European British subjects from alien ('oriental') laws, which were based on different social and legal customs.[87] Extraterritoriality – i.e. the application of English law – was a familiar legal system to British subjects who had been born or raised in the metropole. In this regard, extraterritoriality should not apply to local populations of British subjecthood in the frontier found in Chinese territory, as English law was equally as alien to them as Chinese law. Instead, he believed the Indian criminal codes – which were designed for colonial subjects – were more suitable for criminal jurisdiction.

However, this argument of legal culture and familiarity did not extend to Indian and Burmese migrants in the frontier. Instead, Smith felt that such migrants in the frontier needed to be distinguished from the local populations. As a result, they should therefore be tried by extraterritorial jurisdiction in Chinese territory.[88] A case in 1912 demonstrated this consular position on British Indian subjects in the frontier. Indian-born Jaffar had moved across the frontier from Burma to escape debts.[89] He lived on the Chinese side of the frontier for a few years with his Burmese wife, Ma Yen, in the village of Yinghpan, in Chinese territory. On 12 June 1912, an unidentified person murdered both Jaffar and Ma Yen in their house. The Chinese authorities initially tried to claim jurisdiction over the probate case as Jaffar had paid house tax to the Chinese authorities. The Burmese authorities rejected this Chinese claim stating that the residency rules did not apply to British subjects who were born outside of the frontier region.[90] Eastes felt that as Jaffar and his wife were 'Mohamodan natives of India proper ... subjects of Great Britain', they were therefore different from the indigenous population. This was not only because of the place of their original domicile, but also due to their lifestyle. Jaffar in particular was a British migrant who had settled on the frontier and his life appeared distinct from that of local inhabitants who frequently changed residencies in the frontier.[91] This was a particular 'rule of colonial difference' articulated by consuls that distinguished between Indian subjects and native hill populations, determining which laws should be applicable to which ethnic groups in the context of the frontier.[92]

Whilst visiting the frontier between October and December 1914, Smith took the opportunity to meet with Burma Frontier Officers.[93] They supported his proposal and the Superintendent for the Northern Shan States suggested that Section 188 of the Indian Code of Criminal Procedure (1898) could apply to Kachins who committed offences in China.[94] This provision allowed for the extraterritorial use of the Code of Criminal Procedure over 'Native Indian' subjects of India who had committed offences at any place 'without and beyond the limits of British India', such as the semi-autonomous Princely States.[95] Section 188 already applied to the Northern Shan States and Shans were considered 'native Indian subjects' for the purposes of the law, except in places where the Kachin Hills regulations applied to Kachins.[96] In order to enable the Burma Frontier Officers to exercise extraterritorial colonial authority over the vast stretch of the Kachin Hills frontier, Rose suggested that the Superintendents of the Northern Shan States, the Deputy Commissioner at Bhamo and the Deputy Commissioner of Myitkyina should be appointed as 'political agents for the Tengyueh consular district'.[97]

The Foreign Office and the Ambassador at Beijing both agreed with Smith's proposal.[98] Despite the concern that China might object to this jurisdictional incursion, John Jordan believed that it would not damage Sino-British relations and might be acceptable given precedent of this practice elsewhere.[99] The Russian authorities already exercised similar powers on the Sino-Russian border over Russian subjects in China, including 'native tribesmen' claimed by Russia.[100] Jordan left the issue of how it could be implemented to those in the India Office, who agreed to the proposal and thereafter set out the means by which colonial Indian law could be applied by the Burmese Frontier Officers. The proposal allowed Burmese officials jurisdiction over suspects who had committed offences in China and had returned to Burma, as if the crime had occurred in Burmese territory.[101] The extension of powers proposed by C. D. Smith thus came into effect after 1916, with the application of Sections 188 and 189 of the British Indian Criminal Procedure Code (1898). This provision now applied to the 'hill tribes in the Kachin Hill Tracts' that were directly adjacent to the frontier and the Tengyue district, located within the Bhamo and Myitkyina districts.[102] The colonial government in Rangoon, British consular authorities in Beijing and the Foreign Office had therefore recognised the necessities of creating another type of transfrontier jurisdiction.

Conclusion

This chapter has shown how consuls petitioned for amended legal powers as a response to the transfrontier movement of people. The establishment of borders – although a key part of colonial policy – served to limit jurisdiction as much as to consolidate it. The Tengyue consul was ill-equipped to assume jurisdiction in many instances where a British subject was suspected of committing transfrontier crimes. As a result, the movement of people across arbitrary borders showcased the jurisdictional holes between colonial and consular authority. Three different types of transfrontier migrants highlighted these jurisdictional shortcomings: 'undesirable' Indian and Burmese economic migrants, transfrontier elopers and Burmese subjects suspected of committing criminal offences in China.

Increasing numbers of colonial migrants made their way across the frontier and into the province of Yunnan in the early twentieth century. Consuls successfully petitioned for greater deportation powers to remove such 'undesirable' Indian and Burmese subjects. This created legal and penal connections to British Burma. The Burmese government also deported 'undesirable' Burmese subjects of Chinese heritage, creating a circulation of people across the frontier. As the case of Ramya showed, consuls also often bent existing laws or ignored them ('maskee the law') in order to fit their sense of what was necessary and practical for the frontier.

Consuls also worked alongside Burmese officers, highlighting the jurisdictional 'holes' between colonial and consular authority. Incidents of transfrontier elopement revealed the disjuncture between local custom and imperial law. The contravention of local custom was a serious issue not only to local Kachin groups, but also to British officers who understood the likelihood of social disruption on the frontier. The Tengyue consul alongside Burmese Frontier Officers therefore petitioned for the election of Burmese and Chinese arbitrators. It was a legal resolution that required no changes to legislation, but a rearrangement of local legal practices.

In other instances concerning transfrontier crime, suspects who could be charged under the Orders in Council could not be punished due to practical considerations or the limitations of consular jurisdiction. Consuls were again key to reformulating law in the frontier in order to remedy this jurisdictional shortcoming. By 1915, this resulted in Burmese officers exercising jurisdiction over British subjects who committed crimes in China, and who later returned to Burma or lived on the divide. It was a simple solution, which transferred some of the jurisdiction of consular authority to colonial officials. This allowed Burma to have political borders and transfrontier legal powers. Consular officers were therefore central to working out how to extend British colonial jurisdiction across borders.

Notes

1 IOR: L/PS/10/208/2 C. Smith, acting Tengyue consul, to J. Jordan, Ambassador at Beijing, 6 October 1914.
2 J. Scott, *The Art of Not Being Governed: An Anarchist History of Upland Southeast Asia* (New Haven: Yale University Press, 2009).

3   L. Benton, *A Search for Sovereignty: Law and Geography in European Empires, 1400–1900* (Cambridge: Cambridge University Press, 2010).

4   In some places where larger groups of Kachins, for example, resided in Shan territory, the Kachin Hill-Tribes regulations applied.

5   This was only possible after 'pacifying' certain areas, which often involved using Military Police to force local leaders to accept British sovereignty.

6   L. Shakespear, *History of Upper Assam, Upper Burmah and the North-Eastern Frontier* (London: Macmillan and Co., 1914), p. 172. On the structure of indigenous groups, especially the Kachin, see: E. R. Leach. *Political Systems of Highland Burma: A Study of Kachin Social Structure* (Boston: Beacon Press, 1964).

7   See, amongst others: F. Ward, *In Farthest Burma: The Record of an Arduous Journey of Exploration and Research through the Unknown Frontier Territory of Burma and Tibet* (London: Seeley Service and Co., 1921); J. Anderson, *Mandalay to Momein: A Narrative of the Two Expeditions of 1868 and 1875 under Colonel Edward B. Sladen and Colonel Horace Browne* (London: Macmillan and Co., 1876); G. Scott, 'The wild Wa: a headhunting race', *Asiatic Quarterly Review*, 1 (1896), 138–52.

8   See, for example: A. Rose, *Lisu Tribes of the Burma-China Frontier* (Calcutta: Baptist Mission Press, 1910).

9   W. Geil, *A Yankee on the Yangtze: Being a Narrative of a Journey from Shanghai through the Central Kingdom to Burma* (London: Hodder & Stoughton, 1904), p. 281.

10 *Ibid.*, pp. 281, 284.

11 TNA: FO228/1733 A. Rose, Tengyue consul, to J. Jordan, Ambassador at Beijing, 21 February 1909.

12 Scott, 'The wild Wa'. The British distinguished between the 'tame' Wa in the Shan regions under British jurisdiction and the 'wild' Wa in the autonomous Wa region.

13 See, for example, on the practices of the Kachins: Leach, *Political Systems of Highland Burma*.

14 On the Chinese categorisation of various groups and subgroups, see, for example: P. Giersch, *Asian Borderlands: The Transformation of Qing China's Yunnan Frontier* (Cambridge, MA: Harvard University Press, 2006), pp. 64–97.

15 See: M. Fiskesjö, 'On the "raw" and the "cooked" barbarians of imperial China', *Inner China*, 1 (1999), 139–68.

16 D. Bello, 'To go where no Han could go for long: malaria and the Qing construction of ethnic administrative space in frontier Yunnan', *Modern China*, 31:3 (2005), 288–9.

17 There is an extensive Chinese literature on Chinese frontier politics and the *tusi* system in China's southwest. See, *inter alia*: Y. Wu, *zhongguo tusi zhidu yuanyuan yu fazhangshi* [*A History of the Origins and Development of China's Native Chieftaincy System*] (Chengdu: Sichuan minzu chubanshe, 1988); Y. Gong, *zhongguo tusi zhidu* [*China's Tusi System*] (Kunming: Yunnan remin chubanshe, 1992); Y. She, *zhongguo tusi zhidu* [*China's Tusi System*] (Shanghai: Shangwu shuju reprint, 1947). In other places and at various times, the Chinese had also engaged in a practice of *gaitu guiliu*. This was a practice of replacing *tusi* with imperial officers. However, the Qing gradually used softer methods to inculcate local headmen to Chinese rule, such as though education. See: J. Herman, 'Empire in the southwest: early Qing reforms in the native chieftain system', *Journal of Asian Studies*, 56:1 (1997), 47–74.

18 Giersch, *Asian Borderlands*, p. 61.

19 This did not mean that China did not understand the concept of Western territoriality. In some cases, Chinese officials used Western cartographic tools to try and gain an upper hand in land disputes. See: E. Vanden Bussche, 'Contested Realms: Colonial Rivalry, Border Demarcation, and State-Building in Southwest China, 1885–1960' (PhD dissertation, Stanford University, 2014). On a similar process with the Siamese monarchy and Western border-demarcation, see also: Thongchai Winichakul, *Siam Mapped: A History of the Geo-body of a Nation* (Honolulu: University of Hawaii Press, 1994).

20 Giersch, *Asian Borderlands*, p. 61.

21 *Ibid.*, p. 62.

22   During the 1910s and 1920s, many more headlines focused on foreign imperialism in Mongolia, Manchuria and Tibet. During the early 1940s, writers began giving more attention to the Burma-China frontier with the Japanese presence in 1942.

23   See, for example: T. McGrath, 'A warlord frontier: the Yunnan-Burma border dispute, 1910–1937', *Ohio Academy of History Proceedings* (2003), 7–29; M. Norins, 'Tribal boundaries of the Burma-Yunnan frontier', *Pacific Affairs*, 12:1 (1939), 67–79.

24   On the overlapping claims of Burma and Siam prior to 1886 see Winichakul, *Siam Mapped*.

25   IOR: L/PS/10/208/2 A. Rose to H. Thompson, Chief Secretary to Government of Burma, and J. Jordan, Ambassador at Beijing, 'Burma-China Frontier: Report of Consul's Tour and Frontier Meetings for the Open Season 1910 to 1911', 25 February 1911. There remained at least 241 km of undelimited boundary lying north of 'Manang Pum' along the range of mountains known as the Irrawaddy-Salween Divide, whilst another section lay to the south, with a tract that was located to the east of the Wa states from 'Nalawt-Pang-sang' to the Namting River. George Scott attempted to claim a boundary in this southern region alone after the failure of the Boundary Commission in 1899–1900. His demarcation was known as 'Scott's Line', but the Chinese authorities refused to recognise it.

26   For example, in 1911, following border disagreements and the Pianma incident, consul Archibald Rose reported that a British supplementary boundary pillar was destroyed and a regular frontier pillar was defaced on the orders of the Tengyue *daotai*. The Chinese authorities also retracted their recognition of a number of other pillars falling between the two undelimited sections and the interpreter who helped the Tengyue consul into the unadministered territory was imprisoned. IOR: L/PS/10/208/2 A. Rose to H. Thompson, Chief Secretary to Government of Burma, and J. Jordan, Ambassador at Beijing, 'Burma-China Frontier: Report of Consul's Tour and Frontier Meetings for the Open Season 1910 to 1911', 25 February 1911.

27   *Ibid.*

28   A number of Chinese language works highlight this immigration process and Chinese policy from the Ming Dynasty to the Southwest. See, amongst others: M. Cang, *yunnan biandi yimin shi* [*The History of Migration in the Yunnan Periphery*] (Beijing: minzu chubanshe, 2004); S. Cao, *zhongguo yimin shi, di liu juan* [*The History of Migration in China*], vol. 6 (Fuzhou: Fujian renmin chubanshe, 1997). In English, see amongst others works: U. Theobald and J. Cao (eds), *Southwest China in a Regional and Global Perspective (c.1600–1911): Metals, Transport, Trade and Society* (Leiden: Brill, 2018).

29   J. Lee, 'Food supply and population growth in Southwest China 1250–1850', *Journal of Asian Studies*, 41:4 (1982), 712, 722–24.

30   J. Lee, 'The legacy of immigration in Southwest China, 1250–1850', *Annales de Démographie Historique* (1992), 279–304.

31   On Chinese migration and urbanisation in the frontier, see: Giersch, *Asian Borderlands*, pp. 127–38, 165–66.

32   G. Geary, *Burma after the Conquest: Viewed in its Political, Social and Commercial Aspects, from Mandalay* (London: S. Low, Marston, 1886), p. 27; J. Anderson, *A Report on the Expedition to Western Yunnan via Bhamo* (Calcutta: Asiatic Society, 1871), pp. 216–19.

33   *Census of India, 1901, Volume XII Burma, Part I Report* (Rangoon: Office of the Superintendent of Government Printing, 1902), p. 29.

34   On the use of the highlands as sites of refuge from lowland authority, see: J. Scott, *The Art of Not Being Governed: An Anarchist History of Upland Southeast Asia* (New Haven: Yale University Press, 2009).

35   J. Ma, 'Salt and revenue in frontier formation: state mobilized ethnic politics in the Yunnan-Burma borderland since the 1720s', *Modern Asian Studies*, 48:6 (2014), 1647.

36   TNA: FO228/1598 G. Litton to E. Satow, Ambassador at Beijing, 'Intelligence report, Tengyueh', 30 January 1905.

37   *Ibid.*

38 For some, the decision to migrate was also often contingent upon the seasons, as the rainy season prevented easy travel and there were higher incidences of epidemics in rainy seasons.
39 M. Thampi, *Indians in China 1800–1949* (New Delhi: Manohar, 2005).
40 On Sikh men working in the Shanghai Municipal Police, see: I. Jackson, 'The Raj on Nanjing Road: Sikh policemen in treaty-port China', *Modern Asian Studies*, 46:6 (2012), 1672–704.
41 TNA: FO656/109 E. Fraser, Hankou consulate-general, to J. Jordan, Ambassador at Beijing, 21 November 1906.
42 TNA: FO656/101 H. de Sausmarez, Her Britannic Majesty's Supreme Court for China, to Secretary to the Government of India, Foreign Department, 16 July 1906.
43 *Ibid.*
44 TNA: FO656/109 Municipal Council, Hankou to E. Fraser, Hankou consul-general, 'employment of natives of India as police', 17 November 1906.
45 *Ibid.*
46 See, for example: E. Kolsky, 'The colonial rule of law and legal regime of exception: frontier "fanaticism" and state violence in British India', *American Historical Review*, 120:4 (2015), 1218–46.
47 TNA: FO656/92 E. Satow, Ambassador at Beijing to Foreign Office, 21 July 1903.
48 TNA: FO656/92 F. Bourne, Her Britannic Majesty's Supreme Court for China, to E. Satow, Ambassador at Beijing, 27 May 1903.
49 Chief Judge Nicholas Hannen had rejected a similar suggestion by the first Tengyue consul, J. W. Jamieson in 1899. Jamieson had wanted the Judge of the Sessions Court in Mandalay to have the power to hear certain cases that arose in Tengyue.
50 TNA: FO656/92 E. Satow, Ambassador at Beijing, to Foreign Office, 21 July 1903.
51 TNA: FO656/106 H. de Sausmarez, Chief Judge, to Ernest Satow, Ambassador at Beijing, 14 July 1905.
52 TNA: FO656/92 E. Satow, Ambassador at Beijing, to Foreign Office, 21 July 1903.
53 Lahore was added in the Order in Council 1913 (Amendment), Article 6.
54 China Order in Council (1904), Article 83 and 83(4).
55 China Order in Council (1904), Article 88.
56 China Order in Council (1904), Article 83(3).
57 TNA: FO656/152 H. Harding, Tengyue consul, to W. Carrapiett, Deputy Commissioner, Bhamo, 24 March 1925.
58 TNA: FO656/152 H. Harding, Tengyue consul, to S. Turner, Chief Judge, 5 October 1925.
59 TNA: FO656/152 S. Turner, Chief Judge, to H. Harding, Tengyue consul, 12 August 1925.
60 N. Osada, '"Discovery of outsiders": the expulsion of undesirable Chinese and urban governance of colonial Rangoon, Burma, c. 1900–1920', *Journal of Sophia Asian Studies*, 1:32 (2014), 89.
61 *Ibid.*
62 *Ibid.*
63 TNA: FO228/3275 'Tengyue Intelligence Report for September Quarter, 1920'.
64 *Ibid.*
65 IOR/L/PS/10/208/2 C. Smith to J. Jordan, Ambassador at Beijing, 6 October 1914.
66 *Ibid.*
67 *Ibid.*
68 Geil, *A Yankee on the Yangtze*, p. 295.
69 *Report on the Administration of Burma during 1897–8* (Rangoon: Government Printing, Burma, 1898).
70 Geil, *A Yankee on the Yangtze*, p. 295. The Qing also used native militias to buttress their military; see Giersch, *Asian Borderlands*, pp. 113–16.
71 TNA: FO228/3275 'Tengyueh Intelligence Report for the six months ended March 31st, 1920'; TNA: FO228/3275 'Tengyueh Intelligence Report for the six months ended June 1919'.

72 TNA: FO228/3275 'Tengyueh Intelligence Report for the six months ended March 31st, 1920'.
73 TNA: FO228/3275 'Tengyueh Intelligence Report, ended March, 1919'.
74 Throughout the 1910s and 1920s, there were numerous rebellions and 'political disturbances' in the frontier. One of the largest was the Kannai rebellion in 1924. In 1926 in Tengyue, a coup d'état against Tang Jiyao caused considerable upheaval.
75 IOR: L/PS/10/208/2 W. Cabell, Superintendent of the Northern Shan States, H. Thornton, the Superintendent of the Northern Shan States, and A. Rose, Tengyue consul, to Geng Baogui, Tengyue *daotai*, 21 January 1911.
76 *Ibid.*
77 IOR: L/PS/10/208/2 H. Thompson, Chief Secretary to the Government of Burma, to the Secretary to the Government of India in the Foreign Department, 18 April 1911; IOR/L/PS/10/208/2 J. Jordan, Ambassador at Beijing, to A. Rose, Tengyue consul, 26 July 1911; IOR/L/PS/10/208/2 E. Grey, Foreign Office to J. Jordan, Ambassador at Beijing, 8 July 1911.
78 IOR: L/PS/10/208/2 J. Jordan, Ambassador at Beijing, to C. Smith, 26 July 1911.
79 *Ibid.*
80 *Ibid.*
81 TNA: FO656/139 C. Smith to J. Jordan, Ambassador at Beijing, 6 October 1914; IOR/L/PS/10/208/2 C. Smith to J. Jordan, Ambassador at Beijing, 6 October 1914.
82 TNA: FO656/139 W. Langley, Foreign Office, to A. Rose, Tengyue consul, 10 June 1911; IOR/L/PS/10/208/2 C. Smith, acting Tengyue consul, to J. Jordan, Ambassador at Beijing, 6 October 1914; IOR/L/PS/10/208/2 W. Langley, Foreign Office, to A. Rose, 10 June 1911.
83 TNA: FO656/139 W. Langley, Foreign Office, to A. Rose, 10 June 1911; IOR/L/PS/10/208/2 W. Langley, Foreign Office, to A. Rose, 10 June 1911.
84 IOR: L/PS/10/208/2 C. Smith to J. Jordan, Ambassador at Beijing, 6 October 1914.
85 *Ibid.*
86 *Ibid.*
87 *Ibid.*
88 *Ibid.*
89 TNA: FO228/1952 A. Eastes to Yang Fuzhang, Tengyue *daoyin*, 26 March 1915. The Jaffar case and the issue of nationality of border crossers is also highlighted in: R. Mazumder, 'Illegal border crossers and unruly citizens: Burma-Pakistan-Indian borderlands from the nineteenth to the mid-twentieth centuries', *Modern Asian Studies* (2019), 1–39.
90 TNA: FO228/1952 A. Eastes to J. Jordan, Ambassador at Beijing, 26 March 1915.
91 TNA: FO228/1952 A. Eastes to Yang Fuzhang, Tengyue *daoyin*, 26 March 1915.
92 On the rule of colonial difference in India, and Indian criminal law, see: Elizabeth Kolsky, *Colonial Justice in British India: White Violence and the Rule of Law* (Cambridge, Cambridge University Press, 2010); Elizabeth Kolsky, 'Codification and the rule of colonial difference: criminal procedure in British India', *Law and History Review*, 23:3 (2005), 631–84.
93 IOR: L/PS/10/208/2 C. Smith to J. Jordan, Ambassador at Beijing, 12 January 1915.
94 *Ibid.*
95 IOR: L/PS/10/208/2 'Sections 188 and 189, Indian Criminal Procedure Code', FO minute paper, 'Burma-China Frontier', 8 March 1915. See also: E. Beverley, 'Frontier as resource: law, crime and sovereignty on the margins of empire', *Comparative Studies in Society and History*, 55:2 (2013), 241–72.
96 IOR: L/PS/10/208/2 C. Smith to J. Jordan, Ambassador at Beijing, 12 January 1915.
97 *Ibid.*
98 IOR: L/PS/10/208/2 C. Smith to E. Grey, Foreign Office, 12 January 1915; IOR: L/PS/10/208/2 J. Jordan, Ambassador at Beijing, to E. Grey, Foreign Office, 30 November 1914.
99 TNA: FO656/139 J. Jordan, Ambassador at Beijing, to Foreign Office, 30 November 1914; IOR: L/PS/10/208/2 C. Smith to E. Grey, 12 January 1915; IOR: L/PS/10/208/2 J. Jordan, Ambassador at Beijing, to E. Grey, Foreign Office, 30 November 1914.

100 TNA: FO656/139 J. Jordan, Ambassador at Beijing, to Foreign Office, 30 November 1914; IOR: L/PS/10/208/2 C. Smith to E. Grey, 12 January 1915; IOR: L/PS/10/208/2 J. Jordan, Ambassador at Beijing, to E. Grey, Foreign Office, 30 November 1914.
101 IOR: L/PS/10/208/2 Government of India to Austin Chamberlin, Secretary of State for India, 17 December 1915.
102 TNA: FO656/139 Government of India, Foreign and Political Department to A. Chamberlain, Secretary of State for India, 17 December 1915.

CHAPTER THREE

Consuls and Frontier Meetings, 1909–35

From 1899 to 1943, British consuls played an important role on the Burma-China frontier. They exercised consular jurisdiction and helped the Burmese colonial officials to apply territorial laws over borders in the frontier. They also helped to resolve disputes between British Burmese and Chinese claimed subjects in annual court case hearings. These hearings, known as the 'Frontier Meetings' (huishen/huian), awarded compensation to victims of criminal offences. The defendants and complainants in the Meetings were mostly ethnic frontier inhabitants. They included the ethnic Kachins living in the Shan States as well as other local groups such as the Shans, Lisus and others. The cases reflected the everyday lives of the people and the most common cross-border suspected crimes. From cattle theft to blood feuds, consuls helped negotiate for a settlement that suited British interests. Some cases were politically sensitive involving questions of sovereignty, territoriality and legal authority between China and Britain. In this chapter, I show how consuls worked in the Frontier Meetings as legal mediators and how they promoted colonial sovereignty over disputed lands across parts of the frontier.

The Frontier Meetings were not the only mixed courts in China. In Shanghai, Hankou, Harbin and Xiamen, mixed courts resolved cases involving Chinese defendants and treaty power plaintiffs. Scholars have analysed this 'system' (huishen zhidu), mostly through examining the Shanghai Mixed Court (huishen gongxie).[1] The Frontier Meetings on the Burma-China frontier, however, had an unusual constitution. They had jurisdiction over cases involving local groups and transfrontier crime, used customary law as legal parameters and only had the power to award compensation. Yao Yong has argued that these Meetings strengthened the notion of borders, sovereignty and nationality between the two empires.[2] Local people, especially headmen, became aware of these concepts and were able to utilise the jurisdictional competition between China and Britain to pursue their own interests.[3] This chapter takes a British perspective, examining the role of consuls. As Yao has contended, these Meetings often witnessed political and cultural clashes between British and Chinese officials over claims to the same land, people and resources. Meetings did indeed open up the question of sovereignty in disputed areas and I argue that the Tengyue consuls worked as mediators and promoted Burmese sovereignty claims over disputed lands. Examining the role of consuls in Frontier Meetings can also provide a window onto the ways in which British officials accommodated indigenous law and worked with local headmen and Chinese officials in the exercise of their legal powers. Consuls had to advise, negotiate and bargain with their Chinese colleagues, and at times they delegated authority to local headmen to resolve sensitive cases where there was a stalemate between British and Chinese officials. Tengyue officials therefore used the plural legal environment strategically to bolster British sovereignty in the frontier.

The first section of this chapter examines the establishment of the Frontier Meetings. I then demonstrate the nature of the Meetings and the role of the consuls in these courts. In the third section, I take a closer look at the 'Pianma cases' to demonstrate how consuls advanced Burmese sovereign claims to disputed lands in the frontier. Finally, I show how the Burma officers viewed the consuls in these courts and their role in helping to achieve a 'successful' outcome for British interests through these Meetings.

The establishment of Frontier Meetings

Photographic records can provide powerful visualisations, but their existence in colonial files can also be misleading. Although the first consular court hearing in Tengyue is depicted in the colonial archive (Figure 5, below), the image of holding court was a symbolic display of power. The Tengyue consul presided over few consular court hearings. Consular reports regularly stated 'nil' returns for consular criminal and civil hearings for the Tengyue district.[4] In contrast, the 'major portion' of a consul's time was spent resolving a 'heavy roll' of Sino-British frontier cases.[5] This involved his work in the Frontier Meetings. These courts usually involved only individuals from local ethnic frontier groups, mainly Shans, Lisus and Kachins populating each side of the frontier. The injured party was a subject claimed by either China or

Figure 5   First consular court held at Tengyue, 1909. British Consul (centre) with local Chinese officials (immediate left and right) surrounded by British Sikh and Chinese court assistants (outer right and left)

Burma and the perpetrator claimed by the other. Meetings heard cases involving anything from cattle thefts and petty assaults to village raids and murders. British and Chinese authorities sought to find if the perpetrator was guilty of the offence claimed. When guilt was established, the perpetrator's sovereign (Burma or China), paid according to a mutually agreed scale by the Chinese and Burmese Frontier Officers.

Annual Meetings were set up following the Manai Agreement (1902). It established a court of first instance in Nawngma, a village on the British side of the frontier that lay opposite the Chinese village of Manai. This meeting could also take place at Namhkam, an important market town in the Burmese Shan States, lying approximately 160 km southwest of Tengyue. From 1909, another simultaneous-running court of first instance was established at Sima, which was located 80 km west of Tengyue. These Meetings were intended to hear transfrontier cases that arose further to the north.[6] One or two Burmese officials – usually an Assistant Superintendent and a Deputy Commissioner – sat with a Chinese District Magistrate, an Administrative Deputy and/or the Tengyue *daotai/daoyin* (circuit intendant).[7] Consuls worked with their Burmese counterparts and learned how they could contribute towards transfrontier British interests.[8] A local headman gave advice to Burmese and Chinese officials on local customs and could sit as an assessor.[9] Appeals and unresolved cases went to the Court of Appeal. The *daotai/daoyin* of Tengyue or a District Magistrate presided over this court with either a Burmese Superintendent or Deputy Commissioner. The Meetings continued to take place almost every year until 1925–6 and sporadically thereafter until 1940.[10]

The object of the Meetings was to rectify the 'Kachin problem', in which the Meetings were to 'replace those blood-feuds, in which the Kachins settle such matters amongst themselves, by properly organized Courts and by settlements which would be enforced if necessary'.[11] Consuls considered some local groups, such as the hill-dwelling Kachin, as more 'warlike' and understood inter-community conflict as an endemic part of life.[12] This disruption could negatively affect colonial administration in the two administrative regions on the Burmese side of the frontier: the Kachin Hills and the Shan States. Although initially the Meetings aimed to resolve disputes between Kachin groups, the jurisdiction of the Meetings was extended to include other native inhabitants and even Chinese subjects in the frontier as parties in cases. Consular officials therefore felt that the Meetings would reduce 'lawlessness' along the frontier.[13] This perception of lawlessness and violence of local frontier populations drew many similarities to British Indian discourses of the northwest frontiers of India.[14] In these northwest regions, however, the Indian government was also concerned with attacks upon Europeans. In due course, British officials in the Indian frontiers acquired new draconian powers to combat this perceived unruliness. In the Burma-China frontier, a less intrusive manner of reducing crime was required. Whereas rebellions occasionally rose up against British or Chinese rule in the Burma-China frontier, such as the Kanai rebellion in 1924 against Chinese jurisdiction, everyday instances of crime were mostly between local populations. Furthermore, as both Britain and China could not administer this region without the help of local headmen, the Frontier Meetings appeared to be the most suitable solution. Consular officials also claimed that Frontier Meetings were important due to a well-versed trope about Chinese maladministration, which characterised Chinese officials as incapable or uninterested in governing its frontier districts effectively. For the British, therefore, the Frontier Meetings were established to prevent the escalation of social disruption in the frontier. The Meetings also rebalanced the perceived inadequacies of Chinese administration in territories nearest to Sino-British borders.

Whereas imperial officers presided over the Meetings, local custom guided their assessment of the cases. In 1909, the Chinese and British authorities agreed seven regulations based on local custom. First, the courts applied 'track law'. This meant that villagers on one side of the frontier had a duty to help find stolen cattle belonging to a person from the other side, if it had been traced entering into their village.[15] Second, those found guilty of raiding villages across the frontier were liable to arrest and punishment. China or Burma paid compensation to victims depending on which side claimed jurisdiction over the perpetrators. Transfrontier raids were a common occurrence and were often linked to long-standing blood feuds. This provision was therefore important for peaceful relations between villages. Third, the headmen, Chinese officers and Burmese Frontier Officers had to make stringent efforts to weed out false claims in the courts. This sought to decrease the workload for the officers and dissuade those seeking to use the Meeting for retaliation against individuals for past feuds. Fourth, accusations of petty theft in the absence of 'definite' evidence could not be investigated. There was no indication in this provision of what was considered 'definite' evidence, but the general principle nevertheless reflected the concern that the Meetings could be used as a way to punish innocent individuals. Fifth, cases were to be recorded at the time of the Meeting and reported to administrative superiors. For many of the Meetings, both the Tengyue consular official as well as a Burmese official – such as a Deputy Commissioner – provided short summaries of the proceedings of the Meetings and their outcomes. These reports were sent to the Secretary to the Government of Burma and, occasionally, the Ambassador at Beijing. However, these reports often did not contain the details of how they reached compromises to resolve cases. Sixth, these rules were to be in accordance to 'meet local conditions' (although what this could entail was not described) and the rules were to be 'faithfully observed'. Finally, there was an agreed scale of financial compensation relating to various crimes.[16] In the event that both Chinese and British officials came to an agreement, the aggressor's sovereign paid a compensatory fee to the victim, the victim's family or their headman. These rules were not a comprehensive code for the officials and in due time they were 'gradually supplemented by the "case law" which evolved from precedents established at successive meetings'.[17]

As the Meetings saw the coming together of British and Chinese officers, both sets of imperial officials required the cooperation of the other for the resolution of cases. Although Tengyue consul Archibald Rose felt that the Meetings were 'hedged with difficulties', he believed that these could be 'generally best met by common sense and mutual agreement'.[18] Some of the crimes may have appeared of little importance to new consuls, such as the theft of cattle. However, livestock were important assets to many groups and transfrontier crime involving the theft of animals – or indeed any other offence – had the potential to trigger inter-village or inter-ethnic conflict if the case was left unresolved. In other instances, incidents of crime in places without agreed borders could trigger territorial disputes between Burma and China.

The Frontier Meetings were therefore an important dispute resolution mechanism for both China and Britain. Peace on the frontier was a key part of British policy and framed how the consul approached the Meetings. Drawing upon the principles laid out by his predecessor Ernest Satow, the Ambassador at Beijing, John Jordan, recorded that 'British interests imperatively demand the preservation of peace on the Burma frontier'.[19] Jordan also advised consul Sly, with regard to cases arising from the Shan States, to 'confine your action to interfering, with discretion, in cases where the security of the frontier would seem to be threatened'.[20] This policy was shaped by the recent events in China, where anti-British and anti-foreign sentiment erupted into larger movements against foreign imperialism. This meant that it was important that consuls did not damage Sino-British relations through disputing local political issues with Chinese officials. A peaceful frontier and amicable Sino-foreign relations also helped Sino-British boundary negotiations and frontier administration. This general principle shaped two goals of the consuls in Meetings. First, consuls aimed to resolve all cases, even if this required a rehearing the next year or over successive years. This minimised the likelihood of social disruption on the frontier. The measure of a 'successful' Meeting was therefore one that resolved outstanding cases and preferably resulted in China paying for compensation where consular officers felt it was due. Second, consuls chose carefully which cases to defend when balancing the need to assert British sovereignty claims to disputed lands with the need to maintain amicable relations with Chinese officials.

Roles of the consul

Consuls played several important roles regarding the resolution of transfrontier cases. One of the most important was acting as a linguistic translator and communicative intermediary with the status that the British thought conveyed enough respect in the eyes of the Chinese authorities. The need for communicative mediators was apparent from the opening of the consulate. The British Burmese authorities' initial attempts to communicate with Chinese officials on transfrontier issues before 1899 were woefully inadequate. Letters sent in English from Burma lacked decorum and had the potential to be insulting to their intended Chinese recipients.[21] The first Tengyue consul J. W. Jamieson thereafter insisted that Tengyue consuls should be correspondence intermediaries between Burmese and Chinese authorities.

Although the Burmese officials later used Chinese translators, the Tengyue consul remained a mediator, helping to interpret the coded language of various Chinese officials. A Chinese consular writer assisted the consul, providing much-needed support. Archibald Rose praised his writer, Han Weizu, in the highest terms for his role in helping him and his predecessors.[22] Consuls also forwarded petitions from Burma to the provincial authorities in Kunming. For example, when a Chinese Frontier Deputy did not appear in the Sima Meeting of 1925-6, the Tengyue consul Ivan Harding petitioned the Tengyue *daoyin* on behalf of Burmese officials in order to ensure his return the next year.[23] Although this seems of little importance, the absence of various Chinese officials mattered greatly. Replacement officials often had little frontier experience and held a lower administrative rank. This meant that they were sometimes unable to take decisions on cases that had a more significant bearing on frontier politics. Harding noted that the Sima Meeting of 1925-6 was a 'fiasco', as the absence of the Chinese Frontier Deputy resulted in only one case out of seven being settled.[24] Consuls also feared that such replacement officers without rank would diminish the status of the Meetings in the eyes of the local headmen.[25] Thus, from a British perspective, the success of the Meetings depended on both the Chinese and local headmen attributing importance to the status of Meetings. Within Meetings, consuls helped translate the words of the Chinese officials for the Burmese officers and translated the arguments of the Burmese officials to the Chinese authorities. Whilst there were also other Chinese interpreters who were present, consuls were in a unique position of being both an interpreter and a British representative who was acquainted with British imperial aims.

Consuls were also advisors and negotiators. As the Meetings were more akin to advocates trying to compromise with one another rather than ones that involved a presiding judge, consuls informed the Burmese officers of the different practices and tactics of their counterparts. Chinese practices of adjudication, evidence, witness testimony and jurisprudence often appeared arbitrary, coercive and retributive to Burmese officers.[26] As consul Harding stated disparagingly at the Nawngma Meeting of 1923-4, the Chinese magistrates and Chinese Frontier Deputies were 'all without even an amateurish understanding of the necessities of the most simple western judicial procedure or official method'.[27] In other words, there was a need for someone to be present in the Meetings to help smooth over these differences in procedure. Consuls, who were trained from the China Consular Service and were familiar with Chinese legal practice and jurisprudence, were therefore best placed to explain these differences to Burmese officers. An example of these differences was evident in a 1914 report from the Deputy Commissioner of Myitkyina. One case involved a Han Chinese defendant who had lived on the British side of the frontier, whom the Burmese officers claimed was a British Burmese subject.[28] The Burmese Deputy Commissioner took issue with what he perceived to be the uncompromising attitude of the Chinese Frontier Deputy and described his cross-examination of their defendant as 'bullying'.[29] Such stringent cross-examining was a common feature in Chinese hearings, whereby confession was the chief source of evidence. The Commissioner asked consul C. D. Smith to protest on his behalf. Mediating this difference in legal procedure would have been a difficult task, but with his acquaintance of both British and Chinese legal approaches, alongside his understanding of Chinese decorum and linguistic abilities, Smith was perfectly placed to resolve the issue. Although there is no detail of how Smith undertook this, his achievement was evident. The Deputy Commissioner remarked of the 1914 Meeting that 'the success ... as usual pivoted on the consul' and that it was 'solely due to Mr Smith's untiring patience and courtesy in rather difficult circumstances, and to his intimate acquaintance with Chinese character and language that so many cases were settled'.[30] Using their understanding of Chinese decorum, consuls therefore offered 'invaluable' guidance to Burmese officers on how to come to an agreement with their Chinese colleagues.[31]

Consuls also thought strategically about how to present cases in ways that would help engender an outcome favourable to British interests. Theoretically, the British and Chinese officers in court were two impartial judges who endeavoured to reach a joint decision and common judgment. However, in practice, the two officials acted more like two barristers, who pleaded their suits and bargained for a favourable result. Frequently, consuls arranged cases to maximise the probability of compromise on both sides. Consul Hall summarised this technique:

> Cases must be carefully arranged so that the principle of compromise keeps the ball rolling. Thus if Burma has a sound case where it is felt that China ought to pay compensation, it is as well to place such a case immediately after a strong Chinese case where Burma has already paid, or decided that it will have to pay, compensation of at least an equal amount. Where China has a palpably weak case it is as well to slip in before it a weak Burma case which can, after a few minutes, be withdrawn as a generous gesture. Not infrequently the Chinese will reciprocate, yet without such a gesture they might have argued their case for hours and eventually sent it to the Court of Appeal ... Tactics further demand acceptance of the distasteful curios shop procedure of prior over

or under statement according as to whether one will receive, or will pay, compensation.[32]

Consuls not only thought strategically about how to present cases but also had to comply with Chinese methods of negotiation in order to settle cases. This demonstrated how British officials had to accommodate Chinese legal methods in order to find a compromise.

Tengyue consuls also informed their Burmese counterparts on what they understood to be the motives of Chinese officers. Throughout successive Frontier Meetings, Burmese officers viewed the Chinese officials as primarily concerned with beneficial monetary outcomes rather than settling cases. Consuls did not dispel this view and successive consuls varied on their level of sympathy and acceptance of this attributed Chinese perspective. As Archibald Rose remarked for the 1910–11 Frontier Meeting at Namhkam:

> Our officers are sometimes discouraged at the fact that their Chinese colleagues have so little perception of abstract justice and they find difficulty in resisting a temptation to bargain over the settlements when monetary compensations are awarded by the Court. Such bargaining is, I think, inevitable to the mind of the Chinese magistrate and, when it is remembered that the awards come first of all from his own pocket and that his is dependent on the recovery of his outlay from numerous other officials and loosely-held tribal villages – a process requiring another long and enduring struggle – these shortcomings may perhaps be charitably forgotten.[33]

Although Rose understood some of the financial restraints of the Chinese Frontier Officers, the consul in 1919 was less sympathetic, accusing the Tengyue *daoyin* of:

> regard[ing] the frontier meeting as a kind of annual competition between Burma and China, and that the chief aim and object of which is to extract as much money as possible from the other side, and the success of the meetings, as far as he is concerned, is judged chiefly by this standard. Small claims are usually settled without much difficulty, but anything over 500 Rupees almost invariably becomes the subject of much lying and prevarication on the Chinese side. It is a melancholy fact, but strongly significant of the Chinese official character and only too plainly demonstrated by the history of the frontier meetings in the past.[34]

Despite the perception that Chinese officers were motivated by financial aims, British officers strove to create personal bonds to better understand their counterparts and produce a more harmonious working atmosphere. Certainly, some Chinese officials were considered friendlier towards British officials than others. In 1911 at the Meeting in Sima, for example, all seventeen cases that were heard were settled.

Following this success of resolved cases, Rose commented of Deputy Zhao that there was 'no doubt that he really likes and respects the British Officials with whom his work lies, and that the respect is mutual'.[35] In fact, Rose felt that throughout the two seasons that he worked with Zhao, he 'proved himself an exceedingly able, courteous and straightforward colleague'.[36] In fact, such friendly relations were key to a successful meeting:

> The happy results of personal relations and mutual confidence have shown themselves very clearly during the past year; current cases have been dealt with promptly as they arose, and there was no actual need for a meeting save for the very excellent and most important reason of all – that of renewing and continuing the good work and genial personal relations commenced by last year's gathering.[37]

However, fractious Meetings certainly existed, with personal differences arising between officials. In 1915, consul C. D. Smith protested that the Chinese authorities had failed to secure witnesses for cases and should pay compensation for the omissions. He claimed that 'with no inconsiderable heat, but in language in which there was no impropriety', he had put across his point but that the Chinese Frontier Deputy had retorted that he was a 'savage' (*yeman ren*) and had sarcastically referred to him as hailing from 'a [so-called] civilized country' (*wenming guo*).[38] Smith's consular successor maintained that Smith had clearly been subject to 'gratuitous and insufferable insolence of the Chinese Deputy'.[39] The use of the terms 'savage' and 'civilized country' was a pointed attack on the British imperial narrative that legitimised British imperialism in China. British officials often claimed that the Chinese legal system was not of the required Western standard, which prevented Britain from agreeing to abolish extraterritoriality. Following the exchange, the Meeting came to an abrupt halt.[40] However, the *daotai* had a different version of the events, stating that while they were 'amicably talking things over suddenly the Consul jumped up waving his fists and shouting. Chou Weiyuan [the Frontier Deputy] could not do otherwise than call him to order, and there was nothing improper in his doing so'.[41] Later, the Kunming consul-general had a meeting to discuss the difficulties with a government representative, Chang Yizhu.[42] Chang stated that local Chinese officials had told him that there had been 'an altercation between Chou and Mr Smith during which the latter had thumped the table with his fists'.[43] This short summary of an exchange not only demonstrated that some Meetings could become fractious, but also that cooperation was an important part of the proceedings; a breakdown in friendly relations could end Meetings abruptly.

To help build personal relations (or indeed repair them), the Burmese and Chinese officers hosted social events alongside the Meetings.

These occasions usually comprised a dinner and entertainment. Beatrix Metford, formerly the wife of Tengyue consul Stanley Wyatt-Smith (1927–31), jovially related the entertainment of the Chinese soldier entourage:

> The favourite is the elephant race. Four men form the legs of the beast, two more standing on top as the head, and a seventh on top of the latter as a trunk. A race between two such 'elephants' is very amusing, especially when, as often happens, one of them collapses near the winning post. It is probably all for the best that few of the onlookers understand the remarks of the 'trunk' who has been let down from a height of ten feet or more.[44]

In another Meeting at Sima, Burma officers considered the social events 'exceptionally successful' with Chinese officials competing with the British officials in a rifle shooting competition, while 'Messrs. Carr [Assistant Superintendent of Sadon] and Liu [Liu Guoshu, Administrative Deputy of Santa] entered together in a three-legged race against the Chinese, Indian and Kachin police and soldiers'.[45] After another Meeting at Nawngma, it was reported that the 'Chinese officials had paper crowns out of crackers at the official dinner and all pulled in a tug-of-war … whilst the Chanta [Santa] deputy gave us a song … [and] the Lungling [Longling] Magistrate composed a poem on the spot to celebrate the occasion'.[46] It was certainly a festive occasion, which intended to bring Chinese, Burmese and consular officers together.

For consuls, the opportunity of hosting social events at the Frontier Meetings was also an opportunity to demonstrate British prestige. Consuls could not do this at Tengyue with a consulate that was considered an 'unostentatious little mud house'.[47] Marches were put on to display British imperial status. For example, a military band consisting of Kachins dressed in Scottish kilts and playing the bagpipes accompanied the dinner at one Meeting at Nawngma.[48] The Chinese officials also prided themselves on providing a good reception to the British officers. Metford described the lavish Chinese dinner parties with spoons and forks provided for their 'clumsy' British guests and arranged entertainment, such as 'wonderful displays of ancient wrestling and sword and bayonet fighting'.[49] Consuls had a closer relationship to the Chinese officers than their Burmese counterparts and such social occasions presented an opportunity for them to consolidate amicable relations in an informal setting. As a Burma Office report highlighted in relating consul Ronald Hall's summary of the history of the gatherings, 'in the haggling which takes place in these courts rather after the manner of a bazaar, only the British consul has any influence with the Chinese, and that because he is known personally to them'.[50]

The Frontier Meetings were an integral part of keeping the frontier free from what consuls considered 'lawlessness'. Friendly relations with Chinese officials helped towards the settlement of cases, which in turn reduced the likelihood of a local uprisings caused by an unresolved case. By 1911, Rose claimed that the proof of the value of the Meetings was reflected in the 'striking decrease of serious charges and the practical absence of those armed raids which until recent years formed so grave a factor in our frontier politics'.[51] However, a peaceful frontier was not the only aim of the British officers, as the Pianma cases would show.

The Pianma cases and the importance of the consul to colonial authority

The settling of transfrontier cases was not without political incentives. Consuls aimed to assert and protect British sovereign claims to land, people and resources in disputed areas of the frontier. The Meetings allowed the consul to hear the views of his Burmese colleagues, 'enabling him to gather what is needed in the interests of Burma'.[52] From the 1910s to the 1930s, there were a number of border skirmishes and jurisdictional contestations between Burma and China.[53] However, one of the clearest examples of the consul acting as advisor, negotiator and intermediary for promoting Burmese sovereignty were in cases involving the region known as Pianma to the Chinese and as Hpimaw to the Burmese. Laying between the N'Maikha and Upper Salween Rivers, the Burmese authorities described it in the first decade of the twentieth century as an 'unadministered' region of the northeast part of the Myitkyina District. China claimed sovereignty over the region through a local headman (*sawbwa*) to the east, who had jurisdiction over the lands and paid allegiance to China. The official British policy asserted that the boundary of the Sino-Burmese frontier was the Salween rather than the N'Maikha. The India Office supported this claim and stated that although China had not accepted the watershed boundary, in 1906 Chinese officials had temporarily agreed to give up Chinese sovereignty claims over Pianma in return for compensation.[54] George Forest, a botanist who travelled with the Tengyue consul George Litton to the region, added to the perception that it was British territory. In his 'Journey on Upper Salwin', published in 1908, he stated that Pianma was only 'nominally subject to the Chinese headman of Teng-keng'.[55] As the village was on the Salween, but was situated west of the divide, it was therefore within the British side of the frontier. He further stated that the Pianma headman wished for the British government to claim sovereignty over his village, as representatives of the local *sawbwa* owing allegiance to China had seized his cattle and carried off two girls in lieu of tribute.

[83]

The region drew attention to the British authorities once more two years later. On 15 March 1910, the British representative in Beijing, Max Müller, reported to consul Archibald Rose that he had received through the Government of Burma a petition from certain villages on the Ngaw Chang River, located on the Burmese side of the watershed frontier.[56] The petition noted that the 'Tengkeng' *sawbwa* with a force of 500 men had raided and burnt the village of Pianma. Under instructions from the Ambassador, Rose protested to the Tengyue *daotai*. He demanded the withdrawal of the perpetrators and the punishment of the *sawbwa*, and for compensation to be paid to the villagers. In response, the *daotai* asserted that Pianma was in Chinese territory and that the incident had been perpetrated 'by some lawless headmen in Tengkeng's jurisdiction'.[57] He reported that he had sent a local official to deal with the case. He felt that the incident was the first fruits of the forward policy of the new army in Yunnan and made a tour in the district in April 1910. He verified that the petitions of the villagers were factually correct and contended that the Chinese officials had inspired or helped the *sawbwa* to carry out the raid. He added that in his view, the prevailing impression among the villagers was that they were under the jurisdiction of Burmese authority.

In May 1910, the *waiwupu* – the Chinese External Affairs Department – declared to the Ambassador at Beijing that Pianma was in Chinese territory. In response, the Burmese government sent an expedition to Pianma in December 1910. Military police remained until April 1911, when negotiations began between Chinese officials and John Jordan, the British Ambassador at Beijing. Although most Burmese soldiers left Pianma, some police garrisons remained. In Beijing, the Chinese authorities argued that the boundary should be the N'Maikha. However, they were powerless to stop the occupation of British police. As Burmese officials refused to withdraw its claim to the district, the Chinese officials refused to hear cases from the disputed region in the Meetings, viewing them as non-transfrontier cases.

Thereafter, Chinese officials attempted to assert sovereignty claims through cases. In a burglary case that occurred in May 1916, it was alleged that a Chinese subject, who was temporarily residing in the jurisdiction of Burma, hired six 'ruffians' – three from Burma and three from the Chinese territory – to tie up and beat an old enemy in the Htawgaw (Tuojiao) area.[58] British military police arrested the ringleader in the disputed territory. In turn, the *daotai* claimed jurisdiction over the offenders. As the Burma subjects had committed a crime in what he understood to be Chinese territory, he insisted that Burmese police had to hand over the individuals. Only an extradition request from a Burmese official could thereafter allow their return. The Burmese

Frontier Officers refused to hand them over and noted that Chinese officials were now using these incidents of crime to assert their claims to people, resources and land.

Tengyue consuls supported Burmese claims to Pianma though careful negotiation. During 1917–18, Burmese officials decided to push for a resolution to three cases from the region. Two of the cases concerned petty crime, but the third was of a more serious nature. This case involved a party of villagers from Chikgaw and its district, claimed by Burma. The villagers went across the frontier to a market at 'Ku-T'an-Ho' (Gutanhe) in China.[59] Whilst selling their goods at the local market, a band of seven Lisu men allegedly attacked, stoned and robbed ninety-six rupees' worth of property, approximately two miles within the Chinese side of the Hpimaw pass. Consul Arthur Eastes asked whether it was possible to hear the cases in the next Meeting and tried to find grounds of commonality to convince the Chinese authorities. He stated:

> [I] talked the matter over with Mr. Chang [Chang Qiyin, Tengyue District Magistrate and Appellate officer of the Sima Meeting] on the evening of his arrival at Sima, I put it to him that in all these cases certain persons had been wronged or injured by Chinese citizens hailing from what was indisputably Chinese territory, and that by universal law in every civilized country wrong-doers should be punished and innocent sufferers at their hands should have their wrongs as far as possible redressed.[60]

Although Eastes persuaded the district magistrate to allow the Chinese and British Frontier Officers to hear the case, in the Meeting the Chinese officers refused to discuss it. Eastes tried again, this time appealing to the *daoyin*. Eastes remarked:

> I decided to adopt different tactics. I therefore expressed my appreciation of his admission in previous similar cases of the duty of government to redress the wrongs of all victims of oppression, irrespective of their place of origin; and I requested the issue of strict orders to effect the arrest of the guilty parties and to afford compensation for the losses suffered by the complainants. This had the desired effect of staving off any fatuous repetition of the denial of the British status of Hpimaw and [the] neighbourhood.[61]

Eastes reported five days later that the Tengyue *daoyin*, Yu Renlong, had issued orders to secure the arrest of the perpetrators.[62] Thereafter there would be a strict enquiry and, if found guilty, local headmen would deal with them in accordance with the custom of the locality. It appeared that Eastes's carefully worded letter had secured British sovereignty and the punishment of the individuals, with the perpetrators tried by a local headman using customary law. Although the question of sovereignty over Pianma remained unsettled, Eastes therefore brought a temporary solution to an outstanding impasse.[63] His handling of the case was careful; instead of asserting British sovereignty as pursued by Burmese officers in the Meetings, he appealed with rhetoric that he felt would speak to Chinese notions of universal justice. He chose to raise the issue outside of the Frontier Meeting hearings, allowing for a less confrontational style in a more informal setting.

However, this was not the end of the matter and further cases arose from the region. In July 1919, ten Chinese Lisus raided a village in the Pianma district.[64] The assailants had wounded five local inhabitants and had taken property worth over 1,000 rupees. One suspect was a 'notorious robber' who had a record of committing crimes in China. Consul Affleck claimed the Chinese Frontier Deputy took no steps to arrest the suspect and that the Deputy had instead accused men from the British side for the attack. Before the Sima Meeting in 1920, Affleck sought an interview with the Chinese official before the Meeting, where it was agreed that a local Chinese Frontier Deputy would summon headmen of the village to settle the case by arbitration.[65] Affleck approved of the reversion to local jurisdiction in this instance, but before any action was taken, a new Frontier Deputy, surnamed Wu, reasserted that the region belonged to China.

It is unclear whether the 1919 case in the end reverted to arbitration by local headmen. However, it was clear that consuls attempted to negotiate with Chinese officials before hearings as a tactic to play down tensions in the courtroom. They also appeared willing to allow local leaders to assume jurisdiction in order to avoid the larger question of British sovereignty in the region. British officials were therefore strategic in their meetings with Chinese officials, and utilised local leaders and the plural legal environment to maintain British claims over disputed lands.

The Burmese view of the consular officers

Burmese officers throughout the first three decades of the twentieth century remarked upon the role of consuls in supporting Burmese authority across the frontier. Burmese Frontier Officers were often 'indebted for the cordial assistance' of consuls during Meetings, where they contributed much towards 'the maintenance of harmonious relations'.[66] They not only facilitated the resolution of cases, but in some instances also helped persuade Chinese officials to station more police on the Chinese side of the frontier.[67] This was important to Burmese officers as they saw 'lawlessness' and inadequate policing on the Chinese side of the frontier as compromising their policy of maintaining a peaceful frontier.

Whereas political instability in the first and second decades of the twentieth century gave rise to a perceived increase in the levels of crime in the frontier, by the late 1910s and 1920s, the perception of crime was that it had reached alarming proportions. Burmese officers reported many more incidents of petty robbery on the routes to Bhamo and Myitkyina from western Yunnan, including 'bandits' who attacked caravans and razed villages to the ground.[68] The gratitude of the Burmese officers to the consul for helping to resolve cases was nearly always present in their reports during this era. Reporting on the Meeting at Nawngma in 1919, H. Thornton, the Superintendent of the Northern Shan States, noted that 'the thanks of all British Officers are due to Mr A. E. Eastes for the ready assistance and unfailing courtesy which in five successive meetings have contributed so largely to such success as has been obtained'.[69] A year later, the Superintendent of the Northern Shan States, Major E. Butterfield, stated that 'too much credit cannot be awarded to Mr Affleck the Consul, Têngyüeh, for the patience and skills with which he assisted at the meetings of the Appellate Court and at all deliberations'.[70] It was clear that the mediating work of consuls in the Meetings was important to Burmese officials.

After a brief hiatus in the late 1920s, the work of the consul continued in the next decade. At Sima in 1930, the Burmese Frontier Officer noted that 'such success as has been attained is due to [the Tengyue consul] Mr Wyatt-Smith. A breakdown on the last day would have left several old and five new ... cases untouched and this break-down was averted only by the Consul's tact and patience'.[71] Consuls therefore continued to provide the services that the Burmese officers required of them. Finally, a Burma Office minute from December in 1937 related consul Ronald Hall's view of the importance of the consul to the Burma officers in the Meetings:

> If no British Consul from China were present at the Courts it would be likely to be a very serious disadvantage from Burma's point of view ... All the reports from the Burma officers pay a high tribute to the work of the Consuls and the Consulate clerk in producing friendly relations and helping to reach a solution, after a deadlock has been reached.[72]

Consuls therefore helped Burmese officers in their efforts to maintain peace on the Burma-China frontier through the resolution of cases. In an era often seen as increasingly 'lawless' to Burmese officials, their role was of great importance for British transfrontier authority.

Conclusion

The last Frontier Meeting took place in January 1940, but with the onset of the Second World War and Japanese occupation, consuls no longer worked as intermediaries in transfrontier cases. Three years later, the Sino-British Treaty for the Relinquishment of Extraterritorial Rights formally ended consular rights on 1 January 1943. This concluded the short, but nevertheless important, legal role of the Tengyue consuls in western Yunnan and the Burma-China frontier. In Meetings, consuls worked as mediators, translators, advisors and petitioners. The Meetings reflected the everyday occurrence of people moving across boundaries, travelling between different villages and markets. Transfrontier crime – whether it involved cattle theft, raids, kidnapping or even murder – required British and Chinese officials to work closely together and try to balance opposing interests when they did not see eye to eye. Consuls were therefore key actors who helped enable this cooperation required in Meetings.

Whereas the imperial discourse of 'lawlessness' in frontiers was a commonality throughout much of the British Empire, the creation of the Frontier Meetings as a solution to such 'lawlessness' was a particularity of the Burma-China frontier. Consuls recognised the importance of a court that was based on local custom and could provide some sort of resolution to replace blood feuds. British officials also had to come to terms with, and accommodate, Chinese methods of negotiation and bargaining. Frontier Meetings therefore appeared to reflect the coming together of local custom, Chinese cultural-legal practices as well as British imperial perspectives and practices.

Consuls were not just intermediaries; they also supported the extension and maintenance of colonial authority in disputed lands. In the region of Pianma, consuls supported colonial Burmese claims to the area from 1911. They negotiated with the Chinese frontier officials, district magistrates and *daotai* officials to avoid inflaming transfrontier relations. With careful appeals to universal justice and referral to local arbitration, British consuls helped maintain an uneasy status quo that supported British sovereignty claims. By allowing local headmen to revolve some politically sensitive cases, they also utilised the plural legal environment to their advantage. Although consuls were in many ways on the margins of the British Empire, within the hills and valleys of the frontier, they were also a central link between British Burma and consular authority in China from 1899 until 1943.

Notes

1   See, for example, in English: T. Stephens, *Order and Discipline in China: The Shanghai Mixed Court, 1911–1927* (Seattle: University of Washington Press, 1992); M. Eiichi, 'H. A. Giles v. Huang Chengyi: Sino-British conflict over the Mixed Court, 1884–85', *East Asian History*, 2:1 (1996), 135–57. For Chinese-language works on the Mixed Court and its successor, the 'Special District Court', see, amongst others: Z. Hu, 'qingmo minchu shanghai gonggong zujie huishen gongxie faquan zhi bianqian

1911–1912', ['The transformation of legal rights in the Shanghai Mixed Court in the International Settlement from 1911 to 1912'] *Shixue yuekan*, 4 (2006), 51–6; Y. Yao, *Shanghai gonggong zujie tequ fayuan yanjiu* [*Research on the Shanghai Special District Court in the International Settlement of Shanghai*] (Shanghai: Shanghai renmin chubanshe, 2011).

2 Y. Yao, 'Bianjing yu bianmin de guojia hua: jindai zhong ying huishen dian mian bian an zhidu' ['Nationalization of the frontier and frontier people: the system of the Sino-British Frontier Meetings border cases'], *lishi renlei xue xue kan*, 13:1 (2015), 87–130.

3 *Ibid.*

4 TNA: FO656/149.

5 IOR: L/PS/18/B173 'Burma-China Frontier: Report on Consuls' Tour and Frontier Meetings for the Open Season 1909–1910'.

6 The Meetings sometimes changed to nearby locations if this was deemed more convenient. The Sima Meetings usually heard fewer cases than the Nawngma Meetings.

7 The numbers of Burmese – and especially Chinese – officials present at the Meetings varied from year to year.

8 IOR: L/PS/10/208/2 'Burma-China Frontier, Report of Consul's Tour and Frontier Meetings for the Open Season 1910 to 1911'.

9 Colonial and consular sources provide little information on the role of the headmen in Frontier Meetings. This may be a reflection of the nature of the sources, as British officials highlighted what they thought was of most interest for their superiors, i.e. the contestation between British and Chinese officials rather than the headman's advice on local custom. Headmen (or other local representatives) may also have given advice to British and Chinese officers prior to the Meetings rather than within the courtroom, meaning that the Meeting reports erased their role altogether. British sources refer to these headmen as 'sawbwa', relating to Shan headmen, with most plaintiffs and defendants being Kachins under their jurisdiction.

10 A number of reasons halted Frontier Meetings. For example, disputes over the designated Chinese official dogged the Meetings in the 1920s, and political and social unrest in the frontier and district of Tengyue prevented the Meeting in other years. In 1934 and 1935, there were no Meetings of first instance as Burma refused to a Meeting being held. This followed a dispute from the aftermath of a 1933 Meeting where Burmese officers alleged that the Chinese authorities shot a witness who provided evidence which helped to quash a Chinese claim for compensation. The Burmese authorities thereafter refused to hold the Meetings until China paid compensation.

11 IOR: L/PS/10/208/2 A. Rose to H. Thompson, Chief Secretary to Government of Burma, and J. Jordan, Ambassador at Beijing, 'Burma-China Frontier: Report of Consul's Tour and Frontier Meetings for the Open Season 1910 to 1911', 25 February 1911.

12 IOR: L/PS/12/2237 Prideaux-Brune to E. M. B. Ingram, Ambassador at Beijing, 6 July 1932; TNA: FO228/1733 A. Rose to J. Jordan, Ambassador at Beijing, 21 February 1909.

13 IOR: L/PS/10/208/2 A. Rose to H. Thompson, Chief Secretary to the Government of Burma, and J. Jordan, Ambassador at Beijing, 'Burma-China Frontier: Report of Consul's Tour and Frontier Meetings for the Open Season 1910 to 1911', 25 February 1911.

14 E. Kolsky, 'The colonial rule of law and legal regime of exception: frontier "fanaticism" and state violence in British India', *American Historical Review*, 120:4 (2015), 1218–46; M. Condos, 'Licence to kill: the Murderous Outrages Act and the rule of law in colonial India, 1867–1925', *Modern Asian Studies*, 50:2 (2015), 479–517.

15 TNA: FO228/1733 H. Sly, Tengyue consul to J. Jordan, Ambassador at Beijing, 'Report on Frontier Meeting, 1909', 22 January 1909.

16 TNA: FO228/1733 H. Sly to J. Jordan, Ambassador at Beijing, 'Enclosure I, six rules to be observed in dealing with trans-frontier cases', 22 January 1909.

17 IOR: L/PS/12/2237 H. Prideaux-Brune to E. M. B. Ingram, Ambassador at Beijing, 6 July 1932. Supplementary rules were added over time on specific issues, such as transfrontier cultivation rights in fields immediately adjoining borders.

18 IOR: L/PS/10/208/2 A. Rose to H. Thompson, Chief Secretary to the Government of Burma, and J. Jordan, Ambassador at Beijing, 'Burma-China Frontier: Report of Consul's Tour and Frontier Meetings for the Open Season 1910 to 1911', 25 February 1911.
19 TNA: FO228/1733 J. Jordan, Ambassador at Beijing, to H. Sly, 15 January 1909.
20 Ibid.
21 P. D. Coates, The China Consuls: British Consular Officers in China, 1843–1943 (Oxford: Oxford University Press, 1988), pp. 315–17.
22 IOR: L/PS/10/208/2 A. Rose to H. Thompson, Chief Secretary to the Government of Burma, and J. Jordan, Ambassador at Beijing, 'Burma-China Frontier: Report of Consul's Tour and Frontier Meetings for the Open Season 1910 to 1911', 25 February 1911.
23 IOR: L/PS/10/338 H. Harding to the Chief Secretary to the Government of Burma, 1 February 1926.
24 Ibid.
25 TNA: FO228/3275 'Tengyue intelligence report for December Quarter, 1920'.
26 These perceived characteristics of Chinese justice became an entrenched British imperial narrative, stressing the cultural incompatibility of Chinese and British legal systems. This in turn helped to legitimise British extraterritoriality. On this perception and narrative of the Chinese justice system from the view of Westerners, see, for example: L. Chen, Chinese Law in Imperial Eyes: Sovereignty, Justice and Transnational Politics (New York: Columbia University Press, 2016); T. Brook, J. Bourgon and G. Blue, Death by a Thousand Cuts (Cambridge, MA: Harvard University Press, 2008).
27 IOR: L/PS/10/338 H. Harding to the Chief Secretary to the Government of Burma, Home and Political Department, 15 February 1924.
28 IOR: L/PS/10/337 E. J. Farmer, Deputy Commissioner, Myitkyina, Burma to the Commissioner, Mandalay, 6 January 1915.
29 Ibid.
30 Ibid.
31 IOR: L/PS/10/338 H. Thornton, Commissioner of the North East Frontier Division, to Chief Secretary to the Government of Burma, Home and Political Department, 4 March 1924.
32 IOR: L/PS/12/2237 R. Hall to Chief Secretary to the Government of Burma, Home and Political Department, 22 June 1936.
33 IOR: L/PS/10/208/2 A. Rose to H. Thompson, Chief Secretary to the Government of Burma, and J. Jordan, Ambassador at Beijing, 'Burma-China Frontier: Report of Consul's Tour and Frontier Meetings for the Open Season 1910 to 1911', 25 February 1911.
34 TNA: FO228/3275 'Intelligence Report for the September Quarter 1919'.
35 IOR: L/PS/10/208/2 A. Rose to H. Thompson, Chief Secretary to the Government of Burma, and J. Jordan, Ambassador at Beijing, 'Burma-China Frontier: Report of Vonsul's Tour and Frontier Meetings for the Open Season 1910 to 1911', 25 February 1911.
36 Ibid.
37 Ibid.
38 IOR: L/PS/10/337 C. Smith to W. F. Rice, Chief Secretary to the Government of Burma, 31 January 1915.
39 Ibid.
40 Ibid.
41 Ibid. Translation: daotai to consul, Superintendent of the Northern Shan States and Deputy Commissioner of Bhamo, 17 January 1915.
42 TNA: FO 228/1952 Goffe, Kunming consul-general, to J. Jordan, 31 March 1916.
43 Ibid.
44 B. Metford, Where China Meets Burma: Life and Travel in the Burma-China Border Lands (London: Blackie, 1935), p. 67.

[90]

45 IOR: L/PS/12/2237 S. Wyatt-Smith, Tengyue consul, to the Chief Secretary to the Government of Burma, Home and Political Department, 13 February 1931.
46 IOR: L/PS/10/338 Deputy Commissioner, Myitkyina, to H. L. Cabell, Commissioner, Mandalay, 19 January 1921.
47 IOR: L/PS/10/208/2 'Burma-China Frontier: Report of Consul's Tour and Frontier Meetings for the Open Season 1910 to 1911.
48 IOR: L/PS/12/2237 R. Hall to Chief Secretary to the Government of Burma, Home and Political Department, 22 June 1936.
49 Metford, *Where China Meets Burma*, p. 67.
50 IOR: M/3/373 Burma Office: 'Burma-Yunnan Frontier Meetings', 17 December 1937.
51 IOR: L/PS/10/208/2 A. Rose to H. Thompson, Chief Secretary to the Government of Burma, and J. Jordan, Ambassador at Beijing, 'Burma-China Frontier: Report of Consul's Tour and Frontier Meetings for the Open Season 1910 to 1911', 25 February 1911.
52 *Ibid.*
53 For example, the 'Banhong Incident' in 1935. See: B. Xie, 'Cong Pianma shijian dao Banhong shijian: zhong main bianjie lishi yange wenti' ['From the Pianma Incident to the Banhong Incident: the historical evolution of the Sino-Burmese border'], *Yunnan shehui kexue*, 4 (2000), 208–30.
54 TNA: FO371/27 'Memorandum of information received during the month of May 1906, regarding external affairs relating to the North-East Frontier, Burma, Siam and China'.
55 G. Forrest, 'Journey on Upper Salwin, October–December, 1905', *Geographic Journal*, 32:3 (1908), 241–2.
56 TNA: FO881/9885 'Memorandum respecting negotiations with China with regard to the Undelimited section of the Burma-China Frontier 1897–June 1911'.
57 *Ibid.*
58 IOR: L/PS/10/337 A. Eastes, Tengyue consul to the Chief Secretary to the Government of Burma, 7 March 1917.
59 TNA: FO228/3275 'Tengyueh Intelligence Report for the Quarter ended December 31st, 1918'.
60 IOR: L/PS/10/337 A. Eastes to the Chief Secretary to the Government of Burma, 18 February 1918.
61 TNA: FO228/3275 'Intelligence Report for Tengyue, ending 31st December 1918'.
62 *Ibid.*
63 The issue of sovereignty over Pianma continued in the 1920s, with a stronger Chinese media focus on British encroachment on the region in the leading Chinese newspaper *Shenbao*.
64 TNA: FO228/3275 'Tengyueh Intelligence Report for September Quarter, 1920'.
65 IOR: L/PS/10/338 J. Affleck to Earl Curzon of Kedleston, Secretary of State for Foreign Affairs, 31 January 1921.
66 *Report on the Administration of Burma, for the Year 1904–5* (Rangoon: Office of the Superintendent, Government Printing, Burma, 1905), p. ii; *Report on the Administration of Burma, for the Year 1906–7* (Rangoon: Office of the Superintendent, Government Printing, Burma, 1907), p. 3.
67 *Reports on the Administration of Burma, for the Year 1909–10* (Rangoon: Office of the Superintendent, Government Printing, Burma, 1911), p. 9.
68 TNA: FO228/3275 'Political Report for Tengyueh Consular District for the Three Months ended June 15th, 1925' (no date).
69 IOR: L/PS/10/337 H. Thornton, Superintendent of the Northern Shan States, to the Chief Secretary to the Government of Burma, 6 February 1919.
70 IOR: L/PS/10/337 E. Butterfield, Superintendent of the Northern Shan States, to the Chief Secretary to the Government of Burma, 6 February 1920.
71 IOR: L/PS/12/2237 F. A. Grose, Deputy Commissioner, Myitkyina, 'Frontier Meeting held at Sima, December 15th to 22nd 1930', 30 December 1930.
72 IOR: M/3/373 Burma Office: 'Burma-Yunnan Frontier Meetings', 17 December 1937.

PART II

Through the mountains and across the desert: Xinjiang

CHAPTER FOUR

Isolation and connection: law between semicolonial China and the Raj

As Britain consolidated its authority over Upper Burma from 1885, the Indian government turned towards British India's northern frontier and northwestern China. Xinjiang was a province of the Qing Empire, but as a region bounded by the mountains and vast stretches of desert, it was also a place that topographically defied strong imperial control.[1] Russia had a growing presence in the north of the province and both the Indian government and Foreign Office viewed a British presence in Xinjiang as an essential bulwark against the Czarist Empire. British Indian policy focused on extending economic and political influence from the mountain passes of northern India to Xinjiang. The oasis towns of southern and western Xinjiang, historically part of the Silk Road, drew merchants from across Central Asia and Siberia. This included growing numbers of Indian traders importing, amongst other products, silks, teas and spices. Indian moneylenders joined them, making their fortunes by loaning to Chinese, Russian and other Indian subjects, and supported the transfrontier trade.

From the late nineteenth to the early twentieth centuries, the Indian government used consular representatives in a bid to promote British Indian trade and spy on Russian agents in the region. From 1891, a 'Special Assistant to the Resident in Kashmir for Chinese Affairs' was stationed in Kashgar, before the position became a recognised consular post from 1908 until 1943. Imperial historians who have focused on the British connection to the province have done so through the lens of Anglo-Russian geopolitics of the so-called 'Great Game', or the tripartite competition between Russia, China and Britain.[2] In this chapter, I move away from this traditional political analysis. Law was far from inconsequential in geopolitics, as it helped to underpin the economic and political influence of British imperial power. I examine the contours of this British legal power. I explore the legal connections between the consular district and the consular authorities on the east coast of China, as well as British India.

Although the history of Xinjiang has often been related as one of subservience to Chinese authority, over the past two decades, a number of China historians have shifted this focus towards the cultural, economic and political diversity of the locality and region.[3] They provide a timely reminder that the dynamics of imperial power were interwoven with distinctive features of local social, economic, political and cultural structures of the region. I argue that the British legal presence in Xinjiang was also born out of a mixture of local, regional and transfrontier imperial connections. Consuls created these links through exercising law that was adapted to suit its community of subjects who had Indian heritage. At the same time, whilst the consular district was a part of the broader China consular circuit, the legal basis of consular jurisdiction in Xinjiang was also distinct from that of the treaty ports as the Chinese authorities considered Kashgar a treaty mart. I therefore show how British jurisdiction in Xinjiang was shaped by an amalgamation of local influences, as well as colonial and consular frameworks.

I first outline the foundations of the British presence in Xinjiang and the legal basis of consular rights. I then demonstrate how the first British representative, George Macartney, attempted to consolidate his legal powers amid the debates over the legal status of Kashgar as a 'treaty mart' as opposed to a 'treaty port'. In the final section, I analyse how the British colonial and consular worlds merged with a piece of legislation – the China (Kashgar) Order in Council (1920).

Imperial interests in Xinjiang

For several centuries, the region of Xinjiang was a contested zone between large empires and local factions. Political power oscillated between local *khanates* and the three large competing empires of Mongolia, Russia and China.[4] It was an expansive region, positioned culturally and geographically between China proper to the east, Islamic Central Asia to the west, and the Steppe and Siberia to the north. Unsurprisingly, it was a meeting place of different cultures and peoples. Increasing numbers of Chinese Muslims (*hui*) joined the majority ethnic Turkic-speaking Muslims (*uyghurs*). A number of other smaller ethnic groups lived in various parts of the region, including Mongols, Kazakhs, Kirghiz and Tajiks, amongst others.

As part of the East-West trade route, the merchants in the towns of Yarkand in the south and Kashgar to the west profited from the exchanges in goods at the intersection between China, Central Asia and Russia. A strong Russian merchant presence also existed in the north and east, especially in Urumqi – later the provincial capital – and Ili. Away from these centres, Xinjiang was mostly desert land with small oasis towns ringed by high mountain passes to the south, west and north. These geographical features limited trade to particular trade routes where smaller caravans could cross through mountain passes and sandy terrain.

Politically, the Qing Empire laid claim to Xinjiang after conquest in 1759, but as a distant land far from imperial power in Beijing, Qing rule was always tenuous. Most prominently, a rebellion led by the Khoqandi warlord Yaqub Beg, establishing the independent state of 'Turkestan' (1865–77), demonstrated the fragile central control of Qing power.[5] The Chinese Empire later poured more resources into reconsolidating its sovereignty in a military conquest. It became a province in 1884 and the Qing renamed it 'Xinjiang', meaning the 'New Frontier'.

As a province on the edge of the Qing Empire, the frontier shaped Qing law and administration. Generally, the Qing code was enforced only in cases involving more serious criminal offences and the Qing permitted certain adaptations for convenience in the administration of justice.[6] As Eric Schluessel has explored, officials had the power to enforce the death penalty without referring such cases to higher review.[7] In relation to local administration, although the north, east and south of Xinjiang all had different historical trajectories, most had a mixture of Turkic-speaking local officials under the supervision of Qing military commanders. Much like the *tusi* system in western Yunnan, the region maintained long-standing local elites who were both part of, and separate from, Chinese officialdom. Local officials (*begs*) used local custom to settle minor criminal cases and collected taxes. For the Muslim population, Islamic judges (*qazis*) also adjudicated cases relating to religious custom. This was necessary in a vast region, requiring local expertise and administration where central authority could not penetrate. The Qing also allowed other entities legal powers in the region. In 1833, for example, the Qing allowed representatives of the Khanate of Khoqand powers to resolve cases between members of their community in the province.[8] The Qing also allowed a mixed tribunal over Kazakhs of Russian subjecthood on the Russian-Chinese frontier.[9] This followed the general pattern of allowing various groups, such as the nomadic Kirghiz, forms of autonomy on the frontier.[10] Qing sovereignty therefore relied on the modification of its own legal framework and permitted multiple local institutions and actors to oversee local life in a sprawling region.

Despite the reassertion of Chinese sovereignty, by the late nineteenth century Qing power was in decline.[11] A series of political challenges across China weakened Qing authority. At the same time, a number of foreign nations – chiefly Britain, France and the United States – had forced the Qing to grant a range of privileges for their subjects. This included residence rights in a number of opened treaty ports along or near the east coast. Foreign nations thereafter began to take further advantage of this weakening centralised power as they looked to the interior and far western provinces of the Celestial Empire to enhance their trade and political interests.

To the north, Russia continued to expand its sphere of influence within Xinjiang and across the region. Russia aimed to extract more privileges from the Qing, building on its series of treaties with China on the Sino-Russian frontier. By the 1727 Treaty of Kiakhta (amended in 1768), the two empires agreed upon the obligation to return fugitives and to enforce various joint punitive provisions in transfrontier cases. At this time, the Qing only allowed a limited transfrontier trade route through the border by the town of Kiakhta. By the nineteenth century, however, Russia obtained more wide-ranging privileges, including extraterritorial and trade rights in northern Xinjiang and Mongolia. After the Treaty of Beijing in 1861, alongside claiming formerly disputed lands, Russia established a consulate in 'Urga' (Ulaan Baatar, Mongolia) and through the Treaty of St Petersburg (1881) further consulates and trading rights in Mongolia and Xinjiang. This gave the Russian authorities and traders a great degree of economic influence in Xinjiang.

At the same time, the British Indian government looked to extend its northern frontier in order to counteract the expansion of Russian power across Central Asia. The Indian government first secured access to the mountain trade routes via the semi-autonomous small states on the fringes of British India, such as Hunza and Chitral.[12] The government then scouted the mountain passes between these states and Xinjiang, and sent several Indian missions to the province between 1870 and 1880 to amass information about the region. This included the journey of W. R. Johnson in 1865, Shaw and Haywood in 1869, and the Forsyth mission in 1873. The latter aimed to forge diplomatic relations with Yaqub Beg, to pinpoint possible trade for British interests (especially in silks, cottons and muslins) and to understand the extent of Russian influence. Despite gathering more economic and ethnographic information, the mission failed on the diplomatic front. Forsyth negotiated a treaty with Beg for the stationing of British Commercial Agents with legal powers, but it was never ratified.[13]

In 1890, the Indian government sent another mission to Xinjiang, this one proving more significant for future British interests. The government tasked Francis Younghusband, a military man and explorer, with surveying the region north of India through to Yarkand. This mission aimed to pinpoint geostrategic areas as buffer zones from Russian influence. The government also wanted to learn more about the trade route from the administrative region of the Gilgit Agency (with a stationed Political Agent linked to the northern region of Kashmir) through the small princely states of Hunza and Nagar.[14] Accompanying Younghusband was George Macartney, an interpreter from the Political Department of India (see Figure 6 below). Macartney was born and raised in Nanjing, and with a British father and Chinese mother, he grew up speaking both English and Chinese. He was therefore in a perfect position to work as a Chinese interpreter for the Government of India. He was first sent to southeast China to assist the Burma Commission to delimit the Burma-China frontier. Afterwards, he acted as a Chinese interpreter for a military expedition to Sikkim in 1888, before accompanying Younghusband to Xinjiang. He decided to stay on in Kashgar working for the British Indian government, but he had no official status as a British representative in the eyes of the Russian or Xinjiang officials. This status would define and limit his legal powers in the next decade.

Figure 6   George Macartney c. 1891 (left) and Francis Younghusband (centre right), 1891

Unofficial residency and 'treaty marts', 1891–1904

The aftermath of the Younghusband mission marked the beginning of George Macartney's presence in Kashgar. In 1891, the Indian government recognised Macartney as a 'Special Assistant for Chinese Affairs to the Resident in Kashmir'. His first task was to oversee the increasing volume of British trade from northern India. Many Indian merchants travelled through the Pamirs and Karakoram Pass to Yarkand and Kashgar selling wares. Although some of these traders migrated to and from northern India, many also decided to settle in Xinjiang. Macartney reported these social and economic developments to the Indian government and monitored Sino-British trading relations. It was within the interests of British India to encourage Indian commercial networks, which in turn enlarged the sphere of British Indian economic influence in the region.

This economic influence was an important facet of political power for British India, whose policy-makers intended to create a bulwark against the expanding Russian Empire in Central Asia. The Russian consul stationed in Kashgar oversaw a healthy transfrontier trade, with Siberian merchants travelling to and from the Sino-Russian frontier to Yarkand, Kashgar, Ili and Urumqi. This network of trade helped the Russian Empire maintain economic dominance within the region. The construction of the Trans-Caspian Railway extended from the eastern shores of the Caspian Sea to Samarkand, Tashkent and Andijan, east of Kashgar. Macartney acted as an intelligence man, providing information on the Russian trade in Central Asia and Xinjiang. His role was far from insignificant even at this early stage of his career. His advice helped British policy-makers in their negotiations with Russia, which later resulted in a number of Anglo-Russian accords. This included the 1893 Durand Agreement that defined the border between British India and Afghanistan (then under the sphere of influence of British India). The following 1895 Pamirs agreement created the Afghan Wakhan corridor as a buffer between British India and Russia.[15] Despite these border agreements, the British Indian government predicted that Russia would, if left unchallenged, eventually control the vital northern India trade route of the Karakoram Pass leading to Yarkand. Macartney's role for the Indian government was far from over; indeed, it was just beginning.

In order to strengthen its own hand in the region, the British Indian government wanted the Qing to recognise Macartney as a consul. This position would therefore bestow diplomatic status upon Macartney. It would also enable him to give tax exemption certificates to British merchants, a right which the Russian consular officials already

[100]

exercised for their Russian trading community. Although in principle Britain could exercise extraterritorial rights anywhere within the territory of China, Britain required the Qing to sanction the opening of a British consulate in Kashgar and to recognise Macartney as the consul stationed there. The most convincing legal argument for this right was through the application of Article VIII of the Treaty of the Bogue (1843). This 'Most Favoured Nation' clause entitled Britain to enjoy any right that China granted to other nations through treaties. Of particular interest to Britain were the provisions of the Sino-Russian Treaty of Tianjin (1858) and Treaty of Beijing (1860). Article V of the Treaty of Tianjin gave the Russian government the freedom to 'name Consuls to the ports opened to trade'. There were also specific provisions concerning the northwest of China. Article IV of the Treaty of Beijing provided for open trade all along the Sino-Russian border and a Russian consul in Urga (Ulaan Baatar, Mongolia). Article VI opened Kashgar as an open trade town for Russian subjects alongside the existing consulates at Ili and Tarbagatay. Article VIII stated that Russia should name consuls at Kashgar and Urga. Further, in the Treaty of St Petersburg (1881), Article X allowed Russia to establish additional consulates in the Chinese northwest, including at Turpan, Khovd, Uliastai, Kumul, Urumqi and Qitai. Article XII permitted duty-free trade for Russian subjects in both Xinjiang and Mongolia, reaffirming the provision of Article III of the Treaty of Kuldja (1851). These provisions allowed Russia extensive rights to open consulates, for Russian consuls to exercise extraterritoriality and for its community of merchants to enjoy economic privileges in the province.

British representatives in Beijing had already tried and failed to secure the stationing of British consuls in the region. In 1884, the Ambassador at Beijing, Harry Parkes, presented a note to the Qing on the issue.[16] He argued that Britain had a legal claim to a consular presence in Kashgar and that a consulate was necessary for issuing passports to a growing British Indian population.[17] The Qing representatives remained unconvinced, arguing that the Xinjiang authorities adequately handled the issuing of passports. Furthermore, whereas the Sino-Russian Treaty of Tianjin (1858) granted the right for Russia to establish consuls at 'different ports', the Qing had a different view on what constituted an opened city for foreign commerce; the word 'ports' meant sea ports. This therefore suggested *maritime* towns, located on the coast or with access to the coast via inland waterways. This characterised the dozens of opened places for residence and trade where a number of foreign nationals enjoyed the benefits of extraterritoriality. The Qing therefore distinguished between 'treaty ports' and places opened for inland stations without a direct waterway link to the east coast.

British consuls would later describe the latter as 'treaty marts'. This was significant, as the Qing emphasised a spatialised legal distinction of Xinjiang in relation to the exercise of foreign privileges.

This differentiation of the consular legal framework in Xinjiang was not limited to the discussions in Beijing. Local officials in Xinjiang used this geographically-based legal distinction when attempting to limit the freedom of movement of British subjects. In 1899, Colonel Powell of the Gurkha Rifles requested a visa to pass through Xinjiang on his way home to England via Central Asia.[18] Huang Daren, the Kashgar *daotai* (circuit intendant) was reluctant to grant him free passage. He stated that whereas the Shanghai *daotai* could issue a visa for British nationals to move throughout China, Shanghai was also a treaty port.[19] This therefore meant that he did not have the same powers to grant travel documents to British subjects. After Macartney protested to the Ambassador at Beijing, diplomatic pressure forced Huang to grant Powell a visa. The case highlighted that the Xinjiang authorities could, and did, contest key rights of British subjects based on the legal distinction of Xinjiang. This meant that British consuls could never fully guarantee certain rights, such as freedom of movement and residence for British subjects in the province. Later, Western travellers such as the ethnographer and archaeologist Aurel Stein would encounter the same difficulties.[20] The legal basis of the rights of British subjects in the district of Kashgar was therefore different from that of treaty ports on the east coast, and the Chinese authorities continued to contest British privileges in the province.

While the efforts to force the Qing to recognise Macartney stalled, Macartney focused on trying to exert judicial powers over British subjects in the province. He saw acquiring judicial rights through customary practice as an increasingly important part of British economic and political interests in Xinjiang. Most subjects were Indian transfrontier traders and moneylenders from Shikarpur in the British Indian province of Sind (now in present-day Pakistan). Whilst some of these businessmen (there are no records of Indian women travelling to Xinjiang) sojourned in the oasis towns, increasing numbers began residing in the commercial centres of Kashgar and Yarkand.[21] It was therefore within Macartney's remit and in the interests of British India to have as much influence as possible over British trade and to keep disputes between British Indian subjects and Chinese and Russian subjects to a minimum.

A large amount of Macartney's and his assistants' time during his first decade in office was spent hearing disputes over moneylending.[22] Although his jurisdiction covered the whole province of Xinjiang – stretching over 3,000 km across and over 1,500 km north to south – the majority of these suits arose in towns on the main commercial routes. Most of the towns were on a trade route leading south and west from Kashgar. These towns included Yangi Hissar, Yarkand, Poskam, Qarghaliq, Hotan and Keriya. Outlaying towns included Tashkurghan to the west and Uchturfan, Asqu and Kuchar further north. A Chinese circuit intendant (*daotai*) had jurisdiction over these towns, with magistrates subordinate to them (*amban*) and local officials in the localities (*begs*).[23]

Aside from commercial disputes, one of Macartney's first major tasks was to negotiate with the Chinese officials in order to secure the freedom of British Indian slaves. Forms of bondage had been a part of local life in certain parts of Central Asia.[24] Russian imperial agents had also attempted to eliminate slavery after the Russian conquest of parts of the region in the 1860s and 1870s, but scholars treat the claimed imperial success of these campaigns with scepticism.[25] In Xinjiang, as Laura Newby has shown, in the eighteenth and nineteenth centuries a significant proportion of the population of the province remained in some sort of bondage.[26] This included not only Chinese subjects, but also, as the consular reports highlight, British subjects. Whereas the liberation of slaves was not one of the primary reasons for stationing a British consul in Xinjiang, Macartney made fighting for their freedom one of his first priorities and he appeared to have some success. In one instance in 1894, Macartney persuaded a local *amban* to free 124 British Indian subjects held in bondage.[27] He believed that Hunza tribesman had kidnapped them from the mountain passes and sold them into slavery in Xinjiang.[28] Most of those freed chose to remain in Xinjiang and became Chinese subjects. Macartney's petitions to the Chinese authorities to facilitate the release of individual British Indian slaves continued later in the decade. For example, in July 1899, in response to Macartney's letter to the Kashgar *daotai*, the local *amban* ordered that a Chitrali man named Sher Muhammad Khan be freed from his servitude to an Afghan Wakhi man, Sar Buland Ali Shah. The *amban* also granted Khan a passport in order to enable him to leave Xinjiang and return to India.[29] Throughout the first decade of the twentieth century, Macartney reported that various other *amban* officials continued to order the freedom of British subjects, although it is unclear whether this was due to sustained pressure from Macartney. Macartney clearly took his part in the emancipation seriously and felt the right to liberty an essential part of his legal role and British imperial identity.[30]

Success of this sort for Macartney was never certain. Due to his status, he relied on Chinese cooperation and when tensions arose between him and Chinese representatives, the communication structures made reporting slow. Several incidents reflected the difficulties he faced. In

1896, Macartney claimed that two local Xinjiang military men and a Chinese soldier assaulted him and a Hindu trader.[31] To Macartney's frustration, the local *amban* dismissed the incident, forcing him to report the affair to his administrative superiors in India. The Indian government forwarded it to the India Office in London, which passed on the issue to the Foreign Office (which oversaw consular administration in China). The case then found its way to the British Ambassador at Beijing as the senior British representative for consular interests in China. In turn, he discussed actions with the Qing representatives in the capital city. The Qing officials notified the Xinjiang governor, who passed on the instructions to the local *daotai*. Finally, the *daotai* instructed the local *amban* to hear the assault case. Although Macartney eventually succeeded in forcing the *amban* to hear the trial, the case reflected the awkward and time-consuming structures of colonial-consular administrative networks between India, the metropole and China. The case highlighted a crucial flaw of imperial governance in frontier areas that sat between colonial and consular jurisdictions. It was obvious that it was necessary to have an official invested with power to oversee British legal interests in a place far removed from centres of imperial power. It also became clear to Macartney that he needed a more direct communicative role not only with his Chinese counterparts but also with colonial and consular officials since he straddled both the colonial and consular administrative systems.

As well as administrative and communication problems, *amban* officials often tried to assume jurisdiction in hearings involving British subjects. Shortly before returning to England on home leave in 1898, Macartney settled a trade dispute between two British subjects in Yarkand.[32] On hearing of Macartney's leave from the town, the local *amban* overturned his ruling and threatened British subjects with fines for presenting petitions to Macartney. Macartney suspected that the Russian consul, Nikolai Petrovsky lay behind these moves. He believed Petrovsky had pressed the *amban* to limit Macartney's powers to hear trading disputes, especially those involving Hindu moneylenders and Russian Andijani (Khoqandi) traders who owed them money.[33] When Macartney returned, he launched a complaint through the same means of communication as the assault case in 1896. This time he insisted that Claude MacDonald, the British Ambassador at Beijing, should urge the Qing to allow him some legal powers over disputes involving British subjects.

In due course, the Qing granted some unofficial powers to Macartney. This was a safe option for the Qing. Mounting British cases added a strain on the local justice system. According to the Joint Commissioner of Ladakh, no fewer than six hundred debt-related cases remained outstanding.[34] The Qing could also revoke non-treaty-based rights, allowing Chinese imperial officials to decide what legal arrangements worked best for Chinese interests. The Qing therefore agreed that Macartney could have judicial powers in civil and criminal cases in which both parties were British subjects. In these cases, Macartney or his agent could hear the trial in the presence of an agent appointed by the *amban*.[35] In suits where one party was a British subject and the other a Chinese subject, Macartney or a substitute representative could attend the cases the *amban* tried. If Macartney felt there had been an injustice, he could appeal to the local *daotai*. Criminal and civil cases where both subjects were foreigners and neither British nor Russian were tried by the *amban* in the presence of a British representative.[36] This legal arrangement appeared to be similar to that of treaty-based consular jurisdiction as in elsewhere in China. However, without a treaty, it was an unreliable legal arrangement for Macartney and an anomaly in China, given that during this period, Britain relied upon treaties as legitimising frameworks for British legal rights. In many senses, it appeared to resemble the legal practice on the south China coast before the Sino-British treaties. There, from 1759 to 1842, the Qing conferred an informal power to the British East India Company (EIC) representatives in Canton to adjudicate cases involving British subjects. Therefore, alongside its legal basis, British legal practice in Xinjiang was also distinct from consular jurisdiction elsewhere in China from 1890 to 1904.

Despite the incremental successes of the 1898 agreement, Macartney continued to depend on the goodwill of local *amban* and *daotai* officials who continued to dictate the scope of his powers. Part of his battle was to convince them to hear the cases of British plaintiffs who presented petitions against Chinese subjects. Most of these petitions came from individuals who claimed they were victims of assault or were owed money. Macartney continued to collect these petitions and tried to pressure the local *daotai* to instruct the *amban* to hear the cases.[37] Often, he did not succeed. In his report from early June in 1899, Macartney reported his feeling of powerlessness:

> there are now no less than 12 cases on which I am in correspondence with the different local officials; and I feel no slight difficulty in getting them to take proper action for their disposal. The issue of reminders appears to have but little result; whilst the control exercised by the Taotai [*daotai*] over his subordinates is so slight that complaints addressed to him are productive of little or no good.[38]

It is unsurprising that Macartney felt this way, given the tenuous legal basis of his powers and his relative isolation from colonial and consular administration. Such isolation was common in the colonial world. As Zoe Laidlaw has shown, colonial governors were often left to themselves to assert their power and administer imperial directives.[39] For Macartney, his task also involved battling with a sovereign power, having no guaranteed legal rights and falling administratively between colonial and consular structures of governance.

Even when the Qing granted Macartney informal powers to hear cases involving British defendants, continued Chinese interference meant that he often struggled to perform his legal duties. An example of this struggle was reflected in the reported case in 1899 of a man surnamed Parman, described as a Hindu.[40] The *amban* in Asqu ordered his arrest, suspecting him of theft, fraud and extortion. However, he refused to hand Parman over to Macartney for trial. Macartney subsequently wrote to Claude MacDonald, stating that his jurisdiction was in accord with the recent 1898 informal agreement that bestowed powers upon him to assume jurisdiction. MacDonald negotiated with Qing representatives in the capital, which resulted in the *amban* handing Parman over to Macartney. Macartney felt that without the Ambassador's eventual intervention, the surrender of Parman would have been 'improbable'.[41] Although it was an eventual success, it reflected the difficulty of assuming jurisdiction in everyday 'mundane' cases in Xinjiang.

In other cases, the Chinese authorities denied that detained men were British nationals. *Amban* officials found it easy to claim jurisdiction as many British subjects did not have identification records. British subjects had also integrated themselves into local society by adopting local customs and becoming proficient in local languages. The case of Gul Mohammed in Yarkand in 1899 brings this to light.[42] A local *amban* charged Mohammad for assaulting a Chinese subject, leading Macartney to contest his jurisdiction. Macartney claimed that the *amban* and other local officials tried to induce Mohammad to accept Chinese subjecthood. Mohammad had no identification documents and the question of his nationality was complicated due to his father, Sayad Dost Mohammad Shah. Shah was born in India, but the *amban* stated that a document that had recorded a financial transaction of Shah identified him as Chinese subject. As Shah had also lived for many years in Xinjiang as a resident, the *amban* claimed he and his son were now Chinese subjects. Gul Mohammad rejected this, pointing to the fact that he had not married in Xinjiang, nor had he bought any landed property (merely acquiring property as an exchange of debts owed from a Chinese subject) as proof he was a British subject sojourning in Chinese territory.[43] Such identification problems also plagued hearings of inheritance. Macartney reported to the India Office that he could not dispose of the estate of a British Indian subject who died in Ili in 1904 due to Chinese interference.[44] Following this case, the Indian government urged the Foreign Office to consider making Macartney a consular official and pressurising the Chinese authorities once more for his consular recognition in Kashgar.[45]

A sense of British prestige helped restart negotiations with the Qing for a consular representative. In early 1904, Lieutenant-Colonel Miles toured the province acting in Macartney's absence. He reported the 'humiliation' he suffered at the hands of the local officials, who had refused to open town gates for him.[46] He claimed that it prevented him from carrying out his duties and underlined the general disrespect towards British representatives. He was certain that local officials would not have directed such an insult to him had he been a consular official. At the same time, the British Indian government was keen to have a local official with diplomatic status to negotiate with the Xinjiang political elite on questions regarding Sino-British borders. There existed few man-made borders between the province and the mountain passes where the British claimed some political influence. A diplomatic representative therefore appeared increasingly important for British Indian interests.

By 1904, the question of Macartney's status was therefore of political, economic and legal importance. His limited legal rights restricted his authority over British subjects and, as a result, curtailed British economic power and British political influence. His judicial power was dependent upon the goodwill of local *daotai* and *amban* officials. As an unofficial British Indian political officer, Macartney exercised a non-treaty-based extraterritoriality akin to that accorded to EIC officials before 1833 on the south China coast. It was an uneasy status quo and the difficulties of resolving cases reflected his relative isolation in the frontier as an unofficial representative. On 1 February 1904, the India Office, the British Ambassador at Beijing and the Foreign Office felt the time was right for a change. They decided to throw caution to the wind – knowing that the Qing and Russian authorities would still oppose the move – and announced that both the British colonial and consular authorities now recognised Macartney as a consular officer. This now meant he could communicate more directly with various officials and institutions within both British colonial and consular administration. It also ushered in the start of a new era of consular jurisdiction in the region.

Consular status

A new status gave Macartney administrative guidelines in line with other China consuls. His consulate building was in Kashgar and although his district was also termed 'Kashgar', his jurisdiction encompassed the entire geographical province of Xinjiang.[47] His legal remit was to adjudicate the cases of British defendants and like other China consulates, he heard cases and suits in a 'provincial court', which was also a 'Court of Record'. This required Macartney to report court proceedings to His Britannic Majesty's Supreme Court for China in Shanghai. Although administrative changes accompanied his new status, the nature and scope of his powers did not change. The new Russian consul, Sergei Kolokolov, appeared friendlier than his predecessor towards Macartney, but refused to officially recognise his status.[48] There was also no formal statement from the Qing following the announcement.[49] Ernest Satow, the Ambassador at Beijing, therefore presented a note to Qing representatives attempting to induce Chinese recognition. Satow outlined the economic and political advantages of a British consular agent in Xinjiang and its benefits to the Qing in an era of growing Russian economic domination in the province. Furthermore, Satow emphasised that consuls were beneficial for economic growth in China and pointed to the role played by inland consuls-general stationed at Chengdu in Sichuan and Kunming in Yunnan for facilitating Sino-British trade.[50] This would be important for the Qing given the recent reparations following the Boxer Rebellion (1900–1) and costly Qing reforms to the administrative and judicial structures.

Having received no response, Satow pressed Prince Qing further, sending him a note referring to the treaties – like his predecessor Harry Parkes – to try once more to position consular jurisdiction in Xinjiang within a legitimate legal framework.[51] Prince Qing's response was unequivocal, stating that the 'Most Favoured Nation' clause did not apply with a treaty of peace. The Sino-Russian Treaty of St Petersburg only allowed a Russian consulate to open in Kashgar as a *quid pro quo* for the retrocession of Ili in 1881.[52] Prince Qing further pointed to the example of Yunnan to show that the opening of a consulate at the frontiers of the Chinese Empire required a new treaty.[53] The Chinese position had not changed; there was no legal grounding for the opening of a consulate in Xinjiang. Satow had to admit defeat.

The unexpected Japanese victory following the Russo-Japanese war in 1904–5 temporarily prevented any possibility of restarting negotiations. Russia lost the Liaodong Peninsula on the east coast and an important part of its Eastern Chinese Railway branch, the 'South Manchurian' line to Japan. Thereafter, Russia focused on maintaining its power in Mongolia and Xinjiang in the midst of a 'strategic retrenchment' within East Asia more broadly.[54] The Russian policy dictated that its representatives in China should not recognise Macartney as a consular official in order to limit British influence in Central Asia. Macartney suspected that the Russian Minister in Beijing urged the Qing to do the same.

Despite this setback for Macartney, all was not lost. The Indian government and the Foreign Office proposed that his consular status could be part of a diplomatic concession. In particular, the Indian government would abandon all its claims through Hunza to the river valley of Raskam and the Taghdumbash Pamir in the Sino-British frontier.[55] As a *quid pro quo*, the Qing would sever its tributary claims to Hunza, agree to a delimited frontier and recognise Macartney as consul.[56] Before this draft agreement became finalised, Lord Lansdowne, the Foreign Secretary, and the India Office decided to postpone the negotiations. British interests in Central Asia now centred on the Sino-British negotiations over British rights in Tibet. Tibet was considered more important as potential buffer zone against Russia, whose representatives had not yet gained a foothold there. With Qing power in decline in Tibet, the British Indian government also sensed that the Qing would grant economic privileges to Britain. The outcome of Sino-British negotiations lived up to British expectations. Amongst other rights, the Convention between Great Britain and Tibet (1904) included provisions that granted trading rights for British subjects in Yadong, Gyantse and Gartok. These places became 'trading marts' and another frontier region of China where Britain enjoyed economic and legal privileges. In return, Britain formalised the recognition of Chinese sovereignty over Tibet.

After the ratification of the Tibet convention, negotiations for consular powers in Xinjiang restarted in August 1906.[57] John Jordan, the Ambassador at Beijing, attempted to convince the Chinese External Affairs Department (*waiwubu*) that it was within Chinese interests to recognise Macartney.[58] This time, Jordan did not refer to the controversial topic of treaty rights.[59] Instead, he downplayed the potential change as a 'mere change of title' for Macartney and, as a token of reciprocity, suggested that it could pave the way for China to have consuls in the British Empire, such as in Australia and New Zealand.[60] The Qing appeared more inclined towards recognition of Macartney, and Jordan predicted that Indian commercial interests and the growing numbers of Indian subjects made it necessary to invest Macartney with 'the judicial and other powers of a Consul for the purposes of regulating the affairs of British subjects'.[61]

However, it was not Sino-British negotiations, but Anglo-Russian political relations, which ultimately consolidated Macartney's consular status. Following the decline of Russian power in north China and the Anglo-Russian conventions in 1905 and 1907, Russia dropped its opposition to Macartney's appointment.[62] The path was open to consular recognition after eighteen years of bargaining for legal rights. Soon afterwards, the Chinese authorities officially recognised Macartney's acting deputy Captain Shuttleworth as consul in September 1908 while Macartney was on leave.[63] It appeared as though Russia had played a crucial role in encouraging the Qing to reject Macartney's recognition. Two years later, the Foreign Office made Macartney a consul-general following Russia's promotion of its resident consul, Sokov, to a consul-general in May 1910. This Russian move was due to its plan to add new vice-consulates at Aqsu and Hotan, which required a Russian consul-general to oversee their work.[64] As there were no plans to create new British consulates in the province, Macartney's position of consul-general was a show of status.[65] Alongside economics and judicial powers, geopolitics and the image of British prestige still mattered as part of consular representation in the province.

By 1910, therefore, Macartney had official diplomatic and consular powers, yet the Indian government continued to pay his salary and accommodation expenses. He reported to both the consular and colonial authorities, sending information about the province and British imperial interests. However, his position was not only unusual as a point between two sets of British authorities. Despite the Qing's eventual recognition of Macartney as a consul, foreign rights in Xinjiang still rested upon an uncertain legal basis. The Qing did not agree that the 'Most Favoured Nation' clause allowed Britain a representative in Xinjiang. This would mark Xinjiang as distinct from other places in China and would later play an important role in the demise of consular jurisdiction in the province in the 1920s and 1930s. Yet, during this era, such issues did not plague Macartney and instead he turned to a more pressing concern: convincing his administrative superiors to grant him wider-ranging legal powers.

Consular legal powers and integration with the Raj

From 1904, Macartney represented both consular and colonial British interests in Xinjiang. In his legal capacity as consul, his powers were framed by the Orders in Council that governed consular administration in China. The substance was English law (statutes, case law and principles) as well as various Acts applicable to the colonies. Although his consular status allowed him to hear cases involving British defendants, by 1915 certain limitations in the exercise of these powers became obvious to him. As the British community grew in number, there was a corresponding rising number of suspects as well as those convicted. Yet there existed no consular jail in Kashgar and no satisfactory local solution to housing convicts. Macartney instead sent many prisoners to India. To do this, he followed the procedure laid down by the Order in Council requiring him to obtain the consent of the Chief Judge of His Britannic Majesty's Supreme Court in Shanghai. This was a lengthy procedure unsuited to the exigencies of local governance. Furthermore, the existing legislation limited his options for exercising deportation. The Order in Council (1904) empowered consuls to deport convicts to Hong Kong, England or the place where they were born or originally domiciled.[66] However, British subjects neither born nor domiciled in India – such as second-generation British subjects in Xinjiang – did not meet these criteria.

An additional consideration for Macartney was the ongoing First World War and the extra numbers of those convicted of engaging in anti-British activities and involvement in Indian nationalist movements. The events in India during the late nineteenth and early twentieth centuries signalled new challenges for British Indian colonial authorities. Organised protests against colonial authority and revolts came in multiple forms, from peasant uprisings such as the Munda tribal revolt on the Bengal-Bihar border (1899–1900) to the agitation of native elites in political movements such as the Swadeshi nationalist movement (1905–8) led by urban educated elites. The threat of British Indian nationalism became more prominent as British Indian nationals moved between parts of the British Empire in greater numbers. This transnational nature of networks of communication and organisations presented new dangers to the authority of the Indian government and a threat to the wider British Empire during the war. Both the Indian government and the consular authorities focused on the treaty ports as potential sites for revolutionary movements, such as the *Ghadr* movement (Sikh and Hindu anti-British revolutionaries), which used networks and links between colonial and semicolonial domains.

In light of these circumstances, Macartney called upon the India Office and the Foreign Office to enact a new legal framework governing his jurisdictional powers. He asked for the integration of his district with the Indian legal system, powers to apply colonial laws in force in India upon British subjects in Xinjiang and wider-ranging powers to deport subjects to India.[67] He cited several reasons for the proposed changes.[68] First, he pointed to the British community in Xinjiang. These subjects were nearly all from the Indian subcontinent. He felt that applying colonial law – drafted in consideration of the Indian populace – made more sense than English law. Second, he highlighted the geographical distance from the east coast, especially from the Chief Judge in Shanghai. Although the province was still at a distance from the Raj, Xinjiang was located closer to northern India and its courts of justice. Finally, considering the Indian population and the proximity to northern India, he wanted more wide-ranging powers of deportation to allow him to send subjects to India. In other words, he wanted consular powers that would allow him to apply colonial laws from British India and to send subjects of British Indian heritage back to India.

After a lengthy period of correspondence, the India Office, the Foreign Office and the British consular authorities finally agreed to the proposals. John Jordan had recently reviewed the petitions of consul Smith from Tengyue, on the Burma-China frontier. Smith had argued that the colonial Burmese authorities should have jurisdiction over colonial subjects from Burma who had committed crimes in the district of Tengyue. Jordan therefore saw the similarities between Tengyue and Kashgar. He also observed that it would be 'eminently practical' and would 'relieve His Majesty's Supreme Court for China of duties and responsibilities ... [towards] British Indian subjects and British protected persons in a remote and inaccessible part of China where conditions are entirely different from those ... in the interior of China Proper and in the treaty ports'.[69] He recognised that Kashgar was geographically and socially distinct from other consular districts in China. The Secretary of State of the Foreign Office acknowledged both the practicality and the customary practice of deporting Indian prisoners, stating that a new piece of legislation would therefore 'settle the question of the practice to be followed in the removal of convicts from Kashgar to India'.[70] Both the Foreign Office and Ambassador at Beijing understood the nature of frontier jurisdiction and the need to empower Kashgar consuls with new legislation that provided a stronger legal connection to India.

After five years of consideration and drafting, the China (Kashgar) Order in Council (1920) contained Macartney's proposals. The Order outlined the consul-general's administrative and jurisdictional powers in relation to India and China, providing for greater integration with the Raj. In terms of law-making, the consular district of Kashgar could now be subject to the enactments of the Governor-General of India or of the Lieutenant-Governor of the Punjab in Council.[71] Consuls-general were empowered to use the Indian Code of Criminal Procedure and 'other enactments relating to the administration of criminal justice in British India for the time being'.[72] The consul-general was also a Sessions Judge with the High Court of the Punjab (the Lahore High Court) as the High and Appellate Court.[73] In civil matters, the consul-general could apply the Code of Civil Procedure and other Indian enactments related to insolvency and bankruptcy as a District Judge.[74] The consul-general was a District Judge and his court a District Court, or a Principal Civil Court of Original Jurisdiction in the district.[75] The

High Court of the Punjab had high court and appellate jurisdiction over the Kashgar cases.[76]

As well as integrating the district with the Raj, consuls-general were given greater legal powers than their consular counterparts elsewhere in China. The consul-general was empowered to make and alter regulations ('King's Regulations') for the 'peace, order and good governance' of British subjects in Xinjiang.[77] These powers could be used to enact regulations to prevent arms trafficking, health regulations and for applying, modifying and repealing Acts that applied to Kashgar enacted by the Governor-General in India or the Lieutenant-Governor of the Punjab.[78] The consul-general also had emergency legislative powers, which required only *ex post facto* sanction from the Foreign Office or the Indian Governor-General.[79]

The Order gave the Kashgar consul-general extensive powers to remove Indian suspects and convicts. If deemed expedient, he could deport an accused subject for trial or a convicted individual for imprisonment in Lahore.[80] Thereafter, some individuals were deported after a conviction for smuggling opium. A lively illegal trade existed where many Indians, Afghans and Chinese transported Afghan opium to Yarkand. At times, it could be a lucrative trade, since the geography of the frontier between Afghanistan and China enabled smugglers to avoid customs police.[81] Consuls-general, especially when pressed by the Chinese authorities, readily deported such smugglers. Shortly after the enactment of the Order, the 'notorious smuggler' Sadat Khan, who already had two convictions for trading opium, was deported after the Chinese authorities requested his removal.[82] Other noted deportees included those convicted for assault or 'house-breaking'. For example, Abdul Khalik and Akhtar Muhammad were both convicted of the latter offence in 1914 and were sentenced to serve two years' imprisonment in India.[83] At the same time, there was at least one other man serving a sentence of imprisonment in a Hyderabad jail in Sind for 'culpable homicide'.[84] Others deported for trial in India included those suspected of involvement in Bolshevik movements and promoting anti-British propaganda.[85]

The order also enabled consuls-general to 'prohibit' individuals believed to have committed an offence from remaining in Kashgar and to bar their re-entry for up to two years.[86] Such infractions included the behaviour of a subject deemed to be 'conducting himself so as to be dangerous to peace and good order' or 'endeavouring to excite enmity between the people of China and His Majesty's power and authority'.[87] A failure to provide 'security', i.e. someone to vouch for their future 'good behaviour', could also lead to deportation.[88] Deportees from the consular district could be sent to the Punjab or any place in the British

Empire if the colonial government consented to receive them and the deported had no right of appeal.[89] In practice, consuls-general always deported such individuals to Punjab and reported these deportations to the Indian government only.[90] In short, the consul-general had wide discretionary powers for deporting suspects to India for a range of offences.

Consuls-general used expulsion and deportation powers extensively, including upon British subjects accused of misdemeanours. An insightful example is the case of Ganpat Ram, a man described as being of Indian heritage. As well as convicting him for assault, the consul-general George Gillan added that he had a history of 'misconducting himself' with local women.[91] As they were Chinese subjects, the consul believed such behaviour was done 'in a manner calculated to endanger the peace'.[92] Ram also had outstanding debts and had concealed property and account books.[93] He was expelled from Xinjiang for one year from 30 September 1927. His case reflected how consuls used their powers of expulsion widely upon subjects with minor criminal convictions or histories of misconduct.

Though the consular district of Kashgar became further integrated with the Raj through the consul-general's discretionary powers, British subjects in Xinjiang still remained subject to Chinese laws and regulations. For example, evasion of Chinese tariff regulations was an offence punishable by a sentence of up to six months' imprisonment as well as fines.[94] Local religious laws and customs, especially those of the Islamic tradition, also applied to many of the Muslim faith, as well as local Turkic customs as enforced by *begs*. British regulations contained within the China Orders in Council and the enactments of the Ambassador at Beijing for British subjects in China also applied to British subjects; for example, King's regulations relating to sanitation and policing applied to Xinjiang.[95] The Kashgar Order in Council also contained provisions that were part of the Order in Council for China. For example, insulting any religion established in the consular district was an offence incurring a term of imprisonment of up to two years and/or a fine.[96] Subjects found publishing or possessing seditious matter were also subject to imprisonment and a fine. This seditious matter included both anti-British material and publications that provoked 'enmity' between Britain and China and its subjects.[97] Those who were involved in war or rebellion against the Government of China could be fined, imprisoned and deported.[98]

Aside from these regulations, consuls-general could draw upon various metropolitan Acts and Orders made specifically for China, as the case of Abdul Qarim in 1919 showcased. The Chinese authorities arrested Qarim for smuggling arms and a joint trial between the consul-general and the local Chinese authorities followed. Qarim was found guilty of treason and consul-general Etherton used the emergency China War Powers Order (1917) to deport Qarim to the Peshawar District.[99]

The outcome of the Kashgar Order was a curious legal framework that reflected its place as a frontier region between two British jurisdictions. A number of different laws and regulations applied to British subjects in Xinjiang, from Indian laws, local and religious customs to extraterritorial legislation and Chinese municipal regulations. The legal environment was a product of its locality, imperial structures, diverse community and geographical location.

Conclusion

In this chapter, I have demonstrated how British representatives strove to formalise legal powers in Xinjiang and how they exercised law through legal frameworks. Before 1908, the first British representative in Xinjiang, George Macartney, attempted to carve out his jurisdictional claims in the province. During this period, it was clear that Macartney struggled to enforce legal powers over British subjects. Instead, he bargained with the Chinese authorities to ensure customary rights. Although he represented the Indian government, he remained very much isolated in Xinjiang. In Beijing, the consular authorities tried to claim formal legal rights for him. However, the Qing drew a legal distinction between 'treaty ports' and inland stations such as Kashgar based on geography; as Xinjiang was not connected to the coast or maritime connections through inland waters, the treaties did not confer consular rights to Britain in the province. This made Xinjiang an exceptional place where only some British privileges could be exercised.

After the Qing recognised Macartney's consular status after 1908, he exercised the same extraterritorial rights as other consuls across China. However, both the nature of the British community consisting of mostly Indian-born men or men of Indian heritage and the geographical proximity to British India shaped consular legislation. Through the China (Kashgar) Order in Council (1920), consuls-general had a strong legal connection to the Raj. They could expel British suspects, deport them for trial or send them for terms of imprisonment in India. The Kashgar consul-general became not just an administrative link between the Raj and the China consular administration, but his court and powers also became tied to the legal system of the Raj. Similar to cases of 'undesirables' in western Yunnan, consuls deported not only those suspected of more serious crimes, but also those suspected of merely disrupting the peace. It was a powerful tool of legal governance, and strengthened the legal and penal connections between consular and colonial authority.

Although British communities were subject to consular jurisdiction, British people in the consular district of Kashgar also remained subject to the plural legal environment of the locality. As a territory of China where forms of local laws and foreign privileges also existed, Xinjiang had multiple layers of jurisdictions. British subjects could be subject to colonial laws from India, consular legislation, Chinese regulations and local customary laws, as well as religious norms. As a result, whilst the exercise of law was shaped by colonial and imperial overlaps, it was also shaped by its locality and the British communities from the Indian subcontinent.

Notes

1   The Chinese province of Xinjiang in the late nineteenth and early twentieth centuries was roughly coterminous with the present-day Xinjiang Uyghur Autonomous Region of China.
2   C. Skrine and P. Nightingale, *Macartney at Kashgar: New Light on British, Chinese and Russian Activities in Sinkiang, 1890–1918* (Oxford: Harper & Row, 1987); G. J. Alder, *British India's Northern Frontiers, 1865–95: A Study in Imperial Policy* (London: Longmans, 1963). Also including Japan, see: L. Nyman, *Great Britain and Chinese, Russian and Japanese Interests in Sinkiang, 1918–1934* (Malmö: Esselte studium, 1977).
3   See, for example, I. Bellér-Hann, *Community Matters in Xinjiang, 1880–1949: Towards a Historical Anthropology of the Uyghur* (Leiden: Brill, 2008); D. Brophy, *Uyghur Nation: Reform and Revolution on the Russia-China Frontier* (Cambridge, MA: Harvard University Press, 2016); F. Starr (ed.), *Xinjiang: China's Muslim Borderland* (London: Armonk, 2004).
4   British appellations for the region over the eighteenth, nineteenth and early twentieth centuries reflected these ambiguities and political changes: 'Chinese Tartary', 'Turkestan', 'Eastern Turkestan' (as distinguished from Soviet 'west Turkestan'), 'Chinese Turkestan', 'the New Dominion' and 'Sinkiang' (Xinjiang). British consular officials also used the term 'Kashgaria'. This mainly referred to the British sphere of influence in Kashgar and its surrounding southwest region, although it also became a generic byword for the whole province.
5   In the same period, the 'Dungan revolt' broke out between 1863 and 1877, where Muslim fighters in the western Chinese provinces of Shaanxi, Gansu and Ningxia rebelled against the Qing.
6   Muslims could also bring their civil suits to the Chinese magistrate's *yamen* during and after the 1880s and *begs* could adjudicate cases according to Islamic sources of law or the Great Qing Code where applicable.
7   E. Schluessel, ' "The law and the law": two kinds of legal space in late-Qing China', in J. Bourgon (ed.), *Les Lieux De La Loi En Chine Impériale/Legalizing Space in Imperial China* (Lyon: Presses Universitaires de Vincennes, 2016), pp. 39–58.
8   Merchants from Khoqand played a strong role in the local cross-border economy and were later known as 'Andijani' traders in British sources. On Qing relations with Khoqand, see: L. Newby, *The Empire and the Khanate: A Political History of Qing Relations with Khoqand, c. 1760–1860* (Leiden: Brill, 2005); Z. Pan, *zhongya haohanguo yu qingdai xinjiang* [*Khoqand in Central Asia and Xinjiang during the Qing Period*] (Beijing: zhongguo shehui kexue chubanshe, 1991).
9   D. Brophy, *Uyghur Nation: Reform and Revolution on the Russia-China Frontier* (Cambridge, MA: Harvard University Press, 2016), p. 79.

10 N. Di Cosmo, 'Kirghiz nomads on the Qing frontier: tribute, trade, or gift exchange', in N. Di Cosmo and D. J. Wyatt (eds) *Political Frontiers, Ethnic Boundaries, and Human Geographies in Chinese History* (London: Routledge, 2003), pp. 351–72.

11 For an overview of Qing conquest and decline to the northwest of China, see: P. Perdue, *China Marches West: The Qing Conquest of Central Eurasia* (Cambridge, MA: Harvard University Press, 2005).

12 For a comprehensive history on British Indian imperial policy on its northern frontiers, see, amongst others, Alder, *British India's Northern Frontiers*.

13 On the mission, see: H. W. Bellow, *Kashmir and Kashgar: A Narrative of the Journey of the Embassy to Kashgar in 1873–4* (London: Tribner, 1875); T. D. Forsyth, *Report of a Mission to Yarkund in 1873* (Calcutta: Foreign Department Press, 1875).

14 Hunza and Nagar were princely states, which later became British protectorates from 1893 until 1947, located in the present-day region of Gilgit-Baltistan in north Pakistan. They bordered the Afghan Wakhan corridor and southwestern part of Xinjiang. China claimed that Hunza was a tributary state to China and the Mir of Hunza paid tribute to China until 1937.

15 Later, the Anglo-Russian Convention (1907) would further define these borders.

16 IOR: PS/10/55 Foreign Office to India Office, 10 May 1904, forwarding excerpt from Parkes' letter, 25 January 1884.

17 *Ibid.*

18 IOR: R/2/1075/216 'Diary of the Special Assistant for Chinese Affairs to the Resident in Kashmir for the fortnight ending the 30th April 1899', 30 April 1899.

19 *Ibid.*

20 See: TNA: FO228/4268.

21 On the network of Shikarpuri traders in Central Asia which included Xinjiang, see: C. Markovits, *The Global World of Indian Merchants, 1750–1947: Traders of Sind from Bukhara to Panama* (Cambridge: Cambridge University Press, 2000), pp. 96–8.

22 Although there is little detail on these dispute resolution cases, Macartney frequently refers to his role as an adjudicator.

23 *Amban* (*xianzheng*) was a Manchu word (Chinese transliteration: *an ban*) that had a generic meaning of an 'official'. The *ambans* had similar roles to an Indian District Officer as a judge, revenue collector, governor of the local gaol, registrar and coroner. A *daotai* was his administrative superior, overseeing a district, much like an Indian Commissioner. Above the *daotai* was a Governor stationed in Urumqi.

24 See, for example: J. Eden, 'Beyond the bazaars: geographies of the slave trade in Central Asia', *Modern Asian Studies*, 51:4 (2017), 919–55.

25 *Ibid.*

26 L. Newby, 'Bondage on Qing China's northwestern frontier', *Modern Asian Studies*, 47:3 (2013), 968–94.

27 Skrine and Nightingale, *Macartney at Kashgar*, p. 78.

28 Skrine and Nightingale, *Macartney at Kashgar*, p. 48.

29 IOR: R/2/1075/216 J. Manners Smith, Political Agent, Gilgit to the Secretary to the Government of India, Foreign Department, 17 August 1899, forwarding 'Diary of the Special Assistant for Chinese Affairs to the Resident in Kashmir for the half month ending the 31 July 1889'.

30 On anti-slavery campaigns and British identity, see, for example: R. Huzzey, *Freedom Burning: Anti-slavery and Empire in Victorian Britain* (New York: Cornell University Press, 2012).

31 Skrine and Nightingale, *Macartney at Kashgar*, p. 89.

32 Skrine and Nightingale, *Macartney at Kashgar*, pp. 95–6.

33 Khoqandi merchants were protected by Russian extraterritoriality after the Russian conquest of the former Khanate of Khoqand in 1875.

34 Skrine and Nightingale, *Macartney at Kashgar*, pp. 104–5.

35 F. Piggott, *Exterritoriality: The Law Relating to Consular Jurisdiction and to Residence in Oriental Countries* (Hong Kong: Kelly and Walsh, 1907), pp. 166–7.

36 *Ibid.*

37 See, for example, his Diaries from 1899: IOR: R/2/1075/216.
38 IOR: R/2/1075/216 Political Agent, Gilgit, to the Secretary to the Government of India, Foreign Department, 9 July 1899, forwarding 'Diary of the Special Assistant for Chinese Affairs to the Resident in Kashmir for the half month ending the 15th June 1889'.
39 Z. Laidlaw, *Colonial Connections, 1815–45: Patronage, the Information Revolution and Colonial Government* (Manchester: Manchester University Press, 2005).
40 IOR: R/2/1075/216 Diary of the Special Assistant for Chinese Affairs to the Resident in Kashmir for the half month ending the 15th August 1899; half month ending the 31st August; half month ending 19 September 1899.
41 IOR: R/2/1075/216 J. Manners Smith, Political Agent, Gilgit to the Secretary to the Government of India, Foreign Department, 19 September 1899, forwarding: 'Diary of the Special Assistant for Chinese Affairs to the Resident in Kashmir for the half month, Jan–March; for the half month ending the 31st Aug, 1899'.
42 IOR: R/2/1075/216 G. Macartney to the Resident in Kashmir, 'Diary of the Special Assistant for Chinese Affairs to the Resident in Kashmir for the fortnight ending Jan–March', 15 March 1899.
43 *Ibid.*
44 IOR: L/PS/10/55 A. Godley, India Office to Under Secretary of State, Foreign Office, 25 October 1906.
45 *Ibid.*
46 IOR: L/PS/10/55 E. Satow, Ambassador at Beijing, to the Marquess of Lansdowne, Foreign Office, 15 June 1904.
47 This roughly covered the present-day region of the Xinjiang Uyghur Autonomous Region as well as the region of 'Kobdo', in present-day northwestern Mongolia.
48 Skrine and Nightingale, *Macartney at Kashgar*, p. 142.
49 IOR: PS/10/55 E. Satow, Ambassador at Beijing, to the Marquess of Lansdowne, Foreign Office, 15 June 1904.
50 *Ibid.*
51 IOR: PS/10/55 Foreign Office to E. Satow, Ambassador at Beijing, 'Draft Note to the Chinese Government', 25 August 1904; Foreign Office to Carnegie, Beijing, 10 August 1906.
52 IOR: L/PS/10/55 E. Satow, Ambassador at Beijing, to the Marquess of Lansdowne, Foreign Office, 15 June 1904.
53 IOR: L/PS/10/55 Prince Qing to E. Satow, 6 June 1904. Ernest Satow interpreted Prince Qing's meaning as such in his draft reply letter: IOR: L/PS/10/55 H. Walpole to India Office 'Enclosures: Annex 2', 6 September 1905.
54 See: A. Marshall, *The Russian General Staff and Asia, 1800–1917* (London: Routledge, 2006), pp. 97–9.
55 The Taghdumbash Pamir is today part of China's Xinjiang Autonomous Region, but the name also referred to the mountain range that sits between present-day Afghanistan, Pakistan and Tajikistan.
56 IOR: L/PS/10/55 H. Walpole, India Office, to Under Secretary of State, Foreign Office, 6 September 1905; Marquess of Landsdowne, Foreign Office, to E. Satow, Ambassador at Beijing, 27 September 1905. See also Skrine and Nightingale, *Macartney at Kashgar*, pp. 140–1.
57 IOR: PS/10/55 E. Barrington, Foreign Office, to India Office, [no stated day] July 1906.
58 IOR: PS/10/55 J. Jordan, Ambassador at Beijing, to E. Grey, Foreign Office, 6 July 1908.
59 *Ibid.*
60 *Ibid.*
61 IOR: PS/10/55 'Memorandum' J. Jordan, Ambassador at Beijing, 5 June 1908.
62 Skrine and Nightingale, *Macartney at Kashgar*, pp. 137–73.
63 IOR: PS/10/55 J. Jordan, Ambassador at Beijing, to E. Grey, Foreign Office, 6 July 1908; IOR: PS/10/55 A. R. B. Shuttleworth, Acting Kashgar consul, to J. Jordan, Ambassador at Beijing, 28 August 1908.

64 IOR: PS/10/55 W. Langley, Foreign Office, to the Under Secretary of State, India Office, 15 October 1910.
65 A consulate at Urumqi replaced Kashgar briefly before closing in 1949. The consular official did not have extraterritorial powers after 1 January 1943.
66 China Order in Council (1904), Section III, Article 83.
67 TNA: FO656/139 'Memorandum by Sir George Macartney', 14 September 1915.
68 *Ibid.*
69 TNA: FO656/139 J. Jordan, Ambassador at Beijing, to H. de Sausmarez, His Britannic Majesty's Supreme Court for China, 24 February 1916.
70 TNA: FO656/139 Foreign Office to J. Jordan, Ambassador at Beijing, 3 January 1916.
71 China (Kashgar) Order in Council, 1920, Section II, Article 8(1–4).
72 China (Kashgar) Order in Council, 1920, Section III, Article 11.
73 China (Kashgar) Order in Council, 1920, Section III, Article 11; Article 31.
74 China (Kashgar) Order in Council, 1920, Section IV, Article 33.
75 *Ibid.*
76 *Ibid.*
77 China (Kashgar) Order in Council, 1920, Section VII, Article 61.
78 *Ibid.*
79 China (Kashgar) Order in Council, 1920 Section VII, Article 62(4).
80 China (Kashgar) Order in Council, 1920, Section III, Articles 11–14.
81 The Kashgar Diaries periodically note the existence of this smuggling trade and consular officials associated it with the Afghan community. As David Bello notes for the early nineteenth century, Qing officials were aware of a lively opium smuggling trade in the southern part of the province and identified foreign subjects such as Kashmiri, Badakhshani and Khoqandi Muslim suspects alongside Han farmers as smugglers. See: D. Bello, 'Opium in Xinjiang and beyond', in T. Brook and B. T. Wakabayashi (eds), *Opium Regimes: China, Britain and Japan, 1839–1952* (Berkeley: University of California Press, 2000), pp. 137–9.
82 TNA: FO228/3026 P. Etherton, Kashgar consul-general, to Ambassador at Beijing, 'November Diary, 1921', 1 December 1920.
83 IOR: L/PS/10/825 G. Macartney to the Secretary to the Government of India, Foreign and Political Department, 30 September 1914.
84 *Ibid.*
85 TNA: FO228/3024 Secretary to the Government of India, to J. Jordan, Ambassador at Beijing, 6 September 1919.
86 China (Kashgar) Order in Council, 1920, Section III, Article 18(1).
87 *Ibid.*
88 China (Kashgar) Order in Council, 1920, Section III, Article 19(1).
89 China (Kashgar) Order in Council, 1920, Section III, Article 19(3); Article 21.
90 China (Kashgar) Order in Council, 1920, Section III, Article 19(5).
91 TNA: FO228/3664 G. Gillan to the Secretary to the Government of India in the Foreign and Political Department, 'Prohibition Order against Ganpat Ram', 13 August 1927.
92 *Ibid.*
93 *Ibid.*
94 China (Kashgar) Order in Council, 1920, Section III, Article 27(1).
95 China (Kashgar) Order in Council, 1920 Section III, Article 23(1).
96 China (Kashgar) Order in Council, 1920, Section III, Article 28(1).
97 China (Kashgar) Order in Council, 1920, Section III, Article 24(1–2).
98 China (Kashgar) Order in Council, 1920, Section III. Article 22(1–2).
99 TNA: FO228/3024 P. Etherton, Kashgar consul-general, to the Ambassador at Beijing, 24 February 1920; TNA: FO228/3024 Foreign Office to B. Alston, Ambassador at Beijing, 8 March 1920.

CHAPTER FIVE

Administering justice and mediating local custom

Between 1904 and 1942, the British consular representative and his subordinates in Xinjiang heard thousands of cases involving British defendants. The cases covered a range of issues, from civil suits involving marriage, land ownership and debt payments to criminal cases involving assault, arms and drug trafficking, and murder. Some of the cases were politically and culturally sensitive, raising questions about the nature and scope of British consular jurisdiction. In the previous chapter, I explored the legal frameworks of consular jurisdiction and highlighted some of the cases that reflected the limits and extent of consular power. I now turn to take a closer look at the administration of consular justice and court cases.

In this chapter, I show how the nature of the British community and how the challenges of governing subjects in a vast province shaped legal administration and the resolution of cases. The chapter first outlines the nature of consular administration in Xinjiang. Consular officials were legal mediators between the local community, the Raj and consular justice. Consular officials therefore embodied a legal 'meeting point' between local and imperial actors and institutions.[1] However, consuls-general were also dependent on their subordinates – aqsaqals – who were more experienced in local custom. In a region that encompassed a vast area of arid land and oasis towns distanced far apart from each other, the use of aqsaqals reflected how British administration adapted to the frontier environment and how it modelled justice to best serve the needs of its population. As David Brophy has noted, imperial authority – agents of the Russian, Chinese and British Empires – used indigenous hierarchies to govern their subjects in the province.[2] These actors were essential to imperial authority not just because of the environment, but also because these elites were more familiar with the languages and customs of the local community. In Brophy's analysis, Russian *aqsaqals* were mediators between imperial authority (whom they worked for) and the subject population.[3] They were also a 'hybrid of two institutions', liaising between the Qing and Russian officials.[4] Likewise, Laura Newby has drawn attention to the dual role of local headmen (*begs*) who were 'between two worlds' of Chinese imperial officials and the local population.[5] In this chapter, I not only highlight a similar mediation role of British *aqsaqals*, but also show how the consular organisation of *aqsaqals* reflected an important link to the Indian subcontinent.

I turn next to examine the identity of British registered subjects. As Madhavi Thampi has explored, many British subjects migrated to the province from the three main trade routes through Badakhshan, Kashmir and Ladakh.[6] I take a closer look at the British community and the politics of registration. This provides an insight into how the exercise of consular jurisdiction reflected imperial aims and reveals the identity of its registered community. I then examine court statistics and court cases to show what types of cases were heard by consular officials and *aqsaqals*, and how this reflected the registered community and their interests. Finally, through examining cases involving religious custom, I argue that British consular officials accommodated ideas of local custom when adjudicating cases. I therefore show how consular officials exercised consular justice by balancing the consideration of local custom, British rights and the imperatives of intercommunity peace. The chapter uses the period 1911 to 1928 as a window onto these dynamics. The documents of this era provide a more in-depth view of legal practices, giving the richest data for examining court cases.

Consuls-general and aqsaqals

The consul-general stationed in the western city of Kashgar was the most senior British representative in Xinjiang. Despite the nomenclature suggesting that the consular authorities selected consular service men, the Indian government ran the consulate-general and selected consuls-general. Nearly all appointments were men from the Indian Civil Service rather than the China Consular Service.[7] Since they had both consular powers and direct oversight from the Indian government, Kashgar consuls-general straddled both the colonial and consular administrative worlds. On the consular side, their immediate superiors were the Ambassador at Beijing (the most senior British representative in China) and the Chief Judge of His Britannic Majesty's Supreme Court for China in Shanghai (the most senior consular legal representative in China). On the Indian side, the consuls-general reported to the Political Agent at Gilgit and the Resident at Kashmir (as the nearest Indian officers for regional matters) and to the Secretary for Foreign Affairs to the Indian government (for more important political issues).[8] Correspondence to the various authorities concerned political developments in the region, information on Chinese and Russian officials, Turkic nationalism and Islamic movements, economic reports and legal cases involving British subjects. Consuls-general were therefore key informers to two different administrations, which reflected the geographical overlap of colonial and consular interests.

Occasionally, some of the reports – involving sensitive questions of political policy or legal questions of nationality – made their way to the metropole: the Foreign Office (for Chinese and consular matters) and the India Office (for Indian matters). During the political upheaval of the second decade of the twentieth century, reporting increased significantly. Following the fall of the Qing with the Xinhai Revolution (1911–12), Yuan Shikai established a Republic in China. Political fragmentation characterised the new Republic, with autocratic civil and military commanders emerging in various places within China during the 'warlord' period. In Xinjiang, the Qing governor Yuan Dahua fled from the provincial capital of Urumqi and Yang Zengxin became the first Republican governor of Xinjiang. Over the following years, Yang consolidated his autocratic power from Urumqi across the region with fellow Yunnanese compatriots filling key political positions with local elites. A military commander (titai) aided Yang, who subsequently wielded some autonomy over the southwestern region of Xinjiang. Yang eventually crushed those still loyal to the Qing, including secret societies such as the 'Elder Brother Society' (gelaohui). Both the Indian government and the consular authorities read the reports of the Kashgar consul-general to keep track of the shift in regional political power in an uncertain time.

After the Russian Revolution in 1917, consular reports detailed the activities of the Soviets and the spread of Soviet influence across Central Asia. The creation of the Federation of the Soviet Republics shortly afterwards to Xinjiang's immediate west and north (covering modern-day Uzbekistan, Tajikistan, Turkmenistan and Kyrgyzstan) filled many pages of the consul-general's monthly Kashgar 'diaries'. As the Soviets consolidated their power base in the north and west, British imperial policy was twofold. The first aim was to maintain the British economic sphere of influence and consular activities in the southwest of the province with its connections to northern India. Second, consuls-general formed part of a spy network following the activities of the Russians further north. Consul-general Percy Etherton cultivated an intelligence network and supported missions to Tashkent, including most notably the 1918 mission with Frederick M. Bailey.[9]

The overall volume of reports on the political developments of Russia and China suggests that political information gathering remained important to both colonial and consular authorities. However, reports on the consul-general's judicial role and correspondence between consuls-general and local officials on cases also increased steadily. These accounts were of three primary types: reports on cases resolved by the consul-general (involving British defendants), details of petitions presented to the Chinese authorities on behalf of British plaintiffs, and correspondence between the consuls-general and Chinese (and sometimes Russian) officials that concerned disputed cases.

As resolving many of these legal issues involved cooperation or negotiation with Chinese and Russian officials, consuls-general required diplomatic skills. George Macartney, the first consul-general, was a gifted diplomat. Having served as a British representative since 1891, he accumulated over twenty-four years of experience when the new Chinese republican state bestowed upon him a Chinese decoration for his 'conciliations and justice'.[10] Whilst future consuls-general did not have the accumulated local experience and diplomatic skills that Macartney had acquired, most had experience of serving in various frontier locations for the Indian government. For example, Frederick Williamson (consul-general 1927–30) served as Political Agent for Sikkim, a small British protectorate in the Himalayas. John. W. Thomson-Glover (consul-general 1933–6) served prior to his appointment as a Joint Commissioner for Leh and Political Agent for Dir and Chitral in the mountainous regions of northern Indian. The last consul-general, Eric Shipton (1940–2, 1946–8) did not serve as a Political Officer before his first appointment, but spent ten years as an experienced traveller in the Himalayas. Between his two posts in Kashgar, Shipton spent a short time as a consular official in Iran (1943–4). These postings provided consuls-general with a range of skills that were needed for working in a frontier. Chief among them was the ability to work in remote locations with little administrative support and to negotiate with, or work alongside, local leaders.

Similar to most consular officers in China, consuls-general in Xinjiang did not have any legal training. Instead, they learnt how to perform their legal duties whilst in-post. Until 1913, consuls heard criminal and civil cases that did not exceed twelve months of imprisonment, with or without hard labour, and/or a fine of up to 1,000 dollars. However, after 1913, consuls-general could exercise greater powers, as each incumbent had the added position of being an 'assistant judge' to His Britannic Majesty's Supreme Court for China. This meant they could hear more important and complicated criminal or civil cases. To help them learn in-post, the Foreign Office stocked a library within its consulates. This included handbooks on Chinese customs and tariffs, handbooks on international law and English procedure as well as commentaries on English statutes and case law. When in doubt, the Chief Judge in Shanghai offered advice on particular points of law. Nevertheless, much like their frontier consular counterparts in Tengyue, Kashgar consuls-general relied on their experience of the locality, what they understood to be British interests in the region and their patchy understanding of law in their administration of justice.

To understand petitions from the local British community, consuls-general required some proficiency in other languages. This included a working knowledge of the three main languages of the British community and locality: Turkic, Chinese and 'Hindustani'.[11] George Macartney had an impressive linguistic knowledge, as he was fluent in Chinese and was able to converse in Russian, German, French, Hindustani and Turkic. Macartney's successor in 1918, Colonel Percy Etherton, could read and write 'Hindustani and Hindi', as well as Pashtun.[12] Upon taking up his post, he also started learning Russian and Turkic.[13] His vice-consul Nicholas Fitzmaurice, a 'China hand' with experience of serving at various consulates in China, acted as a Chinese interpreter for him.[14] Later, consul-general Clarmont Skrine noted that in 'any one of our files there might be, and often were, papers in six different languages: English, Chinese, Turkic, Urdu and Russian. As for the "spoken word", Turkic, Urdu and Persian were all in regular use with visitors, litigants and witnesses during office hours'.[15] It was a post where being a polyglot was of great importance.

Despite the need for multilingual consular officers, later consuls-general had a limited knowledge of other languages. Colonel Howard-Bury brought this state of affairs to light in the House of Commons on 21 May 1930, when he queried why the Government of India selected such men and why they left their Kashgar post so quickly. The short response by the Indian government was that the position was difficult to fill and it was a challenge to retain staff because the posting was 'remote and unpopular'.[16] In other words, Kashgar remained very much a frontier, despite attempts made to integrate the consulate into the Indian legal and administrative system since the 1920s.

One curiosity about the selection of consular officers was that only a few officials were chosen from the China Consular Service. Harold Ivan Harding served as vice-consul (1922–4), while Nicholas Fitzmaurice also acted as vice-consul and, for a short period, as acting consul-general (1918–22) and then as consul-general (1931–1933).

Michael Cavenagh Gillett served as both vice-consul (1936–7) and later as consul-general (acting 1938 and 1942–6).[17] All China Consular Service men had Chinese language skills, usually serving as a student interpreter in Beijing before gaining experience in consular and vice-consular roles across China. Given that Chinese was important for diplomatic negotiation with Chinese officials, selecting consuls-general without Chinese language skills appears odd. Consular officers had to exchange letters and met in person most frequently with the Chinese circuit intendant (a *daotai* or, after 1911, a *daoyin*) stationed in the larger towns. Disputes over jurisdiction sometimes required a relay of communication and the *daotai/daoyin* acted as the intermediary between the British representatives, local magistrates and the highest Chinese provincial officer in Xinjiang located in Urumqi.[18] The reason why the Government of India did not select many from the China Consular Service remains uncertain. However, there were suggestions that the government was unimpressed with the first appointed consul-general from the Service, Nicholas Fitzmaurice, and his disinterest in intelligence work.[19]

Despite linguistic limitations, consuls-general still attempted to form relationships with their counterparts and promote a British sense of regal and imperial grandeur. The consulate held regular dinners and parties, especially for the Russian officials and military men who formed the largest group of 'Europeans' in Kashgar aside from the Swedish missionaries. Although lacking in other luxuries, the consulate boasted a 'magnificent hall, dining-room and drawing-room' in order to impress upon the Chinese and Russians 'the dignity of the British Empire'.[20] A cook employed by the consulate helped cater for guests, although some were considered underqualified for important receptions; one, for example, accidentally used arsenic instead of baking powder in buns for a tea party.[21] By far the largest annual event was the King's birthday celebration. Over 250 guests attended a garden party held on 4 August 1928 in Kashgar to celebrate the royal occasion. They included Chinese officials, leading members of the Turkic community, various British subjects and the Swedish missionary community.[22] The Russian consular officials also invited consuls-general to dinner parties which reportedly involved long and elaborate entertainments accompanied by vodka, wine and other liquors served in 'unending succession'.[23] The Chinese officials likewise hosted dinner parties followed by entertainment, including games that bewildered some of their British guests. For example, Ella Sykes, the wife of the acting consul-general Percy Sykes, related the seemingly strange finger game of rock-paper-sack (a modified game of the modern-day 'rock-paper-scissors') at the table.[24] Parties were clearly an important diplomatic occasion, but whereas some consuls-general enjoyed such occasions, others complained of the taxing nature of 'dinners of the most tedious kind'.[25] In just two months in 1930, for example, Frederick Williamson attended twenty-nine parties at various towns accompanied by his vice-consul George Sherriff.[26] Though time-consuming, regular attendance at social occasions promoted British prestige and helped consular officials form friendly relations with their Russian and Chinese counterparts. This appeared to mirror the aims of the social occasions of the annual Sino-British 'Frontier Meetings' held in the Burma-China frontier.

Another essential duty of the consuls-general was going on 'tour' to hear cases. In a vast region like Xinjiang, travelling between the various towns was both tiring and time-consuming. In his annual tour in 1924, for example, Clarmont Skrine made seven journeys around southern Xinjiang. He covered a distance of over 6,000 km, visiting thirty-nine towns in fifteen districts. In total, he spent half of his time as consul-general on tour.[27] Resolving legal disputes was only part of the reasoning for going on tour. As Williamson noted in 1928, British prestige again played an important role:

> the fact that the consulate officers take an active interest in the cases of British subjects, and are prepared to go on long tours has a great effect in maintaining our prestige, which is undoubtedly high in Southern Sinkiang. I greatly doubt whether we have any prestige at all north of the Tian Shan [because of Russian influence], and personal acquaintance with the northern officials would certainly improve our position in this respect.[28]

Although diplomacy and the resolution of cases took up much of the consul-general's time, help was at hand. The consulate staffed a *mir munshi* (head clerk) and, at times, a Chinese secretary/translator, a surgeon, accountant, consular guard and various servants.[29] The Chinese secretary translated letters from the *daotai/daoyin* and some consuls-general sent the secretary to convey messages in legal cases and to gather intelligence. As the majority of the later consuls-general did not have Chinese language skills, the absence of capable interpreters and writers could put them at a diplomatic disadvantage. In 1930, consul-general Williamson lamented the unfortunate situation of his consulate and related how it affected his correspondence with his Chinese counterparts:

> at present there is no member of the Consulate staff who is acquainted with the Chinese language. The person who we employ to write our

Chinese correspondence is a clerk in the local Post Office, who comes for an hour or two every day after his own work is finished. Owing to this fact the greatest inconvenience is constantly experienced in dealing both personally and by letter with the Chinese authorities. From the English translation of the [recent] Taoyin's letter I judge that it is couched in discourteous language. I am, however, not able to make an official complaint to this effect, as I cannot be perfectly certain that it is the case.[30]

This state of affairs compromised the work of the consular officials. Without a means of communication, some consuls-general appeared reluctant to engage personally with their counterparts.

Apart from staffing, the consulate suffered other drawbacks. Visitors remarked upon the inadequate building and the challenges of the climatic conditions of the location. Consul-general Clarmont Skrine described it as 'comfortable enough' on first arriving there, but Ella Sykes described the consulate as distinctly uncomfortable to live and work in. She declared the newly built consulate was now 'agreeably free from scorpions', but still housed plenty of spiders, including venomous species.[31] The pest problem continued in the evenings, as reading lights attracted midges, beetles and other insects.[32] Although seemingly of little importance, it highlighted how the consulate and its environment was far from a welcoming place for consular officials and their foreign visitors. The consulate building (see Figure 7 below)

Figure 7   Kashgar consulate, c. 1915

and its location received a more disdainful summary from Colonel Reginald Schomberg in 1926, who stated that 'probably there is no British consulate worse found or more precariously situated than that of Kashgar'.[33]

Although the consulate was generally understaffed and unwelcoming, from 1918 consuls-general received vital support with the periodic appointment of vice-consuls.[34] Vice-consuls supported the consuls-general with intelligence work and lightened the administrative burden by hearing trials. When the consuls-general went on leave, vice-consuls took on the role of their absentee colleagues. They also went on tour to different towns to try serious or complicated cases between British subjects or observed cases between a British and a Chinese subject in a *daotai*'s courthouse (*yamen*). For example, in 1924, Harold Harding aided Clarmont Skrine by touring the outlying towns of Kuchar in the north and Hotan in the south, which were journeys of 763 and 518 km respectively.[35]

There are very few details about the relationship of consular officials and their Chinese counterparts concerning Sino-British cases. However, a few snippets from the consular record suggest that some of the vice-consuls on tour could develop a good working relationship. George Sherriff, for example, ensured the settlement of a large number of cases due to his amicable relationship with various Chinese officials. Williamson recalled that Feng Daren, the district magistrate (*amban*) of Qarghaliq, was 'very friendly to Mr. Sherriff and anxious to settle cases', although his methods for resolving cases were 'of a dilatory and bargaining kind, and the work took a very long time'.[36] Personal amiability appeared to be more important for the resolution of cases than legal procedure. Sherriff described An Daren, *amban* of Poskam, as an 'official of the old school' (educated in the Confucian classics), but it proved 'possible to settle all outstanding cases with him'.[37] Working relationships were therefore attainable so long as consular representatives looked past the different methods applied by their Chinese counterparts. This appeared to be another similarity shared by Yunnan consuls working with Chinese officials in the Frontier Meetings on the Burma-China frontier.

For mediating the voluminous number of minor disputes, consular administration relied upon *aqsaqals* (also rendered in Chinese as '*shangyue*' by British officials). In Turkic, 'aqsaqal' translated as 'white beard' and referred to an elder male member of the community or an experienced merchant who arbitrated disputes. *Aqsaqals* heard minor civil disputes and criminal cases involving British defendants. They could also be present in mixed cases involving British plaintiffs.[38] If the defendant was a Chinese subject, a local administrator, a *beg* (*shangzong/boke*) or a Chinese-appointed *aqsaqal* heard the case, usually drawing upon customary Turkic norms in decision-making.[39] For civil and revenue cases involving religious custom, such as those involving divorce, inheritance and personal property, a *qazi* (*ahong*) – a religious magistrate – heard the case. The Chinese administration appointed a *qazi* on the recommendation of leading local residents. He exercised his office in a public place, usually the chief local mosque or sometimes his own house, so long as the public had free access. Often, the judgment of the *qazi* and *beg* was not subject to the approval of the Chinese authorities unless the case involved larger amounts of money or had greater political or social significance. Whilst both were part of the Chinese administrative system, Chinese and British consular officials remained sceptical of their intentions and regularly claimed that *begs* accepted bribes.[40] In criminal cases involving more serious charges, a local district magistrate (*amban*) heard cases involving Chinese defendants. Due to the size of the province, legal powers were often devolved to *beg* officials as a matter of practicality. Despite the great political changes wrought by the 1911–12 revolution that overthrew the Qing and the subsequent establishment of the Republic, Governor Yang maintained the *beg* system with only minor changes. By October 1922, *amban* officials now had jurisdiction in cases involving money or assets worth 100 *taels* or more.[41] The *amban* usually had up to three *beg* assistants to settle cases in consultation with the *aqsaqal*.[42] British consuls-general during the second decade of the twentieth century suspected that Yang aimed to limit the influence of British *aqsaqals* by directing more minor cases before *amban* officials, who had greater imperial oversight.[43]

The use of *aqsaqals* was a customary practice across parts of Central Asia where communities relied upon such a person to resolve commercial disputes. Both Russia and China used *aqsaqals* to resolve minor disputes involving Russian and Chinese subjects. Merchants tended to form groups with others through native-place ties in Xinjiang,[44] and therefore the appointment of a senior representative of their group to mediate in disputes was a logical administrative solution. For example, Russian Andijani traders had their own *aqsaqal* representatives in the province. The British use of the *aqsaqal* system therefore followed customary practice of imperial administration in the region. At first, Chinese *amban* officials appeared to appoint the *aqsaqals* who represented various British communities.[45] Macartney protested against this interference in 1898 and by the turn of the century, he reached a compromise with the Chinese authorities by consulting with the local *amban* before one of the candidates was selected.[46] After China recognised Macartney as consul in 1908, there is no indication that consular officials consulted Chinese officials on their selection. Instead, the consul-general declared an *aqsaqal* in post after an election of the local British community. British administration therefore managed the British community through ethnic and native-place categories, and *aqsaqals* enforced local custom in trade disputes. British justice therefore modelled itself on a local institution that was both practical and necessary in Xinjiang.

Aqsaqals were important for consular administration as they heard a voluminous number of cases. They also understood the local customs particular to the regional background of the merchant group as well as their native tongue. Despite this, consular reports rarely mention the role of *aqsaqals*. This is unsurprising given the aim of the reports. The resolution of petty trade disputes were not of interest to either the colonial authorities in India or the consular authorities in China. Instead, cases of political interest, which were normally heard by the consul-general, were more significant to the consul-general's administrative superiors. However, snippets of information in consular reports relate the importance of *aqsaqals* for resolving the large numbers of cases. As Etherton stated in 1919:

> The consulate is always overwhelmed with reports and petitions, mostly in Persian and Turki, and it is absolutely essential to have sound and go-ahead men as one's local representatives. The secret, of course, of satisfactory administration in such a large Consular area as this lies in touring and personal supervision of the work of Aksakals [*aqsaqals*].[47]

In short, *aqsaqals* were crucial for British administration. They were practical, skilled and were a familiar institution to the local populace. Some even lived in the bazaar and owned shops within it – the central trading area for merchants – meaning that they were always on hand when disputes arose.[48] Consular officials also had very little oversight over *aqsaqals*, reflecting the limitations of working in a vast province and the dependence upon these locally stationed representatives. For example, despite working as part of the British consular system, not all *aqsaqals* ever met a consular official.[49] By 1922, there were twelve British *aqsaqals* stationed at the largest towns in the province. These places were: Kashgar, Yangi Hissar, Yarkand, Qarghaliq, Guma, Hotan, Keriya, Cherchan, Maralbashi, Aqsu, Ili and Tashkurghan.[50] Percy Sykes, on his travels in the province, photographed a group of *aqsaqals* (see Figure 8, below). Skyes clearly recognised the importance of photographing the men who represented British interests in the region. However, whilst they represented Britain and were part of consular

Figure 8   British *aqsaqals* in Xinjiang, c. 1915

administration, they were also unofficial representatives, marking a striking difference from consular administration elsewhere in China.[51]

Although British administration relied on the local institution of *aqsaqals*, the consular organisation of this institution drew upon Indian organisational models.[52] In October 1917 in Yarkand, Macartney instituted what he termed a 'punchait' (*panchayat*). This was an unofficial Indian institution that operated like a village council or a council administrating the affairs of a particular caste.[53] In Xinjiang, he assigned to this association a chief *aqsaqal* and four 'naib' *aqsaqals*, a term indicating a subordinate district official in India. *Naib aqsaqals* acted as subordinates and represented different British communities: 'Hindu' (a generic term for non-Muslim traders, usually from non-frontier parts of India), 'Kashmiri' (people from Kashmir), 'Wakhi' (those from Wakhan and valleys of the Hindu Kush) 'Chitrali' (those from Chitral) and 'Balti' (those from the southern valleys of the Karakoram). *Naib aqsaqals* took up petitions on behalf of their community members to Chinese and local officials in disputes involving Chinese defendants. By 1918, many of the *aqsaqals* in the main towns had *naib aqsaqals* who represented other sub-group religious, ethnic and regional communities with divergent cultural beliefs and languages.[54] Therefore, the nomenclature and organisation of the *aqsaqal* institution reflected forms of local Indian administration; the idea of the *panchayat* went beyond the borders of India. Its establishment also indicated the growing diversity of the British community and demonstrated how British justice adapted to these social changes.

George Macartney, the first consul-general, had promised the British communities that an election for the post of *aqsaqal* should be every two years.[55] In practice, many served longer terms. For example, Khan Bahadur Mulla Sabit, *aqsaqal* at Yarkand, remained in post for at least seven years (1910–17) and Islam Khan held his post in Ili for twelve years (1906–18) until his death. Not all remained popular with the local British community after election. Members of the Afghan community petitioned Macartney to remove Mulla Sabit from his post.[56] Instead of inquiring into the matter, Macartney dismissed the petition and attributed the disquiet to ethnic and political differences between the *aqsaqal* and the various members of his community. This suggested that Macartney (and perhaps later consuls-general) preferred to retain individuals in post when it suited them rather than listen to popular opinion.

Aside from their legal duties, *aqsaqals* had two other important roles. First, consular officials relied on their local intelligence on Russian and Chinese political activities. This included reports on pan-Islamic and anti-British movements within the local population. Consular officials also relied on *aqsaqals* to report on the changing attitudes of local Chinese officials towards British privileges. Second, *aqsaqals* issued tax exemption certificates. British subjects – like their Russian counterparts – benefited from the exemption of various tariffs as specified in the Sino-British and Sino-Russian treaties. It was customary when travelling with goods between towns that the foreign subject obtained a goods ownership certificate from his *aqsaqal*. This was later stamped and sealed by the Chinese *lijin* (customs) office.[57] The trading community relied on this procedure to enable them to shift goods from one place to the next. *Aqsaqals* therefore supported British imperial officials by enabling British tax-free trade and providing local knowledge. They thus mediated in local life and imperial bureaucracy, and their system of administration was drawn from both local and Indian administrative structures.

A thorny 'subject': regional and ethnic diversity of the British community

Consular jurisdiction as exercised by consuls-general, vice-consuls and *aqsaqals* in the above-mentioned administration was contingent upon one main concept: nationality. In a place characterised by immigration and the transfrontier movement of people, the concept of nationality was nebulous. There were two inter-related questions for British representatives. First, who could they ascertain to be a British subject through descent or birthplace? Second, who was worthy of British protection?

Most of those who claimed British subjecthood were people born either within the British Empire or with paternal connections to the British Empire in Asia. Very few people classified as 'European', i.e. those who had been naturalised or born in Britain or had a father born in Britain, ever resided in the province. Instead, Indian subcontinental traders working the caravan routes that cut through the Pamirs and the Karakoram Range to Xinjiang formed the majority of the first-generation population. They also formed the majority of the sojourning population, who were usually seasonal traders from Leh in northern India. However, ascertaining who was a subject proved difficult and politically sensitive. Many who claimed British subjecthood following a legal claim or charge had not formally registered as a British subject. Nor did these individuals have documentation to prove their nationality. Before the early twentieth century, the fathers of second-generation men usually held no passport or visa documentation when they crossed from India to Xinjiang.[58] In addition, in a place defined by emigration, integration and cross-cultural encounters, cultural and social identity markers were often blurred. In many instances, as David Brophy notes of Russian Andijani subjects, there was little difference in the religion, speech or dress of these immigrants to distinguish them from local Chinese subjects.[59] In the case of British subjects, most second-generation individuals were sons of an Indian-born father and an ethnic Turkic mother of Chinese subjecthood. This mixed heritage meant that consuls struggled to distinguish (what they considered to be) clear ethnic and cultural markers of people with heritage from northern India. Unsurprisingly, Chinese officials suspected that some people who claimed British nationality for tax exemption purposes did so fraudulently. Local Chinese officials therefore often identified many men who resided locally as Chinese subjects, rejecting their claim of British subjecthood. Consular officials and *aqsaqals* had the difficult task of trying to ascertain the legitimacy of their claims to subjecthood and contest Chinese jurisdiction when they believed there was some indication that they could be men of Indian heritage.

However, British contestation was dependent upon the question of who *should* be a British subject, which was not unique to the setting of Xinjiang, but was debated across the British Empire.[60] Ascribing subjecthood required continuous consideration of what defined nationality and what was beneficial for British imperial interests. Thus, the answer to this question depended upon two considerations: first, the understanding of the ethnic, cultural and social aspects of the community who made up the population of British subjects; and, second, British political and economic aims in Xinjiang.

Early consular policy reflected the British ambition to enlarge its economic sphere of influence in the province through registration. Registered individuals did not necessarily need to provide documents in order to prove subjecthood. In 1907, the official consular policy directed consuls to register 'Asiatic' British subjects, i.e. those born in India and Afghanistan, as well as their children (but not their grandchildren) who asked to be registered.[61] British policy appeared to be that the consulate should automatically register the children of 'Asiatic' British fathers, even if these fathers had never registered as British.[62] Although Afghanistan was not a British colony (yet subject to some British influence), John Jordan, the Ambassador at Beijing, suggested to Macartney that he should register Afghan nationals as 'protected' British subjects.[63] These policies widened the definition of a British subject considerably.

In 1913, Macartney extended this policy by touring the province to find British nationals to register. He feared that unregistered subjects could be lured into becoming Russian subjects in order to receive tax exemption benefits. During his tour, Macartney pressed ahead with a system of registration in joint process with local *amban* officials in each major town. In October, he recorded 120 nationality certificates in cooperation with Xiong Daren, the *amban* of Yarkand.[64] In November, he issued certificates for a further 209 British subjects.[65] The vast majority were second-generation men of Indian parentage, who had been born in Xinjiang and owned land. In Qarghaliq, Macartney registered fifty British subjects, some of whom were Afghan subjects from Wakhan. At Hotan, Macartney enrolled seventy subjects. Nearly half of these individuals were born in Afghanistan or were sons of Afghan-born parents. At the end of his tour, Macartney had enrolled 436 persons from six towns.

This number continued to rise and, by the start of 1914, Macartney had registered just over 480 persons.[66] Six months later, the figure increased to 600 and another six months later to 800.[67] The majority of those registered were men, whose registration automatically conferred British status to their wives and children. Macartney estimated that with an average family size of five, there were approximately 4,000 British subjects under his jurisdiction.[68] To put that figure in context, most inland stations registered single or double-digit numbers of residents. As a 'frontier' post, therefore, the district of Kashgar bore little resemblance to other inland consular districts and many of the residents benefited from consular protection and privileges.

Further distinguishing the British population in Xinjiang from other districts was the occupations of the registered subjects and the numbers of those residing permanently. Most of the population were caravan traders, moneylenders or farmers, whose parents had been traders. The transfrontier trade in legal goods included cottons and spices as well as illicit goods such as opium from India and Afghanistan. In the opposite direction, Indian traders took *charas* (cannabis extract), tea, silk, wool and carpets, amongst other items. One prominent section of the British community was the population of Shikarpuri moneylenders who settled in Xinjiang. As Claude Markovits notes, unlike in other places in Central Asia, Indian Shikarpuri traders often took local wives in Xinjiang.[69] They were therefore more likely to settle in the province rather than return to India. Consular reports also noted that marriages between British Indian subjects and women of the local Turkic race (who were Chinese subjects) was the rule rather than the exception. By 1920, the forward policy in registration continued with the help of the China (Kashgar) Order in Council (1920), where a provision was made that allowed a registered man to register his wife or *wives*. This reflected the customary practice of polygamy among the British community in Xinjiang.[70] The provision also included all females and minors, *in whatever degree*, living under the same roof at the time of registration.[71] Registration policy therefore took into account the large family social structure of many of the Indian communities when registering national subjects.

The ethnic composition of registered subjects was also a distinguishing feature of the district compared to other inland consular districts of China. Whereas missionaries and scientists filled the census sheets for many inland consular districts, nearly all of the estimated 4,000 British subjects in Xinjiang in 1915 were of 'Asiatic' descent (i.e. from India and Afghanistan). In reports, consular officials often described their regional identities (where they could be ascertained) as the primary markers of their cultural and linguistic differences: 'Mohammadans and Hindus from the Punjab', 'Peshinis', 'Swatis', 'Bajouris', 'Kashmiris', 'Ladakhis', 'Gilgitis', 'Chitralis', 'Baltistanis', 'Nagaris', 'Kanjutis' and Afghans from Kabul, Badakhshan and Wakhan.[72] The ethnic communities reflected the regional draw of various communities in Xinjiang. It also demonstrated that consular officials tried to understand their community in terms of ethnic and regional categories.

The economic climate of the region also appeared to have a possible influence of the numbers and nature of the British community during this period. As tax exemption was one of the primary advantages of consular registration, British traders benefited greatly and trade boomed in the 1910s. Despite the outbreak of the First World War in 1914, consular reports show increases in trade from British India to the region.[73] This continued until 1921 and the growth of trade suggests that there may have been a corresponding increase in the number of British subjects in the region, alongside second-generation immigrants.[74] However, by 1924, consul-general Clarmont Skrine noted that there was a decrease in registration numbers to 674.[75] The Soviet Union had by this time started to dominate the provincial economy after a brief lull during 1914–21 with the First World War and the Russian Revolution. There was a clear demographic shift in the British community. Of the 674 registered subjects, just over half had been born in Xinjiang (i.e. they were second-generation subjects) as opposed to being born in India. Of the 674, nearly two-thirds were domiciled in Xinjiang. Both those born in Xinjiang and those born in India and residing in Xinjiang were mostly Muslims with heritage from the northwestern frontier regions of India, including Baltistan, Kashmir, Chitral and Bajaur. This left one-third as temporary residents, who were mostly Punjabi or Shikarpuri Hindu traders. By 1924, therefore, the majority of subjects were first- and second-generation Muslim subjects of regional heritage who resided in Xinjiang. The trading community, consisting largely of sojourning Hindu men, formed a much smaller, albeit still important, population.

Case statistics

With a population of somewhere between several hundred and several thousand, hearing legal cases filled a significant portion of a consul-general's time. The ethnic and religious aspects of this British community and their occupations all shaped the way in which British justice functioned across the province and the ways in which the consular officials understood consular justice when hearing cases.

As the British community consisted of numerous traders, moneylenders and landowners, civil cases were voluminous. Until 1922, there were no recorded case statistics. Consular representatives recorded data inconsistently with undefined units of measurement in their monthly reports to India and China. Consul Etherton claimed that the average number of cases per month was sixty-five.[76] This most likely reflected the total number of cases heard and resolved across the province, either heard by himself or by *aqsaqals*. Later records appear to suggest that the average was lower. In May 1920, the number of cases 'disposed of' totalled forty-one.[77] A month later, the figure amounted to forty-nine.[78] In September, the number of cases was fifty-three.[79] Two years later, the October diary of 1922 reported forty-three cases.[80] Although this might appear to be a small number, the statistics did not include those that were left unresolved and those presumably settled out of court.

There were few, if any, petitions in English. Most were written in Turkic with a smaller number in Persian and 'Hindustani'. For November 1919, Percy Etherton noted that 89 per cent of petitions were in Turkic, 7 per cent in Persian and 4 per cent in Hindustani.[81] Half a year later, he recorded 85 per cent in Turkic and 15 per cent in Persian for the month.[82] The predominance of Turkic suggests that resident subjects used the courts, although their ethnicity cannot be discerned. The use of Persian suggests more strongly that a minority of subjects who used the courts were individuals of Afghan or Chitrali heritage.[83]

After 1922, regular statistical reports made their way to the Ambassador at Beijing detailing cases invoking the China (Kashgar) Order in Council (1920). This category excluded many civil suits heard and resolved by *aqsaqals* without reference to the Order in Council (such as those relating to family law). There were both criminal and civil cases, although few criminal cases made their way to the consulate. For example, in 1921, there were three criminal hearings. Etherton sentenced one man to transportation for life for culpable homicide and deported two for smuggling opium.[84] There was no formal recording of civil cases. In 1922, there were two criminal hearings. One involved a man named Nur Mohamed charged with abetting the import of opium, who was later deported to India.[85] The other case resulted in the acquittal of Anant Ram for manslaughter. Again, there was no formal recording of civil cases, although Skrine reported that the number was high, especially suits involving debt.[86] In 1923, there were another three criminal hearings, this time concerning opium smuggling, wrongful confinement and theft. Each of the accused was found guilty and spent three months serving terms of imprisonment in India. For the first time, the consul-general recorded the number of civil cases involving British defendants, with 111 recorded cases, of which 101 involved 'debt'.[87] In 1924, there were six criminal hearings invoking the Order in Council.[88] By the end of the decade, this trend continued. In 1928, there was one criminal hearing involving a man named Ralla Ram.[89] Williamson convicted him of causing grievous hurt with a deadly weapon and sentenced him to five years.[90] Ram later appealed to the Lahore High Court.[91] Civil proceedings numbered 228, which included 201 debt cases.[92] In 1929, there was just one criminal hearing, where Shah Pasand was acquitted of killing Yusuf Akhun and his two wives.[93] The consul-general noted fifty-one civil proceedings for the year.[94]

In separate statistics not defined by the Order in Council, the consul provided returns for the two years of 1922 to 1924.[95] In 1922 and 1923, thirteen cases involved a British plaintiff against a British defendant. There were 157 civil cases featuring British plaintiffs against Chinese subjects, of which 146 concerned debt. Six cases involved Chinese plaintiffs against British subjects, all of which concerned the recovery of debt. For 1924, there were seventeen civil cases of British plaintiffs against British defendants, 131 civil cases of British plaintiffs against Chinese subjects, of which debt claims numbered 119 of 131. Finally, there were twelve cases involving Chinese plaintiffs against British subjects, nine of which were debt cases.[96]

The statistics provide an insightful snapshot of the number and types of cases typically heard at the consulate. There were no regular recording of cases until 1922 and even after the attempt to record them between 1922 and 1925, later consuls-general noted that they could not find many case figures for previous years.[97] These reported cases are therefore important, but patchy, evidence of the penal link to India; many of those convicted to terms of imprisonment were deported to serve their time in jails of the Raj. The vast majority of all cases involved the recovery of debt, giving an indication of the importance of resolving suits involving moneylending. As hearings concerned with the recovery of debt feature prominently in the statistics, this also reflects how consular justice functioned to resolve disputes relating to the occupations and lifestyles of traders and moneylenders.

There were no records of minor criminal justice trials. Consuls-general attributed the absence of petty crime to two factors. First, consuls-general believed that British Indian men had a 'law-abiding nature'.[98] Second, they encouraged litigants to pursue mediation for minor criminal incidents. Certainly, every effort was made to induce the parties in civil proceedings to engage in arbitration rather than resort to legal proceedings by the *Shariat* (*qazis* with *aqsaqals*) or by *aqsaqals* alone. It is therefore likely that these local officials also resolved cases involving minor crimes.

Prominent cases in detail: religious customs and consular justice

The multitude of different ethnic, religious and national subjects in Xinjiang gave rise to communities with different cultural, economic, social, political and legal beliefs. Consular representatives often had to navigate these different values when adjudicating disputes. The resolution of disagreements served two purposes: first, it eased tensions between individuals and within the community, which prevented the escalation of potential individual and community clashes; and, second, it aimed to protect the rights of subjects. As Etherton states in his monthly reports to India and China in the 'Kashgar diaries', consuls-general only recorded cases deemed to be of a sensitive nature, such as those with a religious conflict or political significance.[99] These included the violation of religious beliefs, which could threaten inter-community peace, as well as cases involving the rights of British subjects, such as tax exemptions on land and goods. Most recorded cases do not detail how consuls-general settled cases, merely noting the key parts of the alleged crime and the finding. However, in mixed cases involving Chinese subjects which were reported, consular representatives often worked with the local *amban* to reach a decision. The British representatives had to work out what seemed fair to them, usually taking into account the need to preserve peace between different ethnic and religious groups, mediating divergent local beliefs and finding a compromise with the *amban*. Although these reported cases provide only a glimpse of how consular officials arrived at settlements, they give an insight into their legal reasoning. I will focus on two of the most detailed types of individual cases reported: inter-religious incidents where consuls-general represented Hindu communities and cases involving discrepancies between Islamic law and local custom involving British subjects of the Islamic faith.

Some incidents did not require a formal hearing, with both parties relying instead on the consul to negotiate with his Chinese and Russian counterparts to ameliorate religious tensions. Such conflicts of belief arose most frequently between the community of the British Hindu population and the Muslim majority population in Xinjiang. A number of incidents seemed to augur inter-religious conflict and therefore required careful mediation. Prominent examples included those pertaining to butcher shops. In September 1913, Macartney intervened on behalf of 'Hushuarpuri Hindus' who lived in two *serais* (inns for travellers) in Yarkand, in a case involving a new butcher shop selling beef.[100] Since Hindus regarded the cow as sacred, the sale of beef in their proximity was repugnant to them. Macartney told the *daotai* that because of the importance of their religious rite and the potential for inter-religious conflict, he should prevent all Chinese subjects from opening butcher shops in the vicinity of the *serais*. The *daotai* agreed and Chinese subjects were reminded of this with boards erected on walls and inscribed with the prohibition.[101] Ella Sykes, the wife of the acting consul Percy Sykes, noted that 'sometimes the Yarkandis tear down the notices and the butchers reopen their stalls, but whenever this occurs a complaint from the Hindus to the authorities is ultimately successful'.[102] She understood this to be 'praiseworthy tolerance of the religious views of other races' by Chinese officials.[103] It was indeed testament to both the Chinese (and British) understanding of religious sensitivity and their management of Sino-British inter-community relations between Muslims and Hindus.

However, the issue of the sale of beef did occasionally resurface in incidents involving Russian subjects. A number of Russian Andijani Yarkand residents – including one named Kara Bai – opened a shop selling beef within 150 metres of the Hindu *serai* door. Macartney petitioned the Russian consul-general, Sokov, who in turn ordered the local Russian *aqsaqal* to close the shop and prevent others from opening.[104] This appeared to stop the escalation into inter-religious conflict. Years later, several other 'beef' incidents occurred, requiring careful mediation. In 1917, Macartney secured the intervention of Prince Mestchersky, then Russian consul-general, when Russian merchants opened a shop selling beef. Two years later, Etherton again raised the issue to the Russian consul-general in yet another case, who directed his *aqsaqal* to close another shop and take steps to avoid further confrontation.[105] Although these incidents were seemingly of little consequence, these timely interventions clearly mattered in a place where people with a multitude of religious beliefs lived and worked together.

Aside from the direct contravention of religious beliefs, inter-community conflict could also become inflected with religious overtones. British Shikarpuri moneylenders had a notorious reputation for requesting usurious rates from their clients. Local *beg* and *qazi* magistrates helped resolve acrimonious disputes between British and Chinese subjects. In 1929, Williamson reported a case involving a Shikarpuri moneylender:

> In February one of them demanded his dues from a local Turki, who is of a somewhat quarrelsome and aggressive nature. The case was referred to the Shariat [Islamic court]. The debtor put a saddle on a cow, dressed it in red cloth, and painted its horns red. He led it through the bazaar followed by a large crowd, estimated at 1000 people, and announced that the Hindu would be required to ride the cow to the Shariat. Fortunately no disturbance occurred. The case was evidently settled and the debtor was required to apologise to the Hindu. He has now given a statement to the Kazis [*Qazis*] to the effect that he was responsible for the cow episode and that, if anything of the kind should occur again, he is willing to submit to severe punishment.[106]

Williamson was content to leave the case to the *qazi* to resolve without intervening. He reported the case as an example of how practices of moneylending by British subjects could foster acrimony between religious groups. The case demonstrates that consular officials also relied on trusted local officials to resolve sensitive local cases involving inter-community relations.

Mixed religious unions could also cause religious and political tensions. In 1922, the Chinese authorities accused a British man,

Anant Ram, of killing a local man by running him over with his cart and running away with a Turkic girl, Zainab Khan.[107] Consul-general Clarmont Skrine found Ram not guilty of murder or manslaughter. However, the *amban* objected to his acquittal and Skrine's failure to punish Ram for his elopement with Khan that contravened local custom. Governor Yang Zengxin argued that although Skrine had acquitted Ram of any responsibility for the death of the Chinese subject, Ram should at least be punished for 'seducing' Khan with intent to run away with him. Their union contravened not only Chinese law on abduction but also religious law, as she was Muslim and he was a Hindu.[108] Skrine interviewed Ram, who attested that Khan's parents had assented to his marriage and that the *mullah* (an Islamic theologian) from the neighbouring village had given his blessing. After the marriage, Ram converted to Islam and changed his name to Sheik Mohd Amin.[109] As he was not a Muslim when they were married, he admitted that they had in fact lived as *faux* husband and wife.[110]

Skrine detailed the reasons for his refusal to punish Ram.[111] First, it was obvious that there was no offence according to the China (Kashgar) Order in Council (1920). He then applied his own understanding of local custom to legitimise his position by pointing out that Indian men of the Hindu faith customarily took local Muslim wives. Skrine argued that the consent of the girl's parents mattered more than its contravention of Islamic custom, with the girl given to Ram in lieu of debt payment.[112] In this sense, it was a simple transaction between two men. Skrine also considered local ethnic relations in justification of his verdict and stated that there was no objection within the local Islamic community in Hotan to such inter-faith marriages.[113] He concluded by noting that he refused to deport Ram for eloping with Khan and that to do so would not only be 'politically inexpedient' (i.e. a concession to Chinese pressure) but also 'flagrantly unjust' (due to the acceptability of the customs).[114] He therefore drew upon local custom and community relations to arrive at a decision rather than simply stating that there was no offence according to the Order in Council. This demonstrates how the consideration of custom played an important part in the administration of consular justice.

Consuls-general tried other cases involving British Muslim subjects, which concerned the conflict between proscribed Islamic law and local custom. One such type of common case involved charitable endowments (*waqf*).[115] In theory, these Islamic religious land endowments were prohibited from being sold or exchanged, but court cases show that custom did not always follow this rule. This resulted in cases that raised questions about religious rights, local practice and monetary compensation.[116] In 1922, Zali Khan, a British subject,

[141]

bought a house and a garden on *waqf* land in Keriya near Hotan from one of the trustees, a *qazi* named Alam Akhun.[117] As Skrine pointed out, *waqf* land could only be rented and renewed on an annual basis. Anyone who rented the land and built upon it, or planted trees, could be turned out at any time. However, they could take their house with them once they were evicted.

Drawing on his knowledge of custom across Central Asia, Skrine claimed that in practice, trustees in Xinjiang regarded *waqf* land as their private property and often let it out on a long lease. In turn, the lessee could build houses and make improvements to existing buildings without fear of eviction. In the present case, Zali Kahn's purchase deeds and lease were not properly attested and he was involved in a boundary dispute with the owners of a neighbouring Chinese cemetery. As it was impossible to establish his title, Skrine advocated that Khan should vacate the whole property on condition that the purchase money paid by him should be refunded, with full compensation awarded to him for all improvements made. The *amban* agreed and thereafter the consul-general and the *amban* spent half a day inspecting the land and buildings to assess the amount of compensation in the presence of all the parties. Khan eventually received 1,040 *taels* and reportedly, he 'was more than content with the amount secured for him'.[118] Although Khan received full compensation, the *amban* clearly believed that Khan had no right to the land in the first place. Subsequently he prosecuted five subjects who sold the property to Khan and sentenced them to work in a local gold mine for sixteen months.[119] The Khan verdict was clearly a compromise reached by the consul-general and the *amban*. Khan had no right to claim compensation for abiding by local custom that contravened Islamic law. However, he received compensation nonetheless, whilst those who sold the land to him were prosecuted. This appeared to show that Skrine supported Khan's right to compensation despite contravening religious law.[120]

The resolution followed precedent established in a case that Macartney heard in 1913. A Chinese subject, Abdur Rahim, mortgaged to Khan Sahib Mulla Sabit, a British subject, twenty-two shops in two streets worth 1,000 *taels*.[121] They abutted the north and west sides of a *madrassa* (an Islamic school). The teachers and scholars of the *madrassa* contended that the shops were *waqf* and that Rahim had no right to mortgage the buildings. In contrast, Rahim argued that they were his personal property as he built the shops with his own money. Macartney and the *amban* decided that the amount repayable to Mulla Sabit was 1,000 *taels* (the mortgage money) plus 281 *taels* for the interest based on the rent of the twenty-two shops for three years. The fourteen shops on the north side of the *madrassa* were *waqf* and the eight on the west side were not *waqf*. The *madrassa* was ordered to purchase the latter for a sum of 556 *taels* payable to the consular court in one month, for delivery to Mulla Sabit. The balance of 725 *taels* due to Mulla Sabit would be repayable in two months by the mortgagor Abdul Rahim.[122] This appeared to be a compromise, which allowed Sabit to recover his mortgage money and interest on the rent. In this case, Macartney had to consider several legal customs. First, religious custom prohibited the sale of *waqf*, but officeholders rented the land and lived off the proceeds. As Bella-Hann notes, local custom in Xinjiang sometimes permitted certain types of *waqf* ownership rights.[123] Macartney would have been familiar with the concept of English compensation and the resolution appeared to be a nod to a satisfactory resolution voiding the transaction based on custom. It also gave Mulla Sabit compensation for the amount owed to him through ownership and the work he had put into the buildings.

In sum, consular officials appeared to mediate several different concerns and values when arriving at a decision in religious cases. Although many of the cases seemed minor, their mediation by consular and Chinese officials indicates the importance of resolving such cases in a place where different religious communities lived and worked together. The reporting of such incidents reflects the significance of maintaining peaceful inter-community relations. Consular officials also drew upon notions of local custom to arrive at decisions they felt made sense to them for preserving the peace and acceptable to those who lived by these customary practices, whilst ensuring the rights of British subjects.

Conclusion

Consular officials were key mediators between imperial authority and the local populace in Xinjiang. Unlike other inland consular stations, the consular officials were kept busy with cases reflecting the large British subject population in the province. British administration was also dependent on the work of *aqsaqals*. This reflected the necessity of having local men with customary knowledge to resolve minor trade disputes amongst their merchant community members. *Aqsaqals*, in particular, were crucial for administering law in a large and remote region by mediating disputes between the individuals of the local community. The consular organisation of the *aqsaqal* institution drew from Indian administrative structures, showing that consular administration was a mixture of the adaptation of local institutions, Indian organisational influences and consular frameworks.

Immigration, emigration and the meeting of different ethnic and religious people characterised life in Xinjiang, and this community shaped the administration of British justice. The policies of registration revealed that these communities were drawn almost entirely from the Indian subcontinent. However, identifying British subjects was complicated by the absence of documentation and because many of those claiming Indian heritage had adopted local cultural, linguistic and social identity traits. Many of those who made up the British community were traders, moneylenders and landowners. The preponderance of civil cases reflected how the machinery of consular justice was exercised most frequently to resolve issues pertaining to debt, traded goods and land.

Finally, in court hearings, consular officials did not simply look to the Orders in Council to arrive at decisions. Instead, they tried to balance the concern of peaceful community relations, the importance of local custom and the rights of British subjects. This drew similarities to the Sino-British Frontier Meetings in the Burma-Yunnan frontier. In other words, local legal norms (as well as those drawn from the Indian subcontinent) were accommodated into the exercise of consular law in Xinjiang.

Notes

1 On the role of the frontiers as important points of interaction between state and local actors, see, for example: P. Crossley, H. Siu and D. Sutton (eds), *Empire at the Margins: Culture, Ethnicity, and Frontier in Early Modern China* (Berkeley: University of California Press, 2006); D. Lary (ed.), *Chinese State at the Borders* (Vancouver: University of British Columbia Press, 2007).

2 D. Brophy, *Uyghur Nation: Reform and Revolution on the Russia-China Frontier* (Cambridge, MA: Harvard University Press, 2016).

3 Brophy, *Uyghur Nation*, p. 76.

4 *Ibid.*

5 L. Newby, 'The begs of Xinjiang: between two worlds', *Bulletin of the School of Oriental and African Studies*, 61:2 (1998), 278–97.

6 M. Thampi, *Indians in China, 1800–1949* (New Delhi: Manohar, 2005), pp. 113–39.

7 The first consul-general, George Macartney, was never formally appointed in the Indian Civil Service. On the particulars of the post in the Indian system, see: M. Everest-Phillips, 'British consuls in Kashgar', *Asian Affairs*, 22:1 (1991), 26–7.

8 Later, consuls-general reported to the 'External Affairs Department'.

9 On the intelligence activities of Etherton, see: D. Waugh, *Etherton at Kashgar: Rhetoric and Reality in the History of the "Great Game"* (Seattle: Bactrian Press, 2007). For first-hand accounts, see: G. Macartney, 'Bolshevism as I saw it at Tashkent in 1918', *Journal of the Central Asian Society*, 7:2–3 (1920), 42–58; P. Etherton, *In the Heart of Asia* (Boston: Houghton Mifflin Company, 1926).

10 IOR: L/PS/11/74 India Office Secret and Political Department, 'Minute: Chinese Turkestan', 7 March 1914; 'Translation of Despatch No. 49, Chang Yung-Ching, Kuan-Cha-Shih of Kashgar and Superintendent of Foreign Intercourse Affairs', 2 December 1913.

11 'Hindustandi' was a generic term for the language used by many British Indian subjects. Today we might consider this to mean a mix of Urdu and Hindi.

12 IOR: L/PS/10/453 G. Macartney to J. Shuckburgh, India Office, 5 April 1920.

13   *Ibid.*
14   Etherton appears to have had some fluency in Chinese later on in his post, as evidenced by his analysis of the Chinese-language version of the Sino–Russian treaties in 1919.
15   C. Skrine, *Chinese Central Asia* (London: Methuen, 1926), p. 63.
16   IOR: L/PS/12/2345 'Report on the House of Commons', 21 May 1930.
17   Gillett also served as consul in Tengyue in 1940.
18   Before 1911, the province was divided into four circuits (*dao*) headed by a *daotai*, with districts (*xian*) headed by an *amban* (*xianguan*) and sub-districts as smaller administrative divisions overseen by *begs*. After 1911, there were six circuits: Urumqi, Chuguchak (Tacheng), Ili, Altai, Asqu and Kashgar. There were forty-seven districts and numerous sub-districts. There also existed a few local leaders in more autonomous areas. For example, in Hami, a local king (*wang*) governed over this small kingdom in northeast Xinjiang until 1929.
19   Everest-Phillips, 'British consuls in Kashgar', 24–5.
20   Skrine, *Chinese Central Asia*, p. 55.
21   E. Sykes and P. Sykes, *Through Deserts and Oases of Central Asia* (London: Macmillan & Co., 1920), p. 41.
22   TNA: FO228/3869 F. Williamson, Kashgar consul-general, to the Secretary to the Government of India in the Foreign and Political Department, Kashgar 'Diary for the Month of August, 1928', 6 September 1928.
23   Sykes and Sykes, *Through Deserts and Oases of Central Asia*, p. 47.
24   *Ibid.*
25   TNA: FO228/4266 F. Williamson to the Secretary to the Government of India in the Foreign and Political Department, 'Kashgar Diary for June 1930', 8 July 1930.
26   TNA: FO228/4266 F. Williamson to the Secretary to the Government of India in the Foreign and Political Department, 'Kashgar Diary for April and May 1930', 7 June 1930.
27   Skrine, *Chinese Central Asia*, p. 62.
28   TNA: FO228/3869 F. Williamson to the Secretary to the Government of India in the Foreign and Political Department, 23 July 1928.
29   On the role of the *munshi* as interlocutor in British India, see, for example: M. Alam and S. Subrahmanyam, 'The making of a Munshi', *Comparative Studies of South Asia, Africa and the Middle East*, 24:2 (2004), 61–72. Humans were also not the only company in the consulate. When Percy Sykes became acting consul-general during Macartney's absence, he was also kept company by 'Beilka' and 'Brownie' – one a 'powerful white animal rather like a wolf' and another a 'fat, easygoing spaniel'. The former acted as a guard dog, keeping the consulate 'free of thieves', whilst the other one can only assume was more for company. Such animals were doubtless of much importance in a place where a consul-general spent much of his time. See Sykes and Sykes, *Through Deserts and Oases of Central Asia*, p. 53. Clarmont Skrine also kept 'a perfect menagerie of pets' at the consulate including three cats that 'ruled the Consulate'. Their names reflected the polyglot life there, named with a mixture of Hindustani, Turkic, Chinese and Scottish dialect: 'Chang Mao' (big cat) 'Chhota Mao' (small cat) and 'Wee Squeakie' (tiny squeak). See Skrine, *Chinese Central Asia*, pp. 69–70.
30   TNA: FO228/4267 F. Williamson to the Secretary to the Government of India in the Foreign and Political Department, 19 February 1930.
31   Skrine, *Chinese Central Asia*, p. 55; Sykes and Sykes. *Through Deserts and Oases of Central Asia*, pp. 88–9.
32   *Ibid.*
33   TNA: FO228/3664 'Notes made by Colonel Schomberg on a journey to the Pamirs, Kashgar and Yarkand in 1926 (received in the Foreign Office, February 23, 1927)'.
34   A vice-consul position was filled from 1922 to 1923. Between 1924 and 1927, there was no vice-consul and from 1927 onwards, there was a vice-consul on an *ad hoc* basis. IOR: L/PS/12/2345.

35 TNA: FO228/3028 C. Skrine, Kashgar consul-general, to J. R. Macleay, the Ambassador at Beijing, 21 August 1924.
36 TNA: FO228/3869 F. Williamson to the Secretary to the Government of India, Foreign and Political Department, 'Kashgar Diary, for the month of December 1927', 19 January 1928.
37 Ibid.; Daren was a Chinese honorific title for officials.
38 There appears to be no definition of an aqsaqal's scope of jurisdiction in the consular records.
39 On the roles of the beg, see, for example: Newby, 'The begs of Xinjiang'. See also I. Bellér-Hann, Community Matters in Xinjiang, 1880–1949: Towards a Historical Anthropology of the Uyghur (Leiden: Brill, 2008), pp. 179–86. As Bellér-Hann notes, there is difficulty in accessing archival sources to know precise details of how local law worked in practice in Xinjiang during this era. There appear to have been many crossovers between different types of Islamic, customary and Chinese law invoked by different legal officials. For an overview on these different laws in Xinjiang, see: D. Wang, qingdai huijiang falü zhidu yanjiu, 1759–1884 nian [A Study of the Legal System of the Muslim Domain, 1759–1884] (Ha'erbin: Heilongjiang jiaoyu chubanshe, 2003).
40 This scepticism was also present in locally published gazetteers: E. Schluessel, 'The Muslim Emperor of China: Everyday Politics in Colonial Xinjiang, 1877–1933' (PhD dissertation, Harvard University, 2016), pp. 131–3.
41 By October 1922, there was also a change of nomenclature for the begs; instead of 'Foreign Affairs Begs' for mixed cases, the amban appointed a '(Chinese) Foreign Affairs Assistant' as his subordinate.
42 TNA: FO228/3027 C. P. Skrine, Kashgar consul-general, to the Ambassador at Beijing, 'Diary for the month of October 1922', 16 November 1922.
43 TNA: FO228/3027 Kashgar consulate to B. Alston, Ambassador at Beijing, 24 November 1922.
44 Brophy, Uyghur Nation, pp. 39–40.
45 C. Skrine and P. Nightingale, Macartney at Kashgar: New Light on British, Chinese and Russian Activities in Sinkiang, 1890–1918 (Oxford: Harper & Row, 1987), p. 99.
46 IOR: R/2/1075/216 J. Manners-Smith, Political Agent, Gilgit to the Secretary to the Government of India, 11 December forwarding: 'Diary of the Special Assistant for Chinese Affairs to the Resident in Kashmir for the fortnight ending the 15th November 1899'.
47 TNA: FO228/3024 P. Etherton to the Ambassador at Beijing and to the Foreign Secretary to the Government of India, Foreign and Political Department, 'Kashgar Diary for the month November 1919', 3 December 1919.
48 Sykes and Sykes, Through Deserts and Oases of Central Asia, p. 197.
49 P. Fleming, News from Tartary: A Journey from Peking to Kashmir (London: Jonathan Cape, 1936), p. 268.
50 TNA: FO228/3026 P. Etherton to Ambassador at Beijing, 'Diary for November, 1921', 1 December 1920.
51 Whereas other community leaders in China may have played a role in dispute mediation of minor disputes amongst British subject communities, such as for the Sikh community in the Shanghai Municipal Police, they were not considered part of the general administration as aqsaqals were in Xinjiang.
52 Markovits also briefly notes that the Shikarpuri community had a type of panchayat organisation in Xinjiang: C. Markovits, The Global World of Indian Merchants, 1750–1947: Traders of Sind from Bukhara to Panama (Cambridge: Cambridge University Press, 2000), p. 97.
53 On the panchayat, see: J. Jaffe, The Ironies of Colonial Governance: Law, Custom, and Justice in Colonial India (Cambridge: Cambridge University Press, 2015).
54 IOR: L/PS/10/825 P. Etherton to H. Grant, Foreign Secretary to the Government of India in the Foreign and Political Department, 'Diary of the month of August 1918', 26 September 1918.

55 IOR: L/PS/10/825 G. Macartney to the Foreign Secretary to the Government of India in the Foreign and Political Department 'Diary for October 1917', 10 November 1917.
56 *Ibid.*
57 IOR: L/PS/10/825 G. Macartney to H. Grant, Foreign Secretary to the Government of India in the Foreign and Political Department, 'Diary of the month of May 1918', 28 June 1918.
58 Passports and visas for those going to and from India and Xinjiang appear to have been established by the 1920s. On passports in British India, see: R. Singha, 'The Great War and a "proper" passport for the colony: border-crossing in British India, c. 1882–1922', *Indian Economic and Social History Review*, 50:3 (2013), 289–315.
59 Brophy, *Uyghur Nation*, p. 79.
60 On the imperial debates concerning race, gender and subjecthood, see, amongst others: A. Stoler, *Carnal Knowledge and Imperial Power: Race and the Intimate in Colonial Rule* (Berkeley: University of California Press, 2002).
61 On various documents regarding registration policy, see: IOR: PS/10/330.
62 See the various reports in IOR: L/PS/10/330. These regulations were taken from the Siamese Registration Agreement (1899), where many 'Asiatic' subjects were claiming British jurisdiction.
63 IOR: L/PS/10/330 G. Macartney to S. Fraser, Resident in Kashmir, 19 June 1913. Afghans were granted consular protection, but they were not considered as subjects with equal rights to those granted subjecthood.
64 IOR: L/PS/10/825 G. Macartney to the Deputy Secretary to the Government of India in the Foreign Department, 31 October 1913.
65 IOR: L/PS/10/330 G. Macartney to the Deputy Secretary to the Government of India, Foreign Department, 'Diary for the month of November 1913', 9 December 1913.
66 IOR: L/PS/10/825 G. Macartney to the Deputy Secretary to the Government of India in the Foreign Department, 'Diary for December, 1913', 10 January 1914.
67 IOR: L/PS/10/825 G. Macartney to the Deputy Secretary to the Government of India in the Foreign Department, 'Diary for June 1914', 27 July 1914; TNA: FO656/139 'Memorandum by Sir George Macartney', 14 September 1915.
68 TNA: FO656/139 'Memorandum by Sir George Macartney', 14 September 1915.
69 Markovits, *The Global World of Indian Merchants*, p. 98.
70 China (Kashgar) Order in Council (1920) Section VI, Article 48(3).
71 *Ibid.*
72 TNA: FO656/139 'Memorandum by Sir George Macartney', 14 September 1915.
73 BPP, HC: 1924, [Cmd 2247] *Statistical abstract for British self-governing dominions, colonies, possessions, and protectorates in each year from 1903 to 1921*, pp. 242–3, 245–6.
74 *Ibid.*
75 TNA: FO228/3028 C. Skrine to J. R. Macleay, Ambassador at Beijing, 21 August 1924.
76 TNA: FO228/3024 P. Etherton to the Secretary to the Government of India, Foreign and Political Department, 'Kashgar Diary for the month of May, 1920'.
77 *Ibid.*
78 TNA: FO228/3024 P. Etherton to the Secretary to the Government of India, Foreign and Political Department, 'Kashgar Diary for the month of June, 1920'.
79 TNA: FO228/3024 P. Etherton to the Secretary to the Government of India, Foreign and Political Department, 'Kashgar Diary for the month of September, 1920'.
80 TNA: FO228/3027 C. Skrine to the Ambassador at Beijing and the Political Agent at Gilgit, 'Diary for October', 16 November 1922.
81 IOR/L/PS/10/825 P. Etherton to the Foreign Sectary to the Government of India, Foreign and Political Department, 'Diary for November, 1919', 13 January 1920.
82 TNA: FO228/3024 P. Etherton to the Secretary to the Government of India, Foreign and Political Department, 'Kashgar Diary for the month of June, 1920'.
83 Skrine, *Chinese Central Asia*, p. 68.
84 TNA: FO228/3026 P. Etherton to the Foreign Secretary to the Government of India, Foreign and Political Department, 31 March 1922.

85 TNA: FO228/3027 C. Skrine to the Foreign Sectary to the Government of India, Foreign and Political Department, 31 March 1923.
86 *Ibid.*
87 TNA: FO228/3027 C. Skrine to the Foreign Sectary to the Government of India, Foreign and Political Department, 26 February 1924.
88 TNA: FO228/3028 C. Skrine to the Ambassador at Beijing, 'Report of 1st April 1922- 31st March 1924', 21 August 1924.
89 TNA: FO228/4039 F. Williamson to the Foreign Secretary to the Government of India, Foreign and Political Department, 'China (Kashgar) Order in Council 1920: Report on the operation thereof up to 31st December 1928', 7 February 1929.
90 TNA: FO228/3869 F. Williamson to the Secretary to the Government of India, Foreign and Political Department, 'Kashgar Diary for the Months of January and February, 1928', 1 March 1928.
91 NIA: Legislative Department: File No. 1216, 1928.
92 TNA: FO228/4039 F. Williamson to the Foreign Sectary to the Government of India, Foreign and Political Department, 'China (Kashgar) Order in Council 1920: Report on the operation thereof up to 31st December 1928', 7 February 1929.
93 TNA: FO228/4267 F. Williamson to the Foreign Sectary to the Government of India, Foreign and Political Department, 7 February 1930.
94 *Ibid.*
95 TNA: FO228/3028 C. Skrine to the Ambassador at Beijing, 'Report of 1st April 1922–31st March 1924', 21 August 1924.
96 *Ibid.*
97 IOR: L/PS/10/1158 N. Fitzmaurice to F. V. Wylie, Deputy Secretary to the Government of India, Foreign and Political Department, 12 October 1931.
98 TNA: FO228/3028 C. Skrine to R. Macleay, the Ambassador at Beijing, 21 August 1924.
99 TNA: FO228/3024 P. Etherton to Ambassador at Beijing, 'Kashgar Diary for the month of May, 1920'.
100 IOR: L/PS/10/825 G. Macartney to the Deputy Secretary to the Government of India, Foreign and Political Department, 17 September 1913.
101 Sykes and Sykes, *Through Deserts and Oases of Central Asia*, p. 186.
102 *Ibid.*
103 *Ibid.*
104 IOR: L/PS/10/825 P. Etherton to H. Dobbs, Foreign Secretary to the Government of India, Foreign and Political Department, 27 October 1919.
105 *Ibid.*
106 TNA: FO228/4039 F. Williamson to the Secretary to the Government of India, Foreign and Political Department, 'Kashgar Diary for the month of March 1929', 18 April 1929.
107 TNA: FO228/3027 *Daoyin* to C. Skrine, forwarding Yang Zengxin, Xinjiang governor to *daoyin*, 15 November 1922.
108 TNA: FO228/3027 *Daoyin* to Kashgar, forwarding Governor to *daoyin*, 15 November 1922; Yang to *daoyin*, 24 November 1922.
109 On marriage practices as retold through Western, Chinese and local sources in the late nineteenth and early twentieth centuries, see: L. Benson, 'A much-married woman: marriage & divorce in Xinjiang 1850–1950', *The Muslim World*, 83:3–4 (1993), 227–47; Bellér-Hann, *Community Matters in Xinjiang*, pp. 235–66.
110 TNA: FO228/3027 C. Skrine, Kashgar consul-general, to R. Macleay, Ambassador at Beijing, 10 January 1923.
111 *Ibid.*
112 *Ibid.*
113 TNA: FO228/3027 C. Skrine to R. Macleay, Ambassador at Beijing, 10 January 1923.
114 *Ibid.*
115 British consuls were not the only imperial agents to deal with such cases in the region. As Paolo Sartori argues, colonial Russian subjects of the Islamic faith in Central Asia also turned readily to Russian legal resources for the annulment

of religious endowments. See P. Sartori, *Visions of Justice: Shari'a and Cultural Change in Russian Central Asia* (Leiden: Brill, 2017), pp. 211–50.

116 Directives on *waqf* were derived from a number of *hadiths* (traditions of Muhammad).

117 TNA: FO228/3027 C. Skrine to R. Macleay, Ambassador at Beijing, 'Kashgar Diary for the month of December, 1922', 11 January 1923.

118 *Ibid.*

119 TNA: FO228/3027 C. Skrine to R. Macleay, Ambassador at Beijing, 'Kashgar diary for January 1923', 9 February 1923.

120 In China, as Philip Huang amongst others have shown, local custom was quite often taken into account in various civil cases. See, for example, P. Huang, *Code, Custom and Legal Practice in China: The Qing and the Republic Compared* (Stanford: Stanford University Press, 2002).

121 IOR: L/PS/10/825 G. Macartney, Kashgar consul-general, to the Deputy Secretary to the Government of India in the Foreign Department, 'Diary for September 1913', 17 September 1913.

122 *Ibid.*

123 Bellér-Hann, *Community Matters in Xinjiang*, pp. 317–18.

CHAPTER SIX

The British end game in Xinjiang: the decline of consular rights, 1917–39

At the start of 1917, Britain appeared to have secured a range of legal rights for its British community in Xinjiang. British subjects received tax exemption benefits and the right, as a defendant, to have their criminal or civil case heard by a British representative. However, the legitimacy of these rights was taken away after the Russian Revolution later that year, when the Soviets announced their intention to rescind extraterritorial privileges for Russian subjects in China. British consuls-general had always maintained that the Sino-Russian agreements conferred the right for Britain to have a stationed consul in Xinjiang who could exercise extraterritorial jurisdiction. Alongside the rise of Chinese nationalism and the determination of the Xinjiang political elite to revoke British privileges, British consular jurisdiction in the province appeared destined to crumble.

In this chapter, I show how consuls-general navigated this process of decline based on the nature of the community, practicality and political objectives. From 1917, consular representatives tried to buffer their most important rights, whilst conceding others, until the final abolition of British privileges by treaty in 1943. The Kashgar consular officials were not alone in their consideration of how to manage the decline of their powers; diplomats and consular officials across China reflected upon the same issue during the 1920s and 1930s. Scholars have attempted to explain this decline of consular legitimacy and the abolition of British extraterritoriality in a number of ways. Turan Kayaoğlu argues that one of the most important reasons was China's modernisation of its legal system. Western nations thereafter had less reason to regard Chinese law as unfit for treaty power foreign subjects.[1] Wesley Fishel points to the significance of the start of the decline after the First World War.[2] This era saw China resume jurisdiction over subjects of Germany and Austria-Hungary, and later Japanese imperialism and war eroded other consular rights in northern China.[3] Other scholars note the stance of British metropolitan authorities, which gradually withdrew their support for British rights in China, before the eruption of the Second World War finally hastened the abolition of British extraterritoriality.[4]

In this chapter, I show how the absence of a treaty-based right for a consular station in the province started the decline of consular jurisdiction in 1917 that followed a different path from the rest of China. Thereafter, Chinese officials dictated this decline process by working away at British privileges. This included the refusal to grant taxation privileges as well as arresting and detaining British subjects. Consular officials attempted to manage this challenge to their legal authority based on what they understood to be the most significant for imperial interests in the region and its local British communities, and what was deemed practical. By 1931, both the British Indian government and the Ambassador at Beijing withdrew their active support for British consular rights in Xinjiang. Consuls-general meanwhile prioritised the subjecthood status of traders as well as the rights of consular criminal justice. Finally, Chinese economic policies forced out many of the Indian traders from the province, leaving consular rights almost a dead letter until their abolition in 1943.

I start by examining the challenges to economic privileges in the 1910s and early 1920s. I then show how British consular officials protected certain members of the community and certain rights. I finish by highlighting instances of Chinese police power and Chinese economic policies that eroded the last remaining rights of British subjects in the 1930s.

Revoking economic rights

From 1891 to 1908, British representatives in Xinjiang claimed extraterritorial privileges which had been granted by the Sino-Russian treaties. The Qing steadfastly rejected these claims, but nonetheless permitted Britain to station a consul in Kashgar. British representatives in Xinjiang thereafter maintained that the Qing had conceded such rights based on the Sino-Russian treaties. The foundations of consular jurisdiction therefore suffered a serious and eventually fatal blow following the 1917 Russian Revolution when the Soviets announced the intention to abrogate the Sino-Russian treaties. Although various Chinese officials had contested British privileges since 1890, with the Soviet announcement, Xinjiang Governor Yang Zengxin saw an opportunity to launch a more concerted assertion of Chinese sovereignty. He proclaimed the revocation of British economic privileges, which had allowed British subjects a range of tax exemptions on the movement of transfrontier goods as well as on land. Aside from political benefits, this campaign against British tax exemption also had economic benefits for Yang. Since the Boxer Rebellion (1900–1) when China was forced to pay indemnities to the foreign powers, central subsidies halved, and after the fall of the Qing in 1911, the provincial authorities relied on its tax base to prop up its economy.[5] Taxation on goods and land therefore became increasingly important for providing provincial economic stability and self-sufficiency.

To the horror of the incumbent consul-general Percy Etherton, following the Soviet announcement, British *aqsaqals* (merchant arbitrators) reported that *amban* officials (magistrates) had followed Yang's orders in various localities. The reports suggested that *amban* officials were imposing tax on both transfrontier goods of British merchants and on their goods taken between various oasis towns in the province. Left uncontested, this would reduce the profits of the India transfrontier trading community. Yang further declared that certificates of tax exemption provided by British *aqsaqals* were illegitimate, as the Sino-British treaties only granted official British representatives the right to provide such documents.[6] Etherton made individual protests, but by 1919, *aqsaqals* continued to report that local Chinese officials imposed various taxes on British-owned assets.

Appalled at the ongoing attack on British trading interests, Etherton looked to the still operational Sino-Russian treaties to support his objection. He pointed to Article XII of the Sino-Russian Treaty of St Petersburg (1881), which authorised duty-free trade in Mongolia and Xinjiang. As Britain's 'Most Favoured Nation' clause conferred the same rights that China conferred on foreign nations, he argued that British subjects were also exempt from such taxation. Drawing attention to the Chinese-language version of the treaty, Etherton emphasised that there was a linguistic distinction between two Chinese words broadly meaning 'trade and commerce'. The first, *tongshang*, was used throughout the treaty, but the provision granting duty-free trade used another word, *maoyi*. He understood this word as having a broader definition, meaning trade and commerce of any kind, whether transfrontier or within the province.[7] Surely, he contended, any taxation on British goods, whether crossing the frontier or not, was illegal. It was a desperate and ultimately futile attempt to draw legitimacy from the Sino-Russian Treaty. Sensing Etherton's powerlessness to prevent local Chinese officials from imposing taxes in the towns far from Kashgar, Yang simply ignored his interpretation of the treaties.

By December 1919, Etherton believed Yang's redoubled 'hostile attitude' to British rights was due to the outcome of the recent Paris Peace Conference.[8] Many Chinese were outraged as the European powers sanctioned the transfer of the former German concession of Shandong to Japan. This came as a shock to Chinese officials, who expected the concession to be recognised as Chinese sovereign land. It also indicated to the Chinese public that the European powers were more interested in supporting the growth of imperialist Japan, which by 1895 had already secured unilateral extraterritorial privileges in China through the Treaty of Shimonoseki. It added to the outpouring of outrage against Yuan Shikai's approval of Japan's so-called '21 demands' in 1915, which many saw as allowing Japan to secure regional hegemony.

Subsequently, Yang intensified his campaign to limit British consular jurisdiction. This time, he focused on land ownership. Many British subjects owned land in the province and, by 1919, many second-generation male subjects claimed land through inheritance. By custom, an Islamic judge (qazi) witnessed and sealed contracts pertaining to the buying, selling and inheritance of land. Yang therefore ordered them to stop attesting the deeds of foreign subjects. The enforcement of this policy depended on the individual qazi, but where they were enforced, it was a serious blow to British rights and freedoms.[9] Etherton summarised the gravity and extent of the policy based on the reports of aqsaqals:

> Foreign subjects can expect neither assistance nor justice from Chinese officials if they are concerned, even indirectly, in a case in which the question of the possession of land arises. Not content with taking measures to prevent the acquisition of land by foreign subjects in future, the officials in some districts give the strongest impression that they will do everything in their power, by fair means or by foul, to dispossess foreigners of land already held by them ... in some places as the result of measures against acquisition of land by foreigners, British traders find it difficult or impossible to lease or rent shops.[10]

The implications of the policy were clear and affected both those settled in Xinjiang and sojourning traders. As consul-general Clarmont Skrine noted, Indian traders in Xinjiang did their business 'almost entirely on credit' and documents of title to land were 'generally speaking the only security available to those with whom they do business'.[11] As a result, the prohibition of the mortgaging of such documents would have a significant effect on the British community. Not all qazis followed protocol and subsequent proclamations from Yang focused on punishing local people and qazis for allowing the transfer of the ownership of land to British subjects. This was addressed in the proclamation that explicitly outlawed the sale of property of Chinese subjects to British subjects, with those attempting to sell the land liable to 'heavy punishment'.[12] Subsequently, Etherton tried to support existing landowners by protesting against the requisition of land owned by British subjects. At the same time, he was also aware of the difficulties that lay ahead for British landowners and privately discouraged British subjects from acquiring new land.[13]

The campaign against foreign land ownership – and against *qazis* who permitted it – included proclamations declaring stricter oversight on land reserved for religious purposes by religious donation (*waqf*). According to Islamic law, such land could not be used for individual profit. A controversial case arose in Poskam, where the *amban* accused a British subject holding *waqf* land of profiteering.[14] Yang thereafter ordered *qazis* to ensure that those nominated as holders of *waqf* land kept it strictly for religious purposes. At the same time, British farmers and landowners had been forced to pay land and grazing taxes.[15] Raising livestock – such as horses, donkeys, cattle, camels, sheep and goats – was an important livelihood for many in Xinjiang.[16] Similar to the taxation of trade goods, Yang's policies depended on the acquiescence of local *amban* and *qazi* officials. Where they were enforced, it amounted to a concerted attack on British economic privileges.

In the meantime, Etherton hoped – somewhat desperately – that an agreement could be reached with the Chinese authorities for a separate treaty to guarantee British legal rights. He wrote to John Jordan, the Ambassador at Beijing, and proposed that Jordan should start negotiations with the Chinese central authorities for a treaty, which would secure the legitimacy of a consulate in Kashgar.[17] Etherton drew inspiration from the 1886 Burma Convention and subsequent provisions, which allowed the Yunnan consulates to open. He noted that 'a close study of that Agreement shows its applicability to Hsin-Chiang, [Xinjiang] in so far as trans-frontier questions are concerned'.[18] He clearly saw the parallels between British frontier governance in southwest China and Xinjiang, which included the necessity of Chinese acquiescence of transfrontier trade of key commodities and the need for a treaty basis for the exercise of his consular powers.

Although Etherton could see the applicability of the treaty for Xinjiang, it was wishful thinking. In spring of 1920, the long-anticipated process of the abrogation of Russian extraterritoriality finally started. In April, members of the newly established Soviet Turkestan Commission pledged to terminate the privileges formally enjoyed by subjects of the Czarist Empire. In return, they asked for the reopening of the northern Xinjiang town of Ili for trading purposes for Soviet representatives. The Soviets allowed the former Sino-Russian treaties to lapse without renegotiation and after a delay, Russian subjects finally lost their extraterritorial status in September 1920.[19] In an era of rising Chinese nationalism, many Chinese heralded it as the first victory of the new era of the Chinese nation state against foreign imperialism.

Immediately following the abolition, the Chinese administration in Xinjiang decided to test the limits of British jurisdiction. The legal rights of Britain were already unclear and the abrogation of the Russian treaties removed the legitimacy for a stationed consulate in Kashgar. However, Britain could still claim the general principle of extraterritoriality within the territory of China due to other treaty rights. Two inter-related questions therefore remained. What privileges, if any, did these existing treaties confer to Britain in Xinjiang? And what privileges currently exercised in the province were based solely on custom and usage?

A key case involving a British subject named Rozi Mahomed Haji provided the perfect context for Yang to work out these two questions.[20] The incident arose in Qarghaliq in a dispute over irrigation water and involved a fight between two parties of villagers. The charge against Haji was that he induced a Chinese subject, surnamed Chawar, to stab another Chinese subject, who subsequently died. At the same time, another British subject, Tokhta Akhun, punched a Chinese man surnamed Said, knocking out his front teeth. Etherton allowed the *Shariat* (Islamic court) to assume jurisdiction over Akhun's assault of Said, with the *qazi* directing that Akhun pay 62½ *taels* as compensation.[21] Etherton felt that the punishment was excessive, but did not think it worth protesting. Instead, as the first affray resulting in murder involved the liberty of the man, this case was a more important battle for him. The local Qarghaliq *amban*, surnamed Gui, assumed jurisdiction and ordered the arrest and detention of Haji. Etherton protested, but Yang intervened, claiming that China was entitled under treaty to detain British subjects in custody pending preliminary investigation by the local official. Etherton knew immediately that Yang was testing the limits of British privileges conferred by the treaties and viewed the arrest and detention as a 'studied attack upon the extraterritorial rights of British subjects'.[22]

The Kashgar *daotai* claimed that Gui's detention of Haji was both necessary and legal.[23] As the incident occurred in Qarghaliq, a town far from Kashgar, the only British representative nearby was a British *aqsaqal*. Up until this case, Chinese police handed such suspects to the nearest British *aqsaqal* and either he heard the case, held the suspect until a consular official arrived on tour or arranged for an escort to accompany the suspect to Kashgar. However, as the *daotai* pointed out, the Sino-British treaties only permitted the handover of British suspects to government officials. As such, when Chinese police arrested a British subject, there were only two legitimate options. Either the suspects were escorted to the consul-general in Kashgar regardless of the location of their arrest, or the *amban* could order the detention of British subjects and conduct preliminary investigations before deciding whether it was necessary to escort them to Kashgar to hand them over to the consul-general. Gui took the latter option. Whilst claiming that the handover of suspects to British *aqsaqals* was not sanctioned by treaty, the *daotai* also suggested that strictly abiding by the treaty was problematic. He stated that Haji's detention was 'an exceptional modification of the treaty procedure made because the distances in Sinkiang [Xinjiang] were so great and it was not easy to send the parties under escort'.[24] Although it appeared contradictory, the *daotai* knew that if Etherton protested to Beijing, he would have to thereafter abide by the treaty regulations and send all suspects to Kashgar, where he had no jail or personnel to deal with them. The actions of Gui and the *daotai* were measured and tactical. They did not challenge Britain's right to hold the trial of Haji; instead, they tested to see if they could assert their police and *prima facie* powers with his detention, and thereafter pointed to the Sino-British Treaty provisions and appealed to notions of practicality to justify their actions.

After holding a preliminary investigation, Gui could not find enough evidence linking Haji with the knife attack and released him. Although the case against Haji was over, it was clear to Etherton that an intensified battle for jurisdiction over British subjects was just beginning. The stark reality of the situation for Etherton was that British administration had relied on men working in a semi-official capacity because of the distances between the oasis towns. *Aqsaqals* did not have legal rights according to the treaties and it was simply through usage and the complicity of local Chinese officials that this practice became customary. There was now little he could do but allow the Chinese to detain suspects pending preliminary investigations in every future case and to demand their handover afterwards.

Alongside holding British suspects, Chinese officials also tested the British resolve to protect the economic privileges of landowning British subjects. A case in 1924 involving a man named Id Akhun showed that British consuls-general were either powerless to stop local officials from imposing such taxes or were more inclined towards conceding tax exemption privileges for rural subjects.[25] Akhun lived for many years as a farmer. As he was exempted from paying grazing tax due to his extraterritorial status, the village headman made up the deficit each year when collecting the village taxes. Frustrated with the accumulated expense, the headman reported the issue to the local *amban*, surnamed Gui, querying Akhun's claim to British nationality.

[156]

THE BRITISH END GAME IN XINJIANG

On hearing the incident, the consul-general Clarmont Skrine asked the local British *aqsaqal* to hold a joint enquiry with Gui to determine Akhun's nationality. In frustration at the delay sorting the issue, Gui stated that he would conduct the investigation alone. Skrine protested, arguing that a joint enquiry must be held, but the *amban* refused.[26] Gui kept Akhun in jail pending his enquiries and later declared him a Chinese subject. Skrine did not appear to follow up the case. Chinese officials were beginning to realise that they could revoke the economic privileges of British-claimed subjects who were not traders with relative ease. Following this incident, Skrine and his vice-consul, Harold Harding, began to consider how to revise the consular policy on the scope of British rights in China. In particular, they began to think about who should be given priority for protection according to British political and economic interests in the face of greater Chinese challenges to consular jurisdiction.

Revising consular policy

In order to assess the value of protecting certain rights, Harding and Skrine considered the interests of their community as it aligned with British imperial objectives. First, there was the number of British subjects to consider. Whereas the numbers of registered subjects increased in the 1910s (consisting largely of subjects from the Indian subcontinent), emigration to Xinjiang rapidly declined by 1920. This may have been due to the tighter Chinese restrictions against Chinese women marrying foreign subjects and promulgations against British subjects owning land.[27] This was significant as it suggested that the numbers of British subjects in Xinjiang would at best plateau, but more likely simply decline. Moreover, it suggested that the number of traders was decreasing. As British subjecthood was limited to those born in India or second-generation subjects of Indian-born fathers, the resident British community would eventually cease when this generation died, leaving only temporary India traders. In many ways, this suited British interests as transient Indian traders represented the commercial interests of Britain and its economic sphere of influence. Non-trading communities with a limited-life consular protection, such as farmers and their families, were not a high priority for British interests.

Second, the consular officials needed to consider the politicisation of British consular jurisdiction in China and popular discontent with foreign privileges. By 1922, Chinese nationalism and ideas of Bolshevism helped draw attention to foreign extraterritoriality as a primary form of national humiliation (*guochi*) and a negation of Chinese national sovereignty. Harding was aware of Yang's staunch anti-British stance and his intention to continue to limit British influence was brought to his attention by the Kashgar *daotai*. Unwittingly, the *daotai* had forwarded a copy of Yang's instructions ordering *ambans* to deal 'severely and strongly' (*yanzhong banli*) with consular officials over Sino-British cases.[28] Harding also suspected that Yang ordered *begs* to demand lists of British subjects from *aqsaqals* and ordered *ambans* to take up more minor cases. This was intended to provide greater administrative oversight over Sino-British cases, removing powers from *begs* and *aqsaqals* to hear certain cases in which they were more amiable to British interests.[29] This followed reports that certain *qazis* were increasingly under the control of *amban* officials. In cases in Yarkand and Qarghaliq where all the important decisions required approval by the *amban*, the *Shariat* reversed a number of decisions formerly given in favour of British subjects without the production of fresh evidence.[30]

Considering the politicisation of cases involving British subjects, it was within British interests to relinquish jurisdiction over subjects who appeared to have tenuous claims to subjecthood. Chief among them were resident subjects who had the same customs and language as the local community and owned land. Chinese officials had contested British jurisdiction over such people more vigorously. Relinquishing jurisdiction over certain subjects already had precedent in Xinjiang as British policy-makers in Beijing and London agreed to no longer protect Afghan nationals. This followed the end of Afghanistan's British protectorate status from 1919 and persistent Chinese claims of jurisdictional rights over Afghan nationals.[31]

Vice-consul Harding was more convinced than consul-general Skrine about limiting British consular policy in Xinjiang. He believed that the demise of consular jurisdiction was inevitable and that political relations with China mattered more than protecting all subjects. In fact, he stressed that the 'one outstanding interest' for Britain in Xinjiang was the maintenance of Chinese authority, with the encouragement of trade as a secondary importance.[32] In particular, the stability of China and ensuring strong Sino-British relations was important in order to prevent the Soviet domination of northern China. He put forward three policy changes. First, he advocated a reversion to the practice of joint investigation for registering new subjects. Formerly, Etherton had conducted these investigations alone. This infuriated various *amban* officials, who saw this procedure as giving the consul-general carte blanche to confer British status liberally. Second, Harding advocated relinquishing jurisdiction over registered subjects who did not freely admit to British heritage and subjects without obvious ties to India. Formerly, the first consul-general, George Macartney, had insisted that those wishing to register as British subjects should have some tangible connection to India, but this had lapsed under Etherton's consulship.[33] This would avoid the difficult questions of what role culture and ethnicity played in defining British nationality, especially where subjects could not be distinguished by their language or customs from the local population. It would also prevent those suspected of claiming British nationality fraudulently from registering. Finally, he suggested adhering to the long-standing policy of refusing to recognise the grandchildren of Indian-born subjects as British. This would mean that after the second generation died out, the numbers of resident families claiming British status would rapidly decrease.

Harding presented his proposal to the Ambassador at Beijing on 31 October 1922, who forwarded it to the Foreign Office. The Ambassador agreed that British policy should aim to restrict subjecthood. He felt that it was particularly important that Britain should not fight for jurisdiction of, or register, descendants of India-born men who married Turkic wives and owned land. Highlighting the importance of culture to the definition of subjecthood, he emphasised that they were 'indistinguishable' from the local Turkic population as they often only spoke Turkic and had no effective connection to India.[34] No doubt taking into account the British policy of supporting China against the Soviet Union, Lord Curzon, the British Foreign Secretary, also agreed with the policies outlined.[35] Skrine, the Kashgar consul-general, held a more ambivalent view on limiting consular jurisdiction. He felt that British subjects in the province 'who are in the position of colonists' (i.e. were landowners) who paid land and water revenue taxes ought to be able to continue to hold and buy land.[36] This right to acquire land by purchase or mortgage had been 'acquired by prescription, in virtue of long established usage'.[37] Furthermore, given that various *aqsaqals* had reported that some British traders paid both transfrontier customs and customs on articles manufactured locally since April 1922, they too ought to have certain landowning privileges.[38] Despite his reservations, Skrine decided to abide by the new consular policies agreed in Beijing.

In Xinjiang, Yang's instructions to the Kashgar *daoyin* were clear. He saw no legal reason to accept consular privileges based on usage and precedent, and he instructed local officials to focus on eliminating these rights, such as land ownership. Drawing upon the recent Washington Conference attended by many of the treaty powers in 1921, the Kashgar *daoyin* added that the Western powers had reneged on their support for Chinese sovereignty.[39] Opposition to British rights in Xinjiang thereafter appeared to increase among the circles of Chinese officials in the province.

Following the revised British agreement over registration and continued Chinese resistance to British rights, court cases bore out the adherence of the consular officials to the new policy. One notable case involved Id Akhund, a second-generation British subject resident in a village fifteen miles from Yarkand. Akhund was accused of attacking and killing his father when the latter was beating his brother. Skrine adjudged that as Akhund was a grandchild of a British Indian subject and was domiciled in Xinjiang, he had effectively 'severed' all ties with India (i.e. contacts and customs). Skrine therefore left the case to the jurisdiction of the *amban* at Yarkand.[40] If there were any lingering doubts about the status of the grandchildren of Indian subjects, they were clarified a few years later. Consul-general George Gillan made an agreement with the Kashgar *daotai* that Britain would not recognise individuals who had been born in Chinese territory and whose fathers were also born in Chinese territory as British subjects.[41]

It was not only British policy that limited jurisdictional powers; British subjects also decided for themselves if it was in their interests to become Chinese subjects. In 1930, Frederick Williamson reported that six or seven British subjects of Yarkand applied for the cancellation of their registration in order to adopt Chinese nationality in just one month.[42] These subjects wanted to acquire land, which was barred to them due to their British subjecthood. Among them was a prominent person, Tilla Khan, formerly British *aqsaqal* of Yarkand between 1920 and 1923. This case signalled the success of Chinese policies against foreign privileges and their aim to limit the size of the British population.

Events in China added further pressure on consular officials to limit their jurisdiction. Since 1902, Article XII of the Mackay Treaty stated that when Chinese laws were modernised, Britain would consider the abolition of British extraterritoriality in China. In 1926, the Washington Conference commission finally toured parts of China, with a remit to investigate the operation of the Chinese administration of justice. The report dedicated many pages to aspects of Chinese legal reform and the difficulties posed to law and order through war and recent political turbulence. Despite some progress in this regard, the commission suggested that legal reforms still fell short of expected standards.[43] If the commission would not provide a way for the Chinese authorities to rescind extraterritoriality, Chinese officials would have to rely on diplomatic negotiation and pressure.

Although the findings of the commission came as a huge disappointment to China, foreign legal powers started to erode more quickly in the late 1920s. After 1927, the new Nationalist government, the Guomindang, pressed for the reduction of foreign privileges. The

British Foreign Office recognised the sensitivity surrounding certain concessions and adopted a more conciliatory attitude towards Chinese demands. Between 1927 and 1931, Britain relinquished a number of concessions: Hankou, Jiujiang, Xiamen, Zhenjiang and the lease of Weihaiwei. In addition, Belgium, Denmark, Italy, Portugal and Spain agreed to revise the treaties for the abolition of extraterritoriality, and Mexico allowed its extraterritorial rights to lapse in 1928. The Guomindang were optimistic that by negotiation and diplomatic pressure, they could recapture full national sovereign powers.

British policy-makers were aware of the impending demise of British consular jurisdiction. A series of Sino-British negotiations began considering the gradual abolition of consular rights. For the British Ambassador in Beijing and the consular officials in China, the main concern was how to stall the abolition and provide temporary legal safeguards for British subjects. By 1930, Miles Lampson, the Ambassador at Beijing, outlined a draft treaty proposing a process of gradual transition.[44] He proposed protections for foreign subjects, such as the use of foreign co-judges in special courts on the east coast and the relinquishment of jurisdiction in stages, starting with civil jurisdiction, then criminal jurisdiction and finally personal status cases (e.g. family law). It was an unsuitable arrangement for Xinjiang, where British subjects would be unable to go all the way to the east coast to have their cases heard in the courts. Nor was excluding Xinjiang from any future agreement possible. For Lampson, it was clear that he did not regard the protection of the British Indian community in Xinjiang to be worthwhile. John Walton, the secretary to the India Office, shortly afterwards became aware of Lampson's position on Xinjiang.[45] However, he did not feel it was desirable to add to the pressure on Lampson to make special arrangements for Xinjiang.[46] The colonial and consular authorities in Beijing and Delhi were therefore clearly distancing their support for the continued exercise of extraterritorial rights in the region.

In light of the unsuitability of Lampson's proposed plan, the Kashgar consul-general Frederick Williamson put forward his own three-stage transition period proposal for consular rights in the province. His proposal was modelled upon his experience in Xinjiang and the unique circumstances for consular jurisdiction there. He proposed the immediate withdrawal of protection for Indian settlers, an incremental withdrawal of the protection of subjects outside the main trade towns and finally total abolition (to be delayed as long as possible). The idea of the immediate withdrawal of consular protection for Indian settlers was not new. Consular officials had made it clear that the transient trading community (and the transfrontier trade) was their priority for consular protection. However, the geographical limiting of jurisdiction added a new method of potentially rescinding powers. It appeared to reflect the geographical location of British trading community, who resided in the major trade centres rather than in the outlying towns, which had few British traders. However, the proposal of how to restrict consular rights was decided by the Chinese authorities in Xinjiang, who forced the issue of an immediate abolition through criminal cases.

Chinese police power: arrests and interrogation

By the 1930s, Chinese political and legal commentators began to highlight the British presence in the province.[47] These commentaries helped to draw attention to the fact that the foreign presence in Kashgar was intimately tied to British India and had been for some time. In terms of law, their commentary was correct, as after the China (Kashgar) Order in Council (1920), Kashgar became 'a district of the Punjab' and the consular district was classified within the same group of British possessions as India under the exercise of the intra-imperial legislation of the Fugitive Offenders Act (1881).[48]

However, although intellectuals began to highlight different aspects of foreign imperialism, it was actions rather than ideas that dictated the scope of British jurisdiction in Xinjiang. The new governor (now styled Chairman), Jin Shuren, continued the anti-British rhetoric of his predecessor. Jin was cautious of both Soviet and British interests in the province, but also had to turn his attention to fighting local movements that claimed the cities of Qumul, Kashgar and Yarkand amongst others for a brief time.[49] As such, the work of diminishing British rights further was left to the *amban* officials, who attempted to wrestle jurisdiction over British-claimed subjects. A notable case was recorded on 13 January 1929 at Hotan and gave an indication of what was to come. The *amban* ordered the arrest of Shah Pasand on suspicion of killing Yusuf Akhun and his two Turkic wives. As Pasand was a British subject, Frederick Williamson informed the *daoyin* that he would try the case. The *amban* refused the initial request, but after Williamson threatened to involve the consular authorities in Beijing, Pasand was handed over to George Sherriff, the British vice-consul. Sherriff heard the case and acquitted Pasand, finding that Akhun killed his wives before committing suicide.[50] In reporting the case to Jin Shuren, Sherriff claimed that the *amban* tried to save face by claiming that he alone settled the case.[51]

Although the *amban* was forced to hand over Pasand, the battle resumed with another case later the same year. The Yarkand *amban* suspected a Bajauri man, Abdul Aziz, of smuggling opium.[52] The *amban* ordered his arrest and charged him with carrying more opium on his person than he claimed. Williamson then requested that the *amban* deliver him to his consulate, but the *amban* refused. Williamson protested to Jin Shuren and, after some delay, the *amban* released Aziz. As he was not sent to Kashgar, Aziz escaped punishment. Following the incident, Williamson concluded in his annual report that there was 'little doubt' that British rights 'will now be disputed in any such case which may arise'.[53] It was clear that criminal cases were the opportunity for Chinese officials to claim their sovereign rights.

In 1931, jurisdictional challenges continued with the renewed unilateral declaration by the Guomindang government abolishing extraterritoriality. Shortly afterwards, Chinese officials continued to assert their jurisdiction in Sino-British cases. In one prominent case, a British Indian man, Mehrban Ali, was arrested on George Sherriff's orders on 27 May 1931.[54] Ali had first come to Kashgar as a private servant to a man named Blainville, who was an accountant of the Kashgar consulate-general in October 1929. He made a short trip to India a year later and, on returning to Kashgar, failed to present a valid visa. George Sherriff, now consul-general, advised him to return to India, but Ali decided to remain. He became friendly with a personal servant of the Kashgar *daoyin* and worked for him as his chef. Sherriff received a letter from Ali shortly afterwards, which stated that he wanted to become a Chinese subject and stay in Xinjiang. On reading his letter, Sherriff took matters into his own hands and sent three *chaprasis* (messengers for the consulate) to find Ali and bring him back to the consulate. If he resisted, they were ordered to bring him by force. They found him outside the city gate in Kashgar, where they arrested him and took him by cart to the consulate-general. On 28 May, Sherriff announced his intention to deport Ali and bar his re-entry for two years under Article 18 of the China (Kashgar) Order in Council (1920). He then asked the *amban* of Kashgar Old City, as was the custom for exercising deportation orders, for one of his *yamen* (courthouse) runners to help escort Ali to the frontier. Instead, on 2 June, the *amban* and the Secretary for the Foreign Affairs Branch of the *daoyin*'s office came to the consulate claiming that they would deal with Ali. Unsurprisingly, Sherriff would not entertain this request.

Concurrently, Ali's wife, a Chinese subject named Hamra Bibi, requested a divorce. She laid a separate charge for the sale proceeds of the dowry her parents gave to Ali worth 500 *taels*.[55] The importance of the case was not lost on the local *amban*, who stated that Ali's arrest by the consulate involved a question of 'face' relating to Chinese sovereign rights.[56] Ali stated he had revoked his citizenship and was a Chinese subject. Therefore, the public arrest, detention and claim of jurisdiction of Ali was in contravention of China's sovereign rights. The *amban* requested the handover of Ali so that he could try the suit between Ali and his wife, and awaited an official apology from Sherriff.[57]

Sherriff appealed to the *daoyin* for a joint investigation for the divorce suit, but the *daoyin* rejected it categorically.[58] The *daoyin* noted that extraterritoriality and joint investigation only existed in a few treaty ports and concessions. As Kashgar was neither a treaty port nor a concession, he could not agree to a joint investigation.[59] Nor could the Xinjiang authorities allow the arrest even if he was a British subject, as he was outside a treaty port.[60] The *daoyin* ordered a guard to be stationed on the road to India to arrest Ali in the event that Sherriff attempted to deport Ali with his men.[61] Sherriff wrote to the Ambassador in Beijing concerning the case, who also forwarded his own report on the issue to the Foreign Office. The position of the Ambassador and the Foreign Office was that it was not in Britain's interests to sour its relationship with China.[62] Sherriff felt there was little he could do and handed over Ali to the *daoyin* of Kashgar.[63] This was a clear victory for Chinese sovereignty. The incident demonstrated the crumbling power of British consuls to arrest, detain and deport subjects. It also showed that British legal authority was reliant on Chinese policing; even in cases where the consul passed a sentence of deportation or expulsion, he normally required Chinese *yamen* runners to escort the subject to the frontier.[64]

As the Ali case demonstrates, the erosion of British consular power did not simply involve Chinese officials claiming more British subjects under their jurisdiction. Many individuals could also take control of their fate by renouncing their nationality to suit their own purposes. Lampson, the Ambassador at Beijing, described one such incident shortly following the Ali case. Sherriff had charged a man of 'bad and insulting behaviour' and of 'refusing to obey the orders of the consul-general'.[65] He was arrested, detained and was due to be deported. However, the man renounced his British nationality and invoked the protection of the local Chinese authorities, who 'intervened by claiming, that his majesty's consul-general had no right to arrest the alleged offender'.[66] Lampson acknowledged the powerlessness of consular officials to act in such circumstances, given British policy that emphasised amicable Sino-British relations. He noted that 'we do not want nowadays, especially in a place like Sinkiang, if we can help it, to challenge the Chinese authorities on the issue of our right to try and punish a British subject who has renounced British nationality and does not desire our protection'.[67] Simply put, political objectives mattered more than protecting the whole spectrum of extraterritorial rights in the province. Likening Xinjiang to other inland consular stations such as Harbin, he believed that it was pointless to contest the jurisdiction of a person involved in such a minor offence. It was clear that although consular jurisdiction in Xinjiang was different from the rest of China in many respects, inland consuls shared the same difficulties, as they were heavily reliant upon local Chinese cooperation or tacit consent to exercise such legal powers.

Although subjects could decide their own fate by renouncing their nationality, consular officials remained sceptical about the extent to which free will motivated such actions. Highlighting the issue of landownership, consul-general Nicholas Fitzmaurice summarised his impressions of Chinese pressure on British individuals to become Chinese nationals:

> the present policy of the Chinese Authorities is proceeding along lines which will reduce the number of persons claiming British nationality in Sinkiang and will consequently lessen the effects of the change of jurisdiction. The arrangement that no land should be acquired by persons of other than Chinese nationality has induced many landowning families to sever their connection with India; and there has undoubtedly been some pressure applied in other ways. Last May, for instance, some regulations were issued from Urumchi to the effect that all foreign nationals would have to pay registration fees amounting to taels 20 per annum; and, though I know of only one case ... in which these charges have actually been collected, it is more than likely that the threat has sufficed in a number of instances to induce British subjects to apply for Chinese citizenship.[68]

In turn, Chinese jurisdictional claims became bolder, encouraged by the position of the British consuls-general who now prioritised political objectives. Fitzmaurice noted that there had been 'occasional instances' in which consuls had 'acquiesced in minor encroachments on our rights' and had conceded jurisdiction when 'there was no evidence of impartiality towards the British subject or other reason to fear injustice'.[69] It was a carefully planned concession of rights allowing Chinese officials powers to hear criminal cases involving British defendants in view of the inevitable abolition of extraterritoriality. A gradual reduction of British rights was also considered the best course of action for the British community. As Fitzmaurice concluded, 'in the interests of British Indian subjects in Sinkiang, our best policy pending conclusion of the Treaty [for abrogation of British consular rights in China] is to refrain from insistence on the whole of our old rights, so that the change may be effected almost imperceptibly'.[70]

Chinese officials also began limiting the ability of consular officials to aid British plaintiffs. In June 1931, acting consul-general Captain Watts encountered difficulties when helping British petitioners. It was customary that *amban* officials of various districts met the consul-general on tour, but Watts was only greeted in two towns. In Kuchar, Watts sent the *aqsaqal* a list of Chinese subjects against whom British subjects had claims and requested that the *amban* call these men and appoint a day for the British subjects' cases so that he could be present in the *yamen*. This was the usual procedure, but the *amban* refused to call the Chinese subjects and informed Watts that he had no need or right to be present during the hearing.[71] Furthermore, the *amban* informed all the resident British traders of Kuchar that petitions were to be sent to him directly rather than the British consular officers or to the British *aqsaqal*.[72]

The consuls understood the reality of their diminishing power. With the abolition of the Russian treaties, British consuls-general could only claim that British defendants in Xinjiang had the right to a consular court hearing. However, there was no legitimacy for the claim that they were the officials to hear it. When China arrested and interred British subjects, the consuls had little recourse. In the annual report for 1931, Sherriff reflected that both he and his predecessor found 'considerable difficulty' in settling British cases.[73] In fact, he felt that the British policy should bypass Williamson's proposed three-stage transition and opt for the voluntary surrender of extraterritorial rights, a view that the Government of India also suspected might be best.[74] The next year, while the negotiations for the abolition of extraterritoriality were put on hold in Nanjing, Fitzmaurice was equally pessimistic about British legal rights in Xinjiang. He predicted more jurisdictional battles following difficulties encountered in hearing a minor civil case of a British subject.[75] He believed that giving up extraterritorial rights for the possibility of Chinese credit and a favourable *quid pro quo* would not work.[76] He noted that consular rights were becoming harder to assert and stated despondently that 'the less use we are compelled to make of the [consular] Court now, the less the change will be felt when extraterritoriality goes'.[77] The end was indeed in sight.

British Indian exodus: the era of Sheng Shicai and the USSR 1933–43

After 1931, despite the pessimistic outlook of the consular officials on their future guarantee of consular rights, consuls-general continued to exercise extraterritoriality and hear some cases of British subjects. However, the Chinese authorities also continued to arrest and detain many British subjects without trial. This was so commonplace that consular reports started to note the *ad hoc* releases of British subjects. Such was the case for Sadi Amin Khan and Said Ahmad Jan in April

1933. The Chinese authorities suspected both of smuggling opium, and the police searched Jan's house and shop without informing the consulate.[78] Both Khan and Jan were detained pending investigation, but were then released unexpectedly. In due course, the consul-general John W. Thomson-Glover held a trial, found the former man guilty of opium smuggling and fined him.[79] Thomson-Glover characterised the Chinese authorities' action as an exceptional gesture of goodwill. The new Chairman of Xinjiang, Sheng Shicai, had recently taken his post and sent a delegation from Urumqi with friendly messages to Thomson-Glover. However, the release was not a sign of good relations to come. Indeed, the incumbency of Sheng Shicai marked a new era of Chinese determination to limit and erase British rights through arrests and detention.

This went hand in hand with Sheng's pro-Soviet policy, leading the Soviets to dominate the province politically and economically. For some time, the Soviets encouraged both Yang and Jin to limit British consular power. The Soviet Union increased its influence across Central Asia and the Kashgar diaries – the monthly report of the consular officials – document the British fear of the Soviet Union's power in Xinjiang. Britain was powerless to stop Soviet influence, and British Indian policy throughout the 1920s was to use its consular network to spy on Soviet activities and monitor Bolshevik propaganda in Central Asia. Information gathering was important because consular officials also suspected that Soviet agents encouraged and harboured anti-British radicals and pan-Islamic movements that sought the downfall of the colonial government in India. This was perceived as particularly dangerous at a time when nationalist movements in India challenged British colonial authority.

In the 1930s, British consuls-general felt that Soviet power had increased dramatically in Xinjiang under Sheng's leadership. They suspected that Soviet political advisors were at the side of Sheng, leading some to see Sheng's Xinjiang as a puppet state of the USSR. British travellers in the region also reported this political power. The journalist Peter Fleming, who travelled alongside the Swiss journalist Ella Maillart, noted that whilst the Comintern was active in China to spread communism, it appeared as though the Russian Foreign Office dictated policy in Xinjiang. In other words, the Soviet presence was more strategic than ideological in the province and that the USSR aimed to eliminate a British presence.[80]

Economically, Soviet goods also flooded the Xinjiang market and hurt British trade. As early as 1927, the consular reports attributed a 50 per cent decline in the India export and import trade from Xinjiang to the arrival of cheap Soviet goods.[81] Thereafter, Indian-Xinjiang trade steadily declined.[82] The key transfrontier imports into Xinjiang were cotton, silk and woollen goods, and the key exports to India were raw cotton, raw silk, felt rugs and *charas* (cannabis extract).[83] By 1933, nearly all the external trade of the province went to the Soviet Union, although as the Russian goods were of poorer quality, there was still a small market for higher-end British goods, such as velvet, muslin and cloth.[84] Nevertheless, Soviet products reduced the Indian market significantly and made the province a less attractive place for Indian traders.

Civil uprisings also disrupted trade. By 1935, after the downfall of the brief independent East Turkestan Republic and the cession of fighting between Sheng's forces and local militiamen, some parts of the bazaar in Yarkand (the biggest trading town in southern Xinjiang) were still in ruins.[85] Uprisings in Xinjiang had closed all outward traffic to India by both of the two main trade routes to Leh and Gilgit.[86] Trading in the province was risky and profits were not guaranteed.

Chinese policies also aimed to diminish the attraction of the transfrontier trade for Indian traders. Fleming reported that Indian merchants were forced to pay three times the transit duty between the Indian frontier and Kashmir.[87] Chinese custom officials could be obstructive and diminish the profits of British traders. Fleming recounted a typical incident:

> a merchant collects his caravan in Kashgar and applies for passports (formerly unnecessary) for himself and his men. Days pass. The British Consul-General makes repeated representations to the authorities, but by the time the passports are issued half the merchant's potential profits on the journey have gone in feeding men and ponies in enforced idleness. And he will be held up at least once more, arbitrarily, indefinitely, and without appeal, before he crosses the frontier into India.[88]

Residence permits and the conditions of marketplaces after the civil uprisings also restricted the movement of British Indian traders. After the disturbances, Hindu traders remained mostly in Yarkand and only occasionally travelled to Qarghaliq and other towns. Consular officials reported that this was because various Chinese authorities prevented or made it difficult for British traders to travel.[89] In effect, Williamson's proposal that British extraterritoriality could be gradually limited to certain geographical locations became a reality. However, it was not planned consular policy, but war, Soviet economic power and Chinese policy that limited the British community within particular geographical limits. As much as migration had shaped the scope of British jurisdiction between the 1890s and the 1930s, the restriction of the movement of people served to curtail extraterritorial power to certain towns.

The final blow to consular jurisdiction came when Sheng banned the cultivation and exportation of *charas*, which formed the backbone of the Indian transfrontier trade from Xinjiang to India. As the transfrontier export trade to India was double that of imports, this measure affected British trade significantly. The Xinjiang authorities further made the application of residence permits a lengthy proceeding for British subjects.[90] Lengthy application processes for visas could also curtail the movement of Indian traders and also Chinese subjects who desired to travel for the Hajj pilgrimage via India. Whereas in 1933 the Chinese authorities issued 300 visas to Chinese subjects, in 1934 they issued 234, in 1935 just 104 and for the first six months in 1936 only ten.[91] By the end of that year, vice-consul Michael Cavenagh Gillett reported that 312 people had applied for a visa to travel through India for Hajj during the year, but the Chinese authorities had ignored the applications entirely.[92]

The decline of the British community and, alongside it, British economic interests was clearly in evidence by 1937. Of the two main trade routes, there were only small amounts imported from the trade route of Leh, including spices and small foreign goods via Chitral.[93] British trade picked up again when a rebellion erupted in south Xinjiang, presenting an opportunity for British traders. Consul-general Kenneth Packman ambitiously proposed the stationing of a commercial agent to the Government of India to help the small trade.[94] He stated that there were 600 British subjects in the province, of which only 130 were traders. The traders were mainly 'Hoshiarpuri Hindus, a few Kashmiris and some Bajauri drug-peddlers', all of whom Packman considered to be a 'low type of person'.[95] As they were all 'incompetent' and 'lack adequate capital', he suggested that the Indian government should establish a post for a commercial agent and support British companies for transfrontier trade.[96] On 5 January, the Secretary to the Government of India replied that it was 'a waste of time to consider trade developments'.[97] India could not compete with the USSR and nor would the USSR tolerate a British Indian attempt to expand its trade interests in the region. No firms were interested in investing in Xinjiang, and Indian businessmen were not prepared to risk capital in a country which was 'both remote and unsettled'.[98] Ultimately, the position of the Indian government was clear, with the secretary underlining that government interests were 'not concerned with Anglo-Sinkiang trade'.[99] Instead, the secretary advised Packman that in future annual reports, he should focus on providing the government with information on the general economic situation in Xinjiang rather than trade development proposals.[100]

As a result of the diminishing trade and cautious British political policy, the Government of India and the consular officials were less willing to defend British subjects in this period. A petition of Indian traders over the illegal seizure of their goods in Xinjiang confirmed this position categorically, signalling the coming end of British legal protection. In the spring of 1938, several traders who worked for the Central Asian Traders in Hoshiarpur notified their employers that Chinese customs officials had illegally seized their *charas*.[101] They claimed that the seizure occurred before the official prohibition. The company petitioned the Indian government, which consulted with the consul-general. However, both the Government of India and the consul-general felt it would be inexpedient to raise the issue of the prohibition on *charas* or about the illegal seizure to the Xinjiang authorities.[102] It was no longer in their interests to protect the rights of British traders.

Exports and imports on both routes ground to a halt in 1939. The economic and political uncertainty produced by the 'Tungan rebellion' and then the resumption of control of Sheng's Provincial government discouraged Indian traders from trading in the province. Thereafter, Sheng's proclamation to Xinjiang residents to boycott British goods was a fatal blow to British economic interests.[103] Many Indian traders, who had the money and were not tied to land, liquidated their assets with a view to returning to India.[104] Consul-general H. H. Johnson described the trade as being at a 'standstill' with no prospect of its revival.[105] Extra tariffs levied on British-owned goods and the increasing difficulty of obtaining passports from the Chinese authorities hastened this exodus. The consular reports stated that there were an estimated twenty Indian traders left in the former Indian merchant hub of Yarkand, half a dozen in Kashgar, four in Yangi Hissar and only a few in the outlying towns.[106] The British trading community was dwindling, British trade interests were almost finished and the abolition of British jurisdictional rights appeared to be imminent.

Conclusion

From 1917, the decline of British consular jurisdiction took a different path from elsewhere in China. As the basis of British consular power rested on the Sino-Russian treaties, 1917 marked the start of the rapid downfall of British extraterritoriality in Xinjiang following the Soviet announcement to abrogate the treaties. Without the legal legitimacy for a stationed consulate in Kashgar, British consular officials tried desperately to protect a range of rights for British subjects. Consular officials had claimed some of these British rights by virtue of the Sino-Russian treaties, whereas others had been claimed by customary usage. Because of this legal basis, the Chinese authorities increasingly challenged British legal rights. This included rescinding tax exemption privileges, refusing to allow British subjects the transfer or sale of land, and detaining British subjects in Chinese jails prior to hearings.

Due to the nature of the British community in Xinjiang and the remote location of the district from the Chinese east coast, Kashgar consular officials put forward their own proposals for managing the end of British privileges. Consuls-general chose to protect British Indian traders (especially those involved in transfrontier trade) and the right for their subjects to have a consular court hearing for criminal cases. Court cases document the pivotal moments in 1930–2, when the Xinjiang authorities contested these last guarded rights. Chinese police powers thereafter diminished British powers to detain suspects, hold trial and deport convicted persons. At the same time, the British Indian government and the consular authorities in Beijing were less inclined to support extraterritorial rights in the region amid the changing political climate in China.

In the last decade of consular jurisdiction, the economic policies of the Chinese government, civil war and the Soviet domination of Xinjiang forced British traders out of Xinjiang. Chinese economic policies and Russian goods in the province decreased British trading incentives in the region. Followed by the destruction caused by civil war, by 1935 the British community was largely contained within particular geographical limits. Just as migration had shaped British jurisdiction during 1891 to 1930, the restriction of the movement of people curtailed extraterritorial power to certain towns. When the numbers of its trading community dwindled, so did British economic interests and, finally, British legal power.

Notes

1 T. Kayaoğlu, *Legal Imperialism: Sovereignty and Extraterritoriality in Japan, the Ottoman Empire, and China* (Cambridge: Cambridge University Press, 2010).
2 W. Fishel, *The End of Extraterritoriality in China* (Berkeley: University of California Press, 1952).
3 *Ibid*.
4 See, for example: E. Fung, *Diplomacy of Imperial Retreat: Britain's South China Policy 1924–1931* (Hong Kong: Oxford University Press, 1991).
5 See, for example: J. Milward and N. Tursun, 'Political history and strategies of control, 1884–1978', in S. F. Starr (ed.), *Xinjiang: China's Muslim Borderland* (New York: M. E. Sharpe, 2004), p. 66.
6 IOR: L/PS/10/825 G. Macartney to H. Grant, Foreign Secretary to the Government of India in the Foreign and Political Department, 'Diary of the month of May 1918', 28 June 1918.
7 IOR: L/PS/10/825 P. Etherton to Bray, Foreign Secretary to the Government of India in the Foreign and Political Department, 'Diary for the month of February 1919', 10 April 1919.
8 IOR: L/PS/10/825 P. Etherton to H. Dobbs, 'Diary for December 1919', 13 February 1920.

9   *Ibid.*
10 IOR: L/PS/10/825 P. Etherton to H. Dobbs, 'Diary for December 1919', 13 February 1920; FO228/4266 P. Etherton, Kashgar consul-general, to the Ambassador at Beijing and the Secretary to the Government of India, Foreign and Political Department, 21 December 1919.
11 TNA: FO228/3027 C. Skrine to B. Alston, Ambassador at Beijing, 9 October 1922.
12 TNA: FO228/3027 Wei, Acting *amban*, to C. P. Skrine, Kashgar consul-general, 19 September 1922.
13 TNA: FO228/3025 Wellesley, Foreign Office, to the Under Secretary of State, India Office, 27 August 1921.
14 TNA: FO228/4266 F. Williamson to the Foreign Secretary to the Government of India in the Foreign and Political Department, 'Diary for July 1930', 7 August 1930.
15 TNA: FO228/3027 Kashgar consulate to the Ambassador at Beijing, 'Rights of British Subjects in Kashgar', 21 February 1923.
16 See, for example: E. Sykes and P Sykes. *Through Deserts and Oases of Central Asia* (London: Macmillan & Co., 1920), pp. 300–7.
17 TNA: FO228/3024 P. Etherton to the Ambassador at Beijing, 1 February 1920.
18 *Ibid.*
19 SMA U1–3–969 'Extraterritorial rights', Shanghai consul-general to the Chairman of the Municipal Council, 6 October 1920. For the details of Chinese jurisdiction over Russians after 1920, see: A. Kotenev, *Shanghai: Its Mixed Court and Council* (Shanghai: North China Daily News and Herald, 1925), pp. 227–37; Fishel, *The End of Extraterritoriality*, pp. 43–9.
20 TNA: FO228/3025 P. Etherton to B. Alston, Ambassador at Beijing, 27 March 1921.
21 *Ibid.*
22 *Ibid.*
23 TNA: FO228/3025 Kashgar *daotai* to P. Etherton, 6 March 1921.
24 *Ibid.*
25 TNA: FO228/3027 C. P. Skrine to the Ambassador at Beijing, 31 October 1922.
26 TNA: FO228/3027 C. P. Skrine to R. Macleay, Ambassador at Beijing, 15 February 1923.
27 TNA: FO228/3028 C. P. Skrine to R. Macleay, Ambassador at Beijing, 21 August 1924. Various intermarriage prohibitions of different ethnic groups as a measure of social control had precedent in Xinjiang. See: J. Millward, *Beyond the Pass: Economy, Ethnicity and Empire in Qing Central Asia* (Stanford: Stanford University Press, 1998), p. 174. Policies against intermarriage and land owner-ship were also applied periodically to Russians. See C. Skrine and P. Nightingale, *Macartney at Kashgar: New Light on British, Chinese and Russian Activities in Sinkiang, 1890–1918* (Oxford: Harper & Row, 1987), p. 234.
28 TNA: FO228/3027 H. Harding to B. Alston, Ambassador at Beijing, 24 November 1922.
29 *Ibid.*
30 FO228/3025 P. Etherton to the Ambassador at Beijing, 'Diary for the month of December, 1920', 1 January 1921.
31 For the British policy and Chinese position of Afghan nationals from the first decade of the twentieth century, see Skrine and Nightingale, *Macartney at Kashgar*, pp. 140, 233, 237.
32 IOR: L/PS/10/1158 F. Williamson, Kashgar consul-general, to the Foreign Secretary to the Government of India, 'Enclosure 1: Memorandum by Mr. Harding', 28 February 1930.
33 TNA: FO228/3027 H. Harding to the Ambassador at Beijing, 31 October 1922.
34 TNA: FO228/3027 R Macleay, Ambassador at Beijing, to Wellesley, Foreign Office, 15 January 1923.
35 TNA: FO228/3027 G. Curzon, Foreign Office, to R. Macleay, Ambassador at Beijing, 2 October 1923.
36 TNA: FO228/3027 C. Skrine to the Ambassador at Beijing, 21 February 1923.
37 *Ibid.*

38 *Ibid.*
39 TNA: FO228/3027 Tengyue *daoyin* to the Kashgar consulate, 7 December 1922.
40 TNA: FO228/3028 C. Skrine to R. Macleay, Ambassador at Beijing, 21 August 1924.
41 TNA: FO228/3664 G. Gillan, consul-general, to the Secretary to the Government of India, Foreign and Political Department, 14 February 1927.
42 TNA: FO228/4266 F. Williamson to the Secretary to the Government of India, Foreign and Political Department, 'Kashgar diary for the month of January 1930', 5 February 1930; FO228/4266 F. Williamson to the Secretary to the Government of India, Foreign and Political Department, 'Diary for December and January and February, 1929'.
43 *Report of the Commission on Extraterritoriality in China* (Washington DC: Government Printing Office, 1926).
44 NAI: External Affairs Department: File No. 131-X, M. Lampson, Ambassador at Beijing, 'Summary on the notes of extraterritorial surrender in China', 10 March 1930.
45 NAI: External Affairs Department: File No. 131-X, J. C. Walton, India Office, to C. W. Orde, Foreign Office, 16 February 1931.
46 NAI: External Affairs Department: File No. 131-X, J. C. Walton, India Office, to C. W. Orde, Foreign Office, 2 July 1931.
47 See, for example: X. Sun and Y. Zhao, *lingshi caipan quan wenti* [*The Problem of Consular Rights*] (Shanghai: shangwu yin shuguan, 1936), p. 111.
48 The China (Kashgar) Order in Council, 1920, Section II, Article 9(iii)(d).
49 This included the establishment of a brief 'First East Turkestan Republic'. The Guomindang forces crushed the polity in the Battle of Kashgar in 1934.
50 TNA: F0228/4267 F. Williamson to the Secretary to the Government of India, Foreign and Political Department, 7 February 1929.
51 IOR: L/PS/10/1158 'Extract from Sinkiang Annual Confidential Report, 1st July 1929 to 30th June 1930'.
52 TNA: FO228/4267 F. Williamson to the Deputy Secretary to the Government of India, Foreign and Political Department, 19 February 1930; TNA: FO228/4266 F. Williamson to the Deputy Secretary to the Government of India, Foreign and Political Department, 'Diaries for October and November, 1929', 1 December 1929.
53 IOR: L/PS/10/1158 'Extract from Sinkiang Annual Confidential Report, 1st July 1929 to 30th June 1930'.
54 IOR: L/PS/10/1158 N. Fitzmaurice, to F. V. Wylie, Deputy Secretary to the Government of India, Foreign and Political Department, 24 December 1931.
55 IOR: L/PS/10/1158 Kashgar *daotai* [no signature] to G. Sherriff, Kashgar consul-general, 4 June 1931.
56 *Ibid.*
57 *Ibid.*
58 IOR: L/PS/10/1158 Kashgar *daotai* [no signature] to G. Sherriff, Kashgar consul-general, 3 July 1931.
59 *Ibid.*
60 IOR: L/PS/10/1158 G. Sherriff to Foreign Secretary to the Government of India, Foreign and Political Department, 24 June 1931.
61 *Ibid.*
62 IOR: L/PS/10/1158 M. Lampson, Ambassador at Beijing, to A. Henderson, Foreign Office, 4 July 1931.
63 IOR: L/PS/10/1158 G. Sherriff to the Foreign Secretary to the Government of India, Foreign and Political Department, 2 July 1931.
64 *Ibid.*
65 IOR: L/PS/10/1158 M. Lampson, Ambassador at Beijing, to A. Henderson, Foreign Office, 4 July 1931.
66 *Ibid.*
67 *Ibid.*
68 IOR: L/PS/10/1158 N. Fitzmaurice to F. V. Wylie, Deputy Secretary to the Government of India, Foreign and Political Department, 24 December 1931.

69 *Ibid.*
70 *Ibid.*
71 IOR: L/PS/10/1158 G. Sherriff to the Foreign Secretary to the Government of India, Foreign and Political Department, 17 June 1931.
72 *Ibid.*
73 IOR: L/PS/10/1158 G. Sherriff to the Foreign Secretary to the Government of India, Foreign and Political Department, 11 June 1931.
74 NAI: External Affairs Department: File no. 131-x, E. B. Howell, Government of India, 4 November 1931.
75 IOR: L/PS/10/1158 N. Fitzmaurice to H. A. F. Metcalfe, Foreign Secretary to the Government of India, Foreign and Political Department, 21 April 1932.
76 NAI: External Affairs Department: File no. 131-x N. Fitzmaurice to the Secretary to the Government of India, 24 December 1931.
77 IOR: L/PS/10/1158 N. Fitzmaurice to H. A. F. Metcalfe, Foreign Secretary to the Government of India, Foreign and Political Department, 21 April 1932.
78 IOR: L/PS/12/2364 J. W. Thomson-Glover to the Foreign Secretary to the Government of India, Foreign and Political Department, 9 April 1936.
79 IOR: L/PS/12/2364 J. W. Thomson-Glover to the Foreign Secretary to the Government of India, Foreign and Political Department, 23 April 1936.
80 P. Fleming, *News from Tartary: A Journey from Peking to Kashmir* (London: Jonathan Cape, 1936), p. 260.
81 TNA: FO228/3869 G. V. B. Gillan, Kashgar consul-general, to the Secretary to the Government of India, Foreign and Political Department, 'Report on the trade of Chinese Turkestan', 21 May 1927.
82 NAI: External Affairs Department, file no. 454-x, K. C. Packman, Kashgar consul-general, to the Foreign Secretary to the Government of India, 1 July 1937.
83 TNA: FO228/3869 G. V. B. Gillan to the Secretary to the Government of India, Foreign and Political Department, 'Report on the trade of Chinese Turkestan', 21 May 1927.
84 Fleming, *News from Tartary*, p. 257.
85 Fleming, *News from Tartary*, p. 310.
86 IOR: L/PS/12/241 K. C. Packman, Kashgar consul-general, to the Ambassador at Beijing, 'Kashgar Diary for November 1937', 9 December 1937.
87 Fleming, *News from Tartary*, p. 257.
88 *Ibid.*
89 IOR: L/PS/12/2364 J. W. Thomson Glover to the Foreign Secretary to the Government of India, 11 June 1936.
90 IOR: L/PS/12/2364 J. W. Thomson Glover to the Foreign Secretary to the Government of India, 23 July 1936.
91 IOR: L/PS/12/2364 J. W. Thomson Glover to the Foreign Secretary to the Government of India, 18 June 1936.
92 NAI: External Affairs Department, File No. 64-x/37: M. C. Gillett, Kashgar vice-consul, to the Secretary to the Government of India, Foreign and Political Department, 'Hajis passing through India', 21 December 1936.
93 IOR: R/12/52 K. C. Packman, Kashgar consul-general, to the Ambassador at Beijing 18. July 1938.
94 NAI: External Affairs Department, File No. 454-x, K. C. Packman, Kashgar consul-general, to Parsons, Foreign Secretary to the Government of India, 1 July 1937.
95 *Ibid.*
96 *Ibid.*
97 NAI: External Affairs Department, File No. 454-x External Affairs Department notes, 29 September 1937.
98 *Ibid.*
99 NAI: External Affairs Department, File No. 454-x, Parsons, Secretary to the Government of India to Packman, Kashgar consul-general, 5 January 1938.
100 NAI: External Affairs Department, File No. 454-x, Secretary to the Government of India to Packman, Kashgar consul-general, 7 March 1938.

101 IOR: R/12/52 Central Asian Traders, Hoshiarpur (Punjab), to Foreign Secretary, Delhi, 8 April 1938; FO371/22205 L. Dogarmal Chunilal Thalwar, Central Asian Traders, Hoshiarpur to the Secretary to the Government of India in the External Affairs Department, 3 February 1938.
102 IOR: R/12/52 W. R. Hay, Deputy Secretary to the Government of India in the External Affairs Department to the Resident in Kashmir, 23 April 1938.
103 IOR: R/12/52 H. H. Johnson, Kashgar consul-general, to the Ambassador at Beijing, 18 July 1938.
104 *Ibid.*
105 IOR: R/12/52 H. H. Johnson to the Ambassador at Beijing, 'Indo-Sinkiang Trade Report for the year 1839', 28 July 1939.
106 *Ibid.*

CONCLUSION

In the late nineteenth and early twentieth centuries, British imperial agents were stationed on the western frontiers of China. The presence of these officials has often been narrated as part of a larger story of geopolitical rivalry and economic imperialism in Central and Southeast Asia. These agents did, of course, act as intelligence reporters and officers who helped oversee British trade interests, but they were also adjudicators, legal mediators and legal informers. This book has focused on British consular officials of the two frontier consular districts of Kashgar (Xinjiang) and Tengyue (western Yunnan). Here, at the periphery of the Chinese and British Empires, consuls exercised law over British communities. Extraterritoriality was a central part of British imperialism in China, but law played out differently on the frontiers compared to the treaty ports on the east coast. This book has provided a new narrative of the British presence in two western regions, demonstrating how the exercise of law was an essential part of British imperialism across frontiers. Through exploring the legal presence and practice of consuls, this book has presented arguments in three broad areas: the connection between consular and colonial jurisdiction; how the movement of people and goods shaped law; and the nature of extraterritoriality at the frontiers of empire.

Colonial connections

Today, the western frontiers of China are often associated with China's connection to other parts of Asia. In 2013, Xi Jinping unveiled the 'Belt and Road' initiative, which included plans to strengthen trading links from its inner provinces such as Xinjiang to Central Asia and beyond. Likewise, Yunnan is often referred to as a gateway or a 'bridgehead' to South and Southeast Asia. Although there is renewed interest in the connectivity of the frontiers, both Xinjiang and Yunnan have always had strong economic, cultural, political and social links to Central and Southeast Asia respectively. During the late nineteenth and early twentieth centuries, British agents in Kashgar and Tengyue were stationed at the periphery of the British Empire. Despite this isolation, their consular districts lay centrally between different British imperial authorities. Consuls represented the crossover of British imperial interests and, as a result, they mediated between, petitioned and advised two sets of British authorities in Delhi and Rangoon, as well as the consular authorities in China, consisting of the Ambassador in Beijing and the Chief Judge in Shanghai. Sometimes petitions and reports went further afield, connecting them to the India Office and the Foreign Office. Frontiers, then, were peripheral and yet globally connected.

As well as information, law in the British Empire moved across borders. In British India, colonial officials applied colonial law extraterritorially across Indian frontiers, including in the semi-autonomous Princely States and around the Indian Ocean. On the western boundaries of China, consuls petitioned for amendments to the Orders in Council, which framed their legal powers, in order to allow forms of transfrontier jurisdiction. Consuls were agents of empire who were often familiar with working in inland districts far from imperial centres. They understood the requirements of working in such places and therefore the need to adapt their powers to cover jurisdictional gaps between colonial and consular jurisdiction. The frontier presented a different question to British authority in the districts of Tengyue and Kashgar compared to other Indian frontiers: how could consuls eliminate the jurisdictional gaps between consular and colonial jurisdiction?

This book has shown that forms of colonial jurisdiction also extended over borders into China through consuls. In Xinjiang, from 1920, the Kashgar consul-general and his court were a part of the legal system of British India. This institutional connection was strengthened by the application of Indian colonial law in consular hearings. In Tengyue, although there were no institutional connections to Burma, the efforts of consuls eventually resulted in Burmese officers exercising a type of transfrontier jurisdiction over British subjects who had committed crimes in China. Tengyue consuls also worked with Burmese officials to further colonial claims to land, people and resources in disputed areas of the Burma-China frontier. In both Kashgar and Tengyue districts, there was a legal and penal connection between consular jurisdiction in China and colonial jurisdiction in India and Burma as consuls deported various British 'undesirables' and prisoners from their districts to the other side of the border.

One advantage of examining two case studies is to highlight not only the similarities of law on the two frontiers, but also their inter-connection. Indeed, it was not a coincidence that the two major legal amendments that created new forms of transfrontier jurisdiction took place at the same time. During 1914–15, the Foreign Office, the India Office and consular authorities on the east coast of China recognised that both Tengyue and Kashgar struggled with similar frontier issues. Growing numbers of people arrived from the Indian subcontinent, but consular administration was ill-equipped to arrest and detain large numbers of suspects. As consular officials from both frontiers outlined the same jurisdictional problems, it convinced the metropolitan author-ities that it was worthwhile and necessary to formulate new frontier legal practices. The resulting transfrontier legal practices demonstrate the shared qualities of transfrontier imperial management and how colonial and consular jurisdiction were not distinct arenas of law and legal practice, but were informed by and connected to each another.

The movement of people and goods shaping jurisdiction

Imperial agents helped create transfrontier legal connections as a response to the perceived challenges brought by people moving across borders. At its height, hundreds, perhaps even thousands of British subjects lived in these consular districts. Most came from parts of the Indian subcontinent, having been born in colonial territory or having resided there. Their transfrontier movement from colonial territory to the consular district highlighted the jurisdictional gaps between colo-nial and consular jurisdiction. On the Burma-China frontier, incidents of salt smuggling forced British consuls to reconsider how to apply their powers over people who supplied a vital – but illicit – com-modity for frontier populations. British officials also thought about how to extend their jurisdictional influence in cases of transfrontier elopement and helped to create a type of mixed court to adjudicate incidents of transfrontier crime. In both Tengyue and Xinjiang, British transfrontier migrants and their trade were a key part of how consular officials understood the scope of their powers in the district.

The movement of the British community also determined how British consuls understood the relationship between law and space. The exercise of extraterritoriality followed a British subject wherever they went within China. Therefore, consuls focused their attention on the places where British subjects resided and where they travelled. In the Burma-China frontier, the treaties focused on the control of trade on specific paths used by migrants and traders, where consuls could monitor the passage of people and goods, both legal and illicit.

In a place where the environment prevented easy administration, this was not only practical, but also necessary. In Xinjiang, British policy-makers looked to control the mountain passes through the Karakoram and Pamirs, following the path of Indian migrants. Consuls toured the oasis towns of resident British traders in the province and stationed subordinates where they could oversee trading disputes. The exercise of extraterritoriality was therefore specifically localised and geograph-ically patchy as the British community – their numbers, lifestyle and transfrontier travel – shaped the contours of British jurisdiction.

Adapting and accommodating in a plural legal environment

Legal practices in the frontiers involved British officials delegating legal power and working with representatives of other legal systems. In Xinjiang and Tengyue, consular officials allowed indigenous elites to resolve local disputes within British communities. They were local administrators whose knowledge of local languages and customs enabled them to administer customary law. Frontier governance drew inspiration from both the local environment and the legal customs of British subjects who were born in or had resided in British India or Burma. In Xinjiang, the organisation of the native institution of *aqsaqals* drew influences from *panchayats* in India, and the customs of various Indian groups as well as colonial Indian laws were deemed suitable for the exercise of law. In Yunnan, consuls reasoned that the English law basis of extraterritorial jurisdiction was likewise unsuit-able for local hill populations, giving rise to the Sino-British mixed courts, which took local customs as their legal basis. Consuls also understood that in certain instances, it was important to accommo-date local customs in consular hearings. This appeared to be due to two reasons. First, it appeared to give legitimacy to consular decisions and ground the consular system into locally accepted institutions and environments. Often consuls considered not only what was socially acceptable to local people, but also what was important for inter-community peace. Whether it was for resolving blood feuds or the settlement of religious conflict surrounding beef, consuls attempted to work towards a solution that fitted the values of local communities. Second, as well as drawing upon local customs, consular officials often delegated legal authority to resolve sensitive jurisdictional clashes between Britain and China. This included claims to disputed lands, such as in the Burma-China frontier, where consuls allowed local elites to apply local laws in criminal cases in certain circumstances. Imperial law in the frontier was therefore not applied monolithically; it was profoundly shaped by local customs, the consideration of the customs of transfrontier British colonial subjects and the imperatives of maintaining peaceful inter-community relations.

The relationship between Britain and China marked a distinctive legal practice compared to other Indian frontiers. British jurisdiction relied upon Chinese cooperation on many fronts: for policing, surveillance, arrests, detention in jails, armed escort, information gathering and sometimes as co-judges. It was cooperation that helped British jurisdiction survive for as long as it did. Sometimes, Chinese assistance was provided half-heartedly or unwillingly, but it was necessary, as part of a treaty duty, or by customary usage. Whether in conflict or cooperation, the encounter between Chinese and British authority was a creative endeavour, resulting in new forms of law. The presence of Chinese officials and jurisdiction also gave rise to new forms of dispute resolution institutions and methods. On the Burma-China frontier, consuls 'bargained' with their Chinese counterparts in mixed courts and in Xinjiang, consular officials worked alongside their Chinese colleagues in cases involving local customs such as religious land endowments (waqf). British consular officers adopted and accepted Chinese legal methods, and balanced the needs of inter-community peace and British rights whilst working diplomatically and judicially with the Chinese authorities. This cooperation and relation with Chinese officials was also important outside of the courtroom. Parties, celebrations and dinners were also ways in which British officials worked to maintain amicable relations with Chinese officials. These relationships went through phases of friendliness and contempt. However, regardless of the state of their relationship, British officials knew they were often reliant on Chinese authority for exercising law.

Whereas British jurisdiction in these two Sino-British frontiers differed from frontiers elsewhere in the British Empire, the legal basis of frontier consular jurisdiction also distinguished it from law as exercised by British officials elsewhere in China. Both the Tengyue and Kashgar consular districts were frontier places, characterised by the term 'treaty mart' to describe the opened town where a consulate was stationed. This was not just because of geography, but also because of a legal distinction. Consular jurisdiction rested on two primary legal bases. The first was the general principal of extraterritoriality provided by the Treaty of Nanjing (1842) and the Treaty of the Bogue (1843). The second key legal basis – and just as important – was Chinese consent to open places to foreign trade and residence, as well as to allow consuls to exercise law in these localities. The Yunnan consulates were opened by virtue of the Sino-British treaties concerning Burma. These frontier treaties therefore framed the understanding of extraterritorial rights, colonial law and the treaties together. Although the provisions were not clear, consuls eventually worked out an uneasy compromise for legal powers between all three forms of law. In Xinjiang, there was no treaty sanctioning a consular presence. Consuls acquired legal rights over time. British consular officials negotiated with the Chinese authorities and usage and custom cemented consular rights, such as land acquirement and taxation exemption rights. This legal basis on usage rather than treaty shaped the decline of consular rights in the province. In other words, Tengyue and Kashgar were fundamentally different consular districts from others in China; they were not 'treaty ports', but 'treaty marts', defined not only by their isolation from the maritime world, but equally by their localised frontier legal arrangements for the exercise of extraterritorial rights.

This book shows that imperial law was not static, abstract or confined by borders. The frontier environment, the movement of people and the passage of goods shaped imperial law and created legal connections. The practice of law was malleable and consular officials helped to create transfrontier legal practices that bridged colonial and consular jurisdiction. The movement of people were key to this legal process, as they highlighted the jurisdictional gaps between imperial authorities across borders and imperial officials reimagined legal practices based on the identities of these people. Finally, consular jurisdiction was also distinct from the open treaty ports on its maritime edge; law and legal administration in treaty marts on the frontier was wholly different from the treaty ports on the east coast. A consular presence in these two frontier regions amounted to less than half a century, but their importance to the British communities there, as well as to British consular and colonial authority, mattered greatly in an era of imperialism across frontiers in Asia.

KEY TERMS

Titles
amban	县长
aqsaqal	商约
beg	商总/(伯克)
daotai/daoyin	道台/道尹
daren	大人
qazi	阿訇

Ethnic group names
Kachin/Jingpo	景颇族
Lashi	茶山人
Lisu	傈僳族
Shan	掸族/傣族
Wa	佤族

Places
Aqsu	阿克苏
Bhamo	八莫
Chefang/Zhefang	遮放
Cherchen	且末
Guma	皮山
Hotan	和田
Hpimaw/Pianma	片马
Htawgaw/Tuojiao	拖角
Ili/Kuldja	伊宁
Kanai/Yingjiang	盈江
Keriya	于田
Kokang	果敢
Kuchar	库车
Lashio	腊戍
Longling	龙陵
Mangshi	芒市
Maralbashi	巴楚
Nawngma	弄马
Poskam	泽普
Qarghaliq	叶城
Sadon	石旦
Sima	昔马
Tashkurghan	塔什库尔干
Uchturfan	乌什
Yangi Hissar	英古沙
Yarkand	沙車

Institutions, companies and associations

gelaohui	哥老会
huishen gongxie	会审公廨
huishen/ huian	会审/会案
shenbao	申报
waijiaobu	外交部
waiwubu	外务部

Phrases

bainian guochi	百年国耻
chi Yunnan ku	吃云南苦
yanzhong banli	严重办理

Terms

gaihuo	该货
haiyan	海盐
ke min	客民
lijin	厘金
liu min	流民
manai (agreement)	蛮爱(条约)
maoyi	贸易
neidi	内地
pingfan	屏藩
suoyou zhihuo	所有之货
tongshang	通商
tusi	土司
waidi	外地

SELECT BIBLIOGRAPHY

Adelman, Jeremy and Aron, Stephen. 'From borderlands to borders: empires, nation-states, and the peoples in between in North American history', *American Historical Review*, 104:3 (1999) 814–41

Alam, Muzaffar and Subrahmanyam, Sanjay. 'The making of a Munshi', *Comparative Studies of South Asia, Africa and the Middle East*, 24:2 (2004), 61–72

Alder, G. J. *British India's Northern Frontiers 1865–95: A Study in Imperial Policy* (London: Longmans Green, 1963)

An, Guosheng. *xifeng luori: lingshi caipan quan zai jindai zhongguo de queli,* 安国胜，西风落日：领事裁判权在近代中国的确立[*Consular Jurisdiction: Its Background and Course of Establishment in China*] (Shanghai: falü chubanshe, 2012)

Aung-Thwin, Michael. 'The British "pacification" of Burma: order without meaning', *Journal of Southeast Asian Studies*, 16:2 (1985), 245–61

Ballantyne, Tony. *Orientalism and Race: Aryanism in the British Empire* (Basingstoke: Palgrave, 2002)

Baud, Michiel and Van Schendel, Willem. 'Toward a comparative history of borderlands', *Journal of World History*, 8:2 (1997), 211–42

Bellér-Hann, Idikó. *Community Matters in Xinjiang, 1880–1949: Towards a Historical Anthropology of the Uyghur* (Leiden: Brill, 2008)

Bello, David. 'The venomous course of Southwestern opium: Qing prohibition in Yunnan, Sichuan, and Guizhou in the early nineteenth century', *Journal of Asian Studies*, 62:4 (2003), 1109–42

'To go where no Han could go for long: malaria and the Qing construction of ethnic administrative space in frontier Yunnan', *Modern China*, 31:3 (2005), 283–317

Benson, Linda. 'A much-married woman: marriage & divorce in Xinjiang 1850–1950', *The Muslim World*, 83:3–4 (1993), 227–47

Benton, Lauren. 'Historical perspectives on legal pluralism', *The Hague Journal on the Rule of Law*, 3:1 (2001), 57–69

'Making order out of trouble: jurisdictional politics in the Spanish colonial borderlands', *Law and Social Inquiry*, 26:2 (2001), 373–401

Law and Colonial Cultures: Legal Regimes in World History, 1400–1900 (Cambridge: Cambridge University Press, 2002)

A Search for Sovereignty: Law and Geography in European Empires, 1400–1900 (Cambridge: Cambridge University Press, 2010)

Bickers, Robert. *Britain in China: Community, Culture and Colonialism, 1900–1949* (Manchester: Manchester University Press, 1999)

Bickers, Robert and Henriot, Christian (eds). *New Frontiers: Imperialism New Communities in East Asia 1842–1953* (Manchester: Manchester University Press, 2000)

Brook, T., J. Bourgon and G. Blue. *Death by a Thousand Cuts* (Cambridge, MA: Harvard University Press, 2008)

Brophy, David. *Uyghur Nation: Reform and Revolution on the Russia-China Frontier* (Cambridge, MA: Harvard University Press, 2016)

Bussche, E. vanden. 'Contested Realms: Colonial Rivalry, Border Demarcation, and State-Building in Southwest China, 1885–1960' (PhD dissertation, Stanford University, 2014)

Cang Ming, *yunnan biandi yimin shi*, 苍铭, 云南边地移民史[*The History of the Migration in the Yunnan Periphery*] (Beijing: minzu chubanshe, 2004)

Cao Shuji, *zhongguo yimin shi, di liu juan*, 曹树基, 中国移民史第六卷 [*The History of Migration in China*, vol. 6] (Fuzhou: Fujian renmin chubanshe, 1997)

Cassel, Pär. *Grounds of Judgment: Extraterritoriality and Imperial Power in Nineteenth-Century China and Japan* (Oxford: Oxford University Press, 2012)

Chan, K. C. 'The abrogation of British extraterritoriality in China 1942–43: a study of Anglo-American-Chinese relations', *Modern Asian Studies*, 11:2 (1977), 257–91

Chang, Yin-t'ang. 'A historical-geographical study of the undemarcated borderland between China and Indo-Burma', *Tsing Hua Journal of Chinese Studies*, 2:1 (1972), 238–73

Chiang, Tao-chang. 'The production of salt in China, 1644–1911', *Annals, American Association of Geographers*, 66 (1976), 516–30

'The salt trade in Ch'ing China', *Modern Asian Studies*, 17:2 (1983), 197–219

Chen, Li. *Chinese Law in Imperial Eyes: Sovereignty, Justice, and Transcultural Politics* (New York: Columbia University Press, 2016)

Clark, Donald. *Gunboat Justice: British and American Law Courts in China and Japan (1842–1943)*, 3 vols (Hong Kong: Earnshaw, 2015)

Clifford, Nicholas. *Spoilt Children of Empire: Westerners in Shanghai and the Chinese Revolution* (Hanover, NH: University Press of New England, 1991)

Coates, P. D. *The China Consuls: British Consular Officers in China, 1843–1943* (Oxford: Oxford University Press, 1988)

Condos, Mark. 'Licence to kill: the Murderous Outrages Act and the rule of law in colonial India, 1867–1925', *Modern Asian Studies*, 50:2 (2015), 479–517

Condos, Mark and Rand, Gavin. 'Coercion and conciliation at the edge of empire: state-building and its limits in Waziristan, 1849–1914', *Historical Journal*, 61:3 (2018), 695–718

Cooper, Frederick and Stoler, Ann Laura (eds). *Tensions of Empire: Colonial Cultures in a Bourgeois World* (Berkeley: University of California Press, 1997)

Crossley, Pamela, Siu, Helen and Sutton, Donald (eds). *Empire at the Margins: Culture, Ethnicity, and Frontier in Early Modern China* (Berkeley: University of California, 2006)

Dai, Yingcong. 'A disguised defeat: the Myanmar campaign of the Qing dynasty', *Modern Asian Studies*, 38:1 (2004), 145–89

Davis, Bradley. *Imperial Bandits: Outlaws and Rebels in the China-Vietnam Borderlands* (Seattle: University of Washington Press, 2017)

Di Cosmo, N. 'Kirghiz nomads on the Qing frontier: tribute, trade, or gift exchange, in N. Di Cosmo and D. J. Wyatt (eds), *Political Frontiers, Ethnic Boundaries, and Human Geographies in Chinese History* (London: Routledge, 2003), pp. 351–72

Everest-Phillips, Max. 'British consuls in Kashgar', *Asian Affairs*, 22:1 (1991), 20–34

Giersch, Patterson. *Asian Borderlands: The Transformation of Qing China's Yunnan Frontier* (Cambridge, MA: Harvard University Press, 2006)

Glover, Denis et al. (eds). *Explorers and Scientists in China's Borderlands, 1880–1950* (Seattle: University of Washington Press, 2011)

Goodman, Bryna and Goodman, David (eds). *Twentieth-Century Colonialism and China: Localities, the Everyday and the World* (London: Routledge, 2012)

Guha, Ranajit. *Elementary Aspects of Peasant Insurgency in Colonial India* (Durham, NC: Duke University Press, 1999)

Fishel, Wesley R. *The End of Extraterritoriality in China* (New York: Octagon, 1974)

Fiskesjö, Magnus. 'On the "raw" and the "cooked" barbarians of imperial China', *Inner China*, 1 (1999), 139–68

'The Fate of Sacrifice and the Making of Wa History' (PhD dissertation, University of Chicago, 2000)

Forbes, Andrew. *Warlords and Muslims in Chinese Central Asia: A Political History of Republican Sinkiang 1911–1949* (Cambridge: Cambridge University Press, 1986)

Ford, Lisa. *Settler Sovereignty: Jurisdiction and Indigenous People in America and Australia, 1788–1836* (Cambridge, MA: Harvard University Press, 2010)

Forsyth, James. *A History of the Peoples of Siberia: Russia's North Asian Colony, 1581–1990* (Cambridge: Cambridge University Press, 1992)

Gong Yin, *zhongguo tusi zhidu* 龔蔭,中国土司制度 [*China's Tusi System*] (Kunming: Yunnan remin chubanshe, 1992)

Herman, John. 'Empire in the Southwest: early Qing reforms in the native chieftain system, *Journal of Asian Studies*, 56:1 (1997), 47–74

Hu, Zhen. 'Qingmo minchu Shanghai gonggong zujie huishen gongxie faquan zhi bianqian 1911–1912' 胡震，清末明初上海公共租界会审公廨法权之变迁 ['The transformation of legal rights in the Shanghai Mixed Court in the International Settlement from 1911 to 1912'], *shixue yuekan*, 4 (2006), 51–6

Jackson, Isabella. 'The Raj on Nanjing Road: Sikh policemen in treaty-port China', *Modern Asian Studies*, 46:6 (2012), 1672–704

Jacobs, Justin. *Xinjiang and the Modern Chinese State* (Seattle: University of Washington Press, 2016)

Jaffe, James. *The Ironies of Colonial Governance: Law, Custom, and Justice in Colonial India* (Cambridge: Cambridge University Press, 2015)

Kayaoğlu, Turan. *Legal Imperialism: Sovereignty and Extraterritoriality in Japan, the Ottoman Empire, and China* (Cambridge: Cambridge University Press, 2010)

Kolsky, Elizabeth. 'Codification and the rule of colonial difference: criminal procedure in British India', *Law and History Review*, 23:3 (2005), 631–84
  Colonial Justice in British India: White Violence and the Rule of Law (Cambridge, Cambridge University Press, 2010)
  'The colonial rule of law and legal regime of exception: frontier "fanaticism" and state violence in British India', *American Historical Review*, 120:4 (2015), 1218–46
Laidlaw, Zoë. *Colonial Connections, 1815–1845: Patronage, the Information Revolution and Colonial Government* (Manchester: Manchester University Press, 2005)
Lamb, Alistair. *British India and Tibet 1766–1910* (London: Routledge, 1986)
Lambert, David and Lester, Alan (eds). *Colonial Lives across the British Empire: Imperial Careering in the Long Nineteenth Century* (Cambridge: Cambridge University Press, 2006)
Lary, Diana (ed.). *Chinese State at the Borders* (Vancouver: University of British Columbia Press, 2007)
Leach, E. R. *Political Systems of Highland Burma: A Study of Kachin Social Structure* (Boston: Beacon Press, 1964)
Lee, James. 'Food supply and population growth in Southwest China 1250–1850', *Journal of Asian Studies*, 41:4 (1982) 711–46
  'The legacy of immigration in Southwest China, 1250–1850', *Annales de Démographie Historique* (1992), 279–304
Lee, Tahirih. 'The United States Court for China: a triumph of local law', *Buffalo Law Review*, 52:4 (2004), 923–1075
Li, Shian. 'The extraterritoriality negotiations of 1943 and the New Territories', *Modern Asian Studies*, 30:3 (1996), 617–50
Lo, Hui-min and Bryant, Helen. *British Consular Establishments in China 1793–1949* (Taipei: SMC Publishing, 1988)
Ma, J. 'Salt and revenue in frontier formation: state mobilized ethnic politics in the Yunnan-Burma borderlands since the 1720s', *Modern Asian Studies*, 48:6 (2014), 1637–69
Malleson, Wilfrid. 'The British military mission to Turkistan, 1918–1920', *Journal of the Central Asian Society*, 9:2 (1922), 96–110
Markovits, Claude. *The Global World of Indian Merchants, 1750–1947: Traders of Sind from Bukhara to Panama* (Cambridge: Cambridge University Press, 2000)
Marshall, Alex. *The Russian General Staff and Asia, 1800–1917* (London: Routledge, 2006)
Maule, R. 'British policy discussions on the opium question in the Federated Shan States, 1937–1948', *Journal of Southeast Asian Studies*, 33:2 (2002), 203–24
McGrath, T. 'A warlord frontier: the Yunnan-Burma border dispute, 1910–1937', *Ohio Academy of History Proceedings* (2003), 7–29
Merry, Sally Engle [review], 'Martin Chanock, Law Custom and Social Order: The Colonial Experience in Malawi and Zambia (New York, 1985)', *Law and Social Inquiry*, 28:2 (2003), 269–90

[187]

Metcalf, Thomas. *Imperial Connections: India in the Indian Ocean Arena, 1860–1920* (Berkeley: University of California Press, 2007)

Miller, Bradley. *Borderline Crime: Fugitive Criminals and the Challenge of the Border, 1819–1914* (Toronto: University of Toronto Press, 2016)

Millward, James. *Beyond the Pass: Economy, Ethnicity and Empire in Qing Central Asia, 1759–1864* (Stanford: Stanford University Press, 1998)

Millward, James, Dunnell, Ruth, Elliot, Mark and Forêt, Philippe (eds). *New Qing Imperial History: The Making of Inner Asian Empire at Qing Chengde* (New York: Routledge, 2004)

Mueggler, Erik. *The Paper Road: Archive and Experience in the Botanical Exploration of West China and Tibet* (Berkeley: University of California Press, 2011)

Newby, Laura. 'The Begs of Xinjiang: between two worlds', *Bulletin of the School of Oriental and African Studies*, 61:2 (1998), 278–97

Newman, R. K. 'India and the Anglo-Chinese Opium Agreements, 1907–1914', *Modern Asian Studies*, 23:3 (1989), 525–60

Norins, M. 'Tribal boundaries of the Burma-Yunnan frontier', *Pacific Affairs*, 12:1 (1939), 67–79

Nyman, Lars-Erik. *Great Britain and Chinese, Russian and Japanese Interests in Sinkiang, 1918–1934* (Malmö: Esselte studium, 1977)

Osada, Noriyuki. 'Discovery of "outsiders": the expulsion of undesirable Chinese and urban governance of colonial Rangoon, Burma, c. 1900–1920', *Journal of Sophia Asian Studies*, 1:32 (2014), 79–96

Pelcovits, Nathan. *Old China Hands and the Foreign Office* (New York: King's Crown Press, 1948)

Perdue, Peter. *China Marches West: The Qing Conquest of Central Eurasia* (Cambridge, MA: Harvard University Press, 2005)

Richards, J. 'Opium and the British Indian Empire: the Royal Commission of 1895', *Modern Asian Studies*, 36:2 (2002), 375–420

Rodriguez, Andres. 'Building the nation, serving the frontier: mobilizing and reconstructing China's borderlands during the War of Resistance (1937–1945)', *Modern Asian Studies*, 45:2 (2011), 345–76

Ruskola, Teemu. 'Canton is not Boston: the invention of American imperial sovereignty', *American Quarterly*, 57:3 (2005), 859–84

'Colonialism without colonies: on the extraterritorial jurisprudence of the U.S. Court for China', *Law and Contemporary Problems*, 71:1 (2008), 217–42

Saha, Jonathan. *Law, Disorder and the Colonial State: Corruption in Burma c.1900* (Basingstoke: Palgrave Macmillan, 2013)

Schendel, W van. 'Geographies of knowing, geographies of ignorance: jumping scale in Southeast Asia' *Environment and Planning D: Society and Space*, 20:6 (2002), 647–68

Schluessel, Eric. 'The Muslim Emperor of China: Everyday Politics in Colonial Xinjiang, 1877–1933' (PhD dissertation, Harvard University, 2016)

Scott, James, C. *The Art of Not Being Governed: An Anarchist History of Upland Southeast Asia* (New Haven: Yale University Press, 2009)

Scully, Eileen. *Bargaining with the State from Afar: American Citizenship in treaty port China, 1844–1942* (New York: Columbia University Press, 2001)

She Yize, *zhongguo tusi zhidu* 余贻泽,中国土司制度 [*China's Tusi System*] (Shanghai: Shangwu shuju reprint, 1947)

Singha, Radhika. 'The Great War and a "proper" passport for the colony: border-crossing in British India, c.1882–1922', *Indian Economic and Social History Review*, 50:3 (2013), 289–315

Spencer, Joseph Earle. 'Salt in China', *Geographic Review*, 25:3 (1935), 353–66

Skrine, C. P. and Nightingale, Pamela. *Macartney at Kashgar: New Light on British, Chinese and Russian Activities in Sinkiang, 1890–1918* (Oxford: Oxford University Press, 1987)

Starr, S. Frederick (ed.). *Xinjiang: China's Muslim Borderland* (London: M. E. Sharpe, 2004)

Stephens, Thomas. *Order and Discipline in China: the Shanghai Mixed Court 1911–27* (Seattle: University of Washington Press, 1992)

Stoler, Ann Laura. *Carnal Knowledge and Imperial Power: Race and the Intimate in Colonial Rule* (Berkeley: University of California Press, 2002)
Along the Archival Grain: Epistemic Anxieties and Colonial Common Sense (Princeton: Princeton University Press, 2009)

Sutton, Donald. 'Violence and ethnicity on a Qing colonial frontier: customary and statutory law in the eighteenth-century Miao pale', *Modern Asian Studies*, 37:1 (2003), 41–80

Tagliacozzo, Eric. 'Ambiguous commodities, unstable frontiers: the case of Burma, Siam, and imperial Britain, 1800–1900', *Comparative Studies in Society and History*, 46:2 (2004), 354–77
Secret Trade, Porous Borders: Smuggling and States along a Southeast Asian Frontier, 1865–1915 (New Haven: Yale University Press, 2005)

Tejada, Jamie Moreno and Tartar, Bradley (eds). *Transnational Frontiers of Asia and Latin America since 1800* (New York: Routledge, 2017)

Thampi, Madhavi. *Indians in China 1800–1949* (New Delhi: Manohar, 2005)

Thampi, Madhavi (ed.). *India and China in the Colonial World* (New Delhi: Social Science Press, 2005)

Theobald, Ulrich and Cao, Jin (eds), *Southwest China in a Regional and Global Perspective (c.1600–1911): Metals, Transport, Trade and Society* (Leiden: Brill, 2018)

Trocki, Carl. *Opium, Empire and the Global Political Economy* (London: Routledge, 1999)

Tripodi, Christian. *Edge of Empire: The British Political Officer and Tribal Administration on the North-West Frontier 1877–1947* (Farnham: Ashgate, 2011)

Walsh, W. 'The Yunnan myth', *Far Eastern Quarterly*, 2:3 (1943), 272–85

Wang, Dongping. *Qingdai huijiang falü zhidu yanjiu, 1759–1884 nian*, 王东平, 清代回疆法律制度研究, 1759–1884 年 [*Study of the Legal System of the Muslim Domain, 1759–1884*] (Ha'erbin: Heilongjiang Jiaoyu Chubandshe, 2003)

Waugh, Daniel. *Etherton at Kashgar: Rhetoric and Reality in the History of the "Great Game"* (Seattle: Bactrian Press, 2007)

Whewell, Emily. 'British Extraterritoriality in China: The Legal System, Functions of Criminal Jurisdiction and its Challenges, 1833–1943' (PhD dissertation, University of Leicester, 2015)

Wiens, Herold. *China's March towards the Tropics* (Hamden: Shoe String Press, 1954)

Winichakul, Thongchai. *Siam Mapped: A History of the Geo-body of a Nation* (Honolulu: University of Hawaii Press, 1994)

Winther, P. *Anglo-European Science and the Rhetoric of Empire* (Oxford: Lexington Brooks, 2003)

Wright, Ashley. *Opium and Empire in Southeast Asia: Regulating Consumption in British Burma* (Basingstoke: Palgrave Macmillan, 2013)

Wu Yongzhang. *zhongguo tusi zhidu yuanyuan yu fazhangshi* 吴玉章,中国土司制度渊源与发展史 [*A History of the Origins and Development of China's Native Chieftaincy System* (Chengdu: Sichuan Minzu Publishing House, 1988)]

Wyman, Judith. 'The ambiguities of Chinese antiforeignism: Chongqing, 1870–1900', *Late Imperial China*, 18:2 (1997), 86–122

'Opium and the state in late-Qing Sichuan', in T. Brook and B. T. Wakabayashi (eds), *Opium Regimes: China, Britain and Japan, 1839–1952* (Berkeley: University of California Press, 2000), pp. 212–27

Xie Benshu, 'Cong Pianma shijian dao Banhong shijian: zhong main bianjie lishi yange wenti', 谢本书, 从片马事件到班洪事件--中缅边界历史沿革问题 ['From the Pianma incident to the Banhong incident – the historical evolution of the Sino-Burmese border'] *Yunnan shehui kexue*, 4 (2000), 208–30

Yao, Yong. 'bianjing yu bianmin de guojia hua: jindai zhong ying huishen dian mian bian an zhidu', 姚勇: '边境与边民的国家化:近代中英会审滇缅边案制度, ['Nationalization of the frontier and frontier people: the system of the Sino-British Frontier Meetings border cases'], *lishi renleixue xuekan*,13:1 (2015), 87–130

INDEX

EU authorised representative for GPSR:
Easy Access System Europe, Mustamäe tee 50,
10621 Tallinn, Estonia
gpsr.requests@easproject.com